Social Thought in American Fundamentalism, 1918–1933

Robert E. Wenger

Wipf and Stock Publishers
199 W 8th Ave, Suite 3
Eugene, OR 97401

Social Thought in American Fundamentalism, 1918-1933
By Wenger, Robert E.

ISBN 13: 978-1-55635-397-0
ISBN 10: 1-55635-397-9
Publication date 4/3/2007
Previously published by University Microfilms, 1974

INFORMATION TO USERS

This material was produced from a microfilm copy of the original document. While the most advanced technological means to photograph and reproduce this document have been used, the quality is heavily dependent upon the quality of the original submitted.

The following explanation of techniques is provided to help you understand markings or patterns which may appear on this reproduction.

1. The sign or "target" for pages apparently lacking from the document photographed is "Missing Page(s)". If it was possible to obtain the missing page(s) or section, they are spliced into the film along with adjacent pages. This may have necessitated cutting thru an image and duplicating adjacent pages to insure you complete continuity.

2. When an image on the film is obliterated with a large round black mark, it is an indication that the photographer suspected that the copy may have moved during exposure and thus cause a blurred image. You will find a good image of the page in the adjacent frame.

3. When a map, drawing or chart, etc., was part of the material being photographed the photographer followed a definite method in "sectioning" the material. It is customary to begin photoing at the upper left hand corner of a large sheet and to continue photoing from left to right in equal sections with a small overlap. If necessary, sectioning is continued again – beginning below the first row and continuing on until complete.

4. The majority of users indicate that the textual content is of greatest value, however, a somewhat higher quality reproduction could be made from "photographs" if essential to the understanding of the dissertation. Silver prints of "photographs" may be ordered at additional charge by writing the Order Department, giving the catalog number, title, author and specific pages you wish reproduced.

5. PLEASE NOTE: Some pages may have indistinct print. Filmed as received.

Xerox University Microfilms
300 North Zeeb Road
Ann Arbor, Michigan 48106

TABLE OF CONTENTS

LIST OF TABLES

LIST OF ILLUSTRATIONS

CHAPTER I

INTRODUCTION

Somewhere in every volume on the colorful twenties is a section, ranging from a few paragraphs to a chapter, on a religious phenomenon known as fundamentalism. It is usually mentioned in the same context as prohibition, nativism, and the Ku Klux Klan. After a brief explanation of the "backwardness" of segments of American society, attention is quickly focused on William Jennings Bryan and the Scopes trial. Although Scopes loses his case, Bryan is humiliated, fundamentalism subsides, and the reader passes on, smiling patronizingly at the outworn remnants of a folk religion.

This stereotype is not new. During the religious controversies of the twenties, modernist opponents feared, denounced, and ridiculed the fundamentalists, but, like many a present reader, understood them only imperfectly. And since then historians have contributed relatively little to a better understanding of this movement.

To begin with, fundamentalism has until recently been largely ignored, and only two full-length works on the period of controversy have appeared. Stewart G. Cole's <u>The</u>

History of Fundamentalism,[1] published in 1931 as the heat of battle was subsiding, is a fairly accurate representation of the events of the fundamentalist-modernist struggle, but its interpretive value is limited by the author's proximity to those events and his personal antagonism to fundamentalism. A more recent work, Norman F. Furniss' The Fundamentalist Controversy,[2] is also basically a narrative account and owes a heavy debt to Cole, both in factual material and interpretation. Historians who allude to fundamentalism more briefly usually cite one or both of these works as their major source of information.

Furthermore, interpretations of fundamentalism have often focused on alleged social, cultural, or psychological determinants of the movement and have minimized its theological characteristics. For example, some see it as a rural revolt against the big cities, centered largely in the South and Midwest, and incited by economic depression or alienation from cultural power. In the words of Winthrop Hudson,

> Whatever the intentions of its more moderate wing, Fundamentalism can probably best be understood as a phase of the rural-urban conflict, representing the tendency of many who were swept into a strange new urban environment to cling to the securities of their

---

[1]Stewart G. Cole, The History of Fundamentalism (New York: Harper & Row, 1931).

[2]Norman F. Furniss, The Fundamentalist Controversy, 1918-1931 (New Haven: Yale University Press, 1954).

childhood in rural America.[3]

Some reason that an orthodox faith made sense to persons who depended on nature and divine intervention for their livelihood, while city dwellers, with their rational methods of production, came to depend on human solutions to their problems.[4]

Others see in fundamentalism an expression of post-World War I disillusionment and a form of "crowd behavior" akin to that of the Ku Klux Klan and other nativist, anti-radical, anti-Catholic, anti-Semitic hate groups. Writing in 1929, Clifford Kirkpatrick reasoned that

> When men are used to joining in such a crowd as is constituted by a nation at war, or by the Ku Klux Klan, it is easy for them to embark upon a Fundamentalist Crusade to drive evolution from the schools.[5]

Stewart Cole similarly maintained that "exploiters of the masses" sublimated war hates into organized outbursts of

---

[3]Winthrop Hudson, American Protestantism (Chicago: The University of Chicago Press, 1961), p. 148. This has been perhaps the most widely held interpretation. Nearly all historians dealing with the subject have accepted it as at least a partial explanation. Many take their cue from H. Richard Niebuhr, "Fundamentalism," Encyclopaedia of the Social Sciences (15 vols.; New York: Macmillan Company, 1931), VI, 526-27. Both Cole and Furniss have given this thesis a prominent place, as also have Henry F. May in The End of American Innocence (New York: Alfred A. Knopf, 1959), pp. 128-29, and William E. Leuchtenburg in The Perils of Prosperity, 1914-32 (Chicago: The University of Chicago Press, 1958), pp. 217-18.

[4]Niebuhr, "Fundamentalism," VI, 527; Leuchtenburg, Perils of Prosperity, p. 222.

[5]Clifford Kirkpatrick, Religion in Human Affairs (New York: John Wiley & Sons, Inc., 1929), p. 402.

social and religious prejudice, and more recent historians have echoed the same theme.[6]

Many also regard fundamentalism as a reaction of the uneducated masses, isolated from the centers of learning, against the unsettling discoveries of scientific and theological research. As Walter Lippmann reflected on the Scopes trial, he ventured this dogmatic opinion:

> These assaults upon the freedom of teaching have been supported by the ignorant part of our population, the spokesmen of these new inquisitions have often been mountebanks, and invariably they have been ignoramuses.[7]

Not all writers concur with Lippmann's blanket indictment, but most tend to support Kirsopp Lake's judgment of the fundamentalist, that ". . . being half educated, he has no doubts."[8] Some go farther and assert that he assumed a positively anti-intellectual stance. According to Furniss, "Ignorance . . . became a badge the orthodox often wore proudly," and to compensate for their own inferior educa-

---

[6]Cole, Fundamentalism, p. 25; cf. Robert Moats Miller, American Protestantism and Social Issues, 1919-1939 (Chapel Hill: The University of North Carolina Press, 1958), p. 155; John Higham, Strangers in the Land: Patterns of American Nativism, 1860-1925 (New Brunswick, N.J.: Rutgers University Press, 1955), p. 293; and Richard Hofstadter, The Paranoid Style in American Politics (New York: Alfred A. Knopf, 1965), p. 73, note.

[7]Walter Lippmann, American Inquisitors (New York: Macmillan Company, 1928), p. 9.

[8]Kirsopp Lake, The Religion of Yesterday and Tomorrow (London: Christophers, 1925), p. 69.

tion they heaped scorn upon the intellectuals.[9]

The fundamentalist has further been pictured as a psychologically insecure person, clinging for assurance to an infallible Bible. Ray Ginger, in an interpretation reminiscent of Erich Fromm's Escape From Freedom, attributes this alleged insecurity to rapid social change. Industrialization, urbanization, immigration, and the war bred a sense of national guilt and led to "a desperate flight backward to old certainties."[10] William G. McLoughlin, Jr., on the other hand, speaks of economically-induced insecurity among the "unsuccessful middle class," many of whom had drifted into cities but had failed to find prosperity.

> For solace and a sense of belonging they sought to recreate in various store-front churches and gospel tabernacles . . . the simple, enthusiastic, friendly religion which had been part of their community life in the country.[11]

This economic and social insecurity, says McLoughlin, bred a sense of inferiority which led fundamentalists to reject the worldly pleasures of the well-to-do and to assert their own position of divine favor.[12]

---

[9]Furniss, Controversy, pp. 39-40; cf. Kirkpatrick, Religion, pp. 402-403.

[10]Ray Ginger, Six Days or Forever? Tennessee v. John Thomas Scopes (Boston: Beacon Press, 1958), pp. 10-12.

[11]William G. McLoughlin, Jr., Modern Revivalism: Charles Grandison Finney to Billy Graham (New York: Ronald Press Company, 1959), pp. 466-67; cf. Furniss, Controversy, p. 35.

[12]McLoughlin, Modern Revivalism, p. 471.

A final ingredient in the fundamentalist stereotype is the ambitious but frustrated preacher who, sensing his loss of status in a mechanized and secularized age, resorts to the spectacular and even the unscrupulous to regain a following. John Roach Straton, J. Frank Norris, and Edgar Young Clarke are often singled out for notoriety, along with the aging William Jennings Bryan. Kirkpatrick also maintained that the South abounded in "half-starved evangelistic preachers," ignorant and eager for gain and fame.[13]

The cumulative picture emerging from the foregoing interpretations is similar to that painted by George E. Mowry as he describes the two sides at the Scopes trial:

> Stripped of politics, the contending forces at Dayton were those of 1896, the countryside versus the big city, the West and South against the East, Anglo-Saxondom against the polyglots, traditional Protestantism versus the nonbelievers and the wrong believers, Prohibitionists against the sybarites, the simple innocents against the sophisticates.[14]

In addition a few writers, both during the twenties and more recently, have discerned a relationship between fundamentalism and capitalism. Some have attributed to the earlier fundamentalism the political characteristics of the

---

[13]Kirkpatrick, <u>Religion</u>, p. 402; cf. Ginger, Six Days, p. 13; Furniss, Controversy, pp. 29-30. Richard Hofstadter speaks of a loss of status and its results without being specific about individuals in Anti-Intellectualism in American Life (New York: Alfred A. Knopf, 1963), p. 121.

[14]George E. Mowry, The Urban Nation, 1920-1960 (New York: Hill and Wang, 1965), p. 30.

"radical right" of more recent years.[15]

The utility of any interpretive device depends on the degree to which it simplifies a complex reality so that it can be better understood. The traditional stereotype of fundamentalism fails to improve understanding, for it fails to answer several significant questions raised by stubborn historical facts. For example, if fundamentalism was primarily rural, how can one account for urban-born fundamentalist leaders or large urban fundamentalist churches? If it was southern and midwestern, why did Boston, New York, and Philadelphia figure so prominently in the movement? If World War I bred the bitterness out of which fundamentalism arose, whence came its opposition to German higher criticism and Roman Catholicism *before* the war, and why was its post-war attitude toward foreigners, socialists, Jews, and Catholics so divided? If it represented the backward, isolated, and ignorant, what accounts for the scholars in fundamentalism? If it was a psychological reaction of certain social classes to their conditions, why did professional and business people join the crusade against modernism? Or if it catered to the capitalist, what explains its strong

---

[15]Lake, *Religion of Yesterday and Tomorrow*, p. 161; Ginger, *Six Days*, pp. 12-13; Hofstadter, *Paranoid Style*, pp. 73-78. Erling Jorstad, *The Politics of Doomsday: Fundamentalists of the Far Right* (Nashville, Tenn.: Abingdon Press, 1970), while not arguing for an identity of political beliefs between older and newer fundamentalists, does show similarities and connections. See pp. 24, 27-28.

appeal to other classes? Finally, is it fair to judge the motives of fundamentalist leadership by the actions of several colorful and controversial individuals? Surely these questions point to the need for further investigation.

Several historians have recently sensed this need and have undertaken limited revisions. In reappraisals of William Jennings Bryan, for example, Lawrence W. Levine and Willard H. Smith have found him to be a political, social, and economic liberal while retaining his Christian orthodoxy.[16] A more direct and sweeping challenge to earlier interpretations has been issued by Paul A. Carter, who concludes that fundamentalism can not be reduced to "economic, regional, political, or psycho-social categories," but was just what its advocates claimed--a militant reaffirmation of orthodox Christianity after a period of eclipse by scientism and modernism.[17] Willard B. Gatewood, Jr., while retaining much from the older interpretations, offers a better balanced and more sophisticated summary of the move-

---

[16] Lawrence W. Levine, *Defender of the Faith. William Jennings Bryan: The Last Decade, 1915-1925* (New York: Oxford University Press, 1965), pp. 197-210, 358-59, 362-64; Willard H. Smith, "William Jennings Bryan and the Social Gospel," *Journal of American History*, LIII (June, 1966), 41-60.

[17] Paul A. Carter, "The Fundamentalist Defense of the Faith," in *Change and Continuity in Twentieth-Century America: The 1920's*, ed. by John Braeman, Robert H. Bremner, and David Brody (Columbus, Ohio: Ohio State University Press, 1968), pp. 179-214.

ment,[18] as also does Milton L. Rudnick, who stresses the importance of theological factors and asserts that "To view Fundamentalism from any other perspective is to see only a part of the picture--and that in distortion."[19]

Of particular importance are the contributions of Ernest R. Sandeen, who has explored in detail the theological origins of fundamentalism. In a 1967 article he pictures the movement as an alliance between dispensationalism, which emphasized literal interpretation of Scripture, especially as applied to future prophetic fulfillment, and the "Princeton theology," which stressed the doctrine of biblical inerrancy. Sandeen challenges the stereotype by asserting that fundamentalist leadership was reputable, intelligent, vigorous, forward-looking, and urban-oriented.[20] In a later book-length study he more thoroughly traces the movement back to nineteenth-century millenarianism in Great Britain and America.[21] While

---

[18] Willard B. Gatewood, Jr. (ed.), Controversy in the Twenties: Fundamentalism, Modernism, and Evolution (Nashville, Tenn.: Vanderbilt University Press, 1969), pp. 3-46.

[19] Milton L. Rudnick, Fundamentalism and the Missouri Synod (St. Louis, Mo.: Concordia Publishing House, 1966), p. 15.

[20] Ernest R. Sandeen, "Toward a Historical Interpretation of the Origins of Fundamentalism," Church History, XXXVI (March, 1967), 66-83.

[21] Sandeen, The Roots of Fundamentalism: British and American Millenarianism 1800-1930 (Chicago: The University of Chicago Press, 1970).

Sandeen's studies do not adequately explain the controversial twenties, they give a long-range theological perspective which earlier treatments lacked.

These recent works thus suggest the thesis for the present study, that fundamentalism is more complex socially and culturally than historians have generally recognized, and that much of the usual stereotype can be maintained only by ignoring a large body of historical data. But revision is a matter of degree, and it becomes necessary to determine to what extent previous interpretations are inadequate. I have therefore examined the social orientation of fundamentalists from 1918 to 1933 to discover to what extent they constituted a distinct social, political, ideological, or economic "type."

I have assumed that if such a unity existed among fundamentalists, this would be evident from a similarity of background or a consensus on particular issues. I have also assumed that a lack of such a similarity or consensus or the sharing of their views with other Americans must lead us to seek their common denominator elsewhere.

This study, then, is not a new narrative history of fundamentalism but an analysis of fundamentalists' thinking on the life of their times. The period from 1918 to 1933 is especially appropriate for this purpose for at least two reasons. First, it embraces the era of the fundamentalists' greatest militancy, when they expressed themselves freely on the issues that concerned them most. Secondly, the period provided a multitude of issues for discussion as the nation whirled through change and upheaval. The total involvement in war, the painful transition to peace, the absorption with technology and materialistic pursuits, the revolution in morals, the challenge of Al Smith's candidacy, the numbing impact of the Depression, and the experimentalism of the early New Deal all provided abundant fuel for mind and pen.

This study reveals, however, that among all the issues facing them, fundamentalists reached a consensus only on those that were in some way related to two points of reference. The first and more important of these was their biblical faith. When an issue either threatened or called forth an application of biblical teaching they were likely to voice general agreement on that issue. The second point of reference was their nation. Few fundamentalist spokesmen were chauvinists, but most of them placed a strong emphasis on Christian patriotism, and an issue which they felt would affect America's welfare would likely call forth a strong, unified response. In practice these two identifications were usually combined thus: the greatest service to his country a fundamentalist could perform was to preserve and propagate biblical teaching and to apply it to national problems.

But fundamentalism was never monolithic in its

approach to national issues. While men who could agree on the core of Christianity had joined together to fight the common foe of modernism, they sometimes differed widely on a philosophy of history and the proper application of their faith to American life. Neither were fundamentalists always unique in their interpretation of national trends. Non-fundamentalist religious conservatives and even modernists often agreed with them in principle, if not always in detail. So in the final analysis fundamentalism's distinctiveness did not lie in its relationship to its social and cultural milieu. It lay rather in a set of theological agreements and a method of defending them, a point to be developed more fully in the next chapter.

But in analyzing social and political thought in fundamentalism, whose thinking is to be analyzed? Most historians have understandably focused on prominent leaders who gained national recognition through the secular press, such as Bryan, Straton, Norris, and Riley. But a more balanced picture can be obtained by considering the ideas of the larger but less known group of ministers and educators who served in pulpits, educational institutions, itinerant evangelism, and literary work. While the thinking of many of these, like that of the lay members of fundamentalist churches, is inaccessible, a considerable number wrote books and contributed articles to the religious press. I have sought, therefore, to discover from such sources the opinions of the lesser lights as well as those of the well-known spokesmen.

CHAPTER II

"THE FAITH ONCE DELIVERED"

The historiography of fundamentalism has chronically suffered from an inadequate definition of the movement it has purported to analyze. Too often writers have ignored or minimized the theological characteristics of fundamentalism on the assumption that theology was merely a vehicle to express the "real" problems--psychological, social, political, or economic.[1] The result has usually been either an amorphous series of loose and even contradictory descriptions[2] or an arbitrary sociologically-oriented definition only partially consistent with historical facts.

Richard Hofstadter's treatment illustrates this sociological viewpoint. He chooses to deal with fundamentalism as a movement which, due to loss of influence and respectability, developed "a religious style shaped by a desire to

---

[1]Some even imply that the "fundamentals" were spurious. Cole, e.g., charges that they varied according to denomination and "were subject to change as the seasonal problems of discordant parties necessitated." The History of Fundamentalism (New York: Harper & Row, 1931), p. 324.

[2]See, e.g., Sandeen's incisive critique of Furniss on this point, The Roots of Fundamentalism: British and American Millenarianism 1800-1930 (Chicago: The University of Chicago Press, 1970), pp. 285-86.

strike back against everything modern--the higher criticism, evolutionism, the social gospel, rational criticism of any kind." Admitting that this definition can not accommodate "the more thoughtful critics of modernism," Hofstadter excludes them rather than revising his definition.[3] Yet a study of the historical data reveals that many "thoughtful critics" identified themselves with fundamentalism--W. H. Griffith Thomas, Melvin Grove Kyle, J. Gresham Machen, and James M. Gray, to name only a few.

The definition of any movement must be somewhat artificial, for it is, as Darrett B. Rutman reminds us, "a formulation of reality rather than a reality itself, a part of the framework by which the historian orders his data."[4] Yet the historian does well to construct a framework that is not only useful to him and consistent with itself but also able to accommodate the data available. In the case of the fundamentalists the data consists mainly of theological ideas, and these ideas must be taken seriously, for,

---

[3]Richard Hofstadter, Anti-Intellectualism in American Life (New York: Alfred A. Knopf, 1963), pp. 121, 123, note. Joseph R. Gusfield departs even farther from historical fact when he uses the term to describe Protestant, old middle-class, small town Americans fighting a rearguard action against social change. Symbolic Crusade: Status Politics and the American Temperance Movement (Urbana, Ill.: University of Illinois Press, 1963), pp. 9-10, 140, 165.

[4]Darrett B. Rutman, American Puritanism: Faith and Practice (Philadelphia: J. B. Lippincott Company, 1970), vi.

as Rush Welter has pointed out, ideas are autonomous entities, not mere reflections of the circumstances in which they flourish.[5] Thus a proper understanding of fundamentalism must include an understanding of its theological presuppositions.

But we must also understand the presuppositions of fundamentalism's opponent, modernism, for the friction of these two contrasting sets of ideas produced the superheated atmosphere of the twenties and helped to make fundamentalism what it became. Thus it is necessary to explore briefly the origins of this conflict in American religion.

American Protestantism occupied a dominant but vulnerable position after the Civil War. On one hand, it had "Christianized" America to the last frontier and, though divided into many denominational groupings, had achieved a modus vivendi within itself that had assured it supremacy over the nation's religious life. But at the same time much of Protestantism had become the victim of its own success. In the absence of any sharp challenge, it had failed to define its fundamental assumptions and, satisfied with the "heart religion" of nineteenth-century revivalism, it experienced what Winthrop Hudson has called "theological erosion." In the midst of its success and activity, it

---

[5]Rush Welter, "The History of Ideas in America: An Essay in Re-definition," Journal of American History, LI (March, 1965), 599-614.

lost its identity and became captive to the culture it had helped to form.[6]

Among the clergy this cultural captivity became evident in the "New Theology," a religion which identified Christ with the highest cultural institutions and ideals. Practically erasing the distinction between the church and the world, the New Theology invested American cultural development with intrinsic redemptive tendencies. In a society which was about to become "the best of all possible worlds," little need was felt for supernatural redemption through Christ, for the environment would improve the individual. Such a concept meshed easily with and fortified the earlier ideas of Horace Bushnell, who had minimized the need for the conversion of a person growing up in a Christian environment. Because of its lack of a fixed normative content, the New Theology became an umbrella large enough to accommodate both a Russell Conwell and a Walter Rauschenbusch, but at the same time was ineffective as a guide to the individual church member.[7]

So the laity, fed on a bland theological diet, became even more captive culturally than their pastors. It is not

---

[6]I am indebted for this interpretation primarily to Winthrop Hudson, American Protestantism (Chicago: The University of Chicago Press, 1961), pp. 131-37.

[7]Ibid., pp. 137-41; Jerald C. Brauer, Protestantism in America (Philadelphia: Westminster Press, 1953), pp. 196-98.

surprising that when Robert and Helen Lynd asked "Middletown" residents in 1925 what a Christian believes many thought the question was a joke. To them "being a Christian" was somewhat synonymous with being civilized, honest, or reputable. Although they considered church membership to be very important and professed a generally orthodox creed, their attitude toward religion was only one of "unalert acceptance."[8] Another study has revealed that three-fourths of all British visitors to the United States between 1900 and 1935 lamented the "sham, superficiality, and hypocrisy" in American worship, a near reversal of opinion expressed before 1885. The era from 1885 to 1900 is thus marked as the center of a period of drift toward secularization in American churches.[9]

But American Protestantism was being affected not only by its cultural surroundings but also by its contact with new ideas from Europe, among them the evolutionary hypothesis and the higher critical theories of biblical literature. To assert that the "intellectually alert" American Christians accepted these views while the ignorant or uninformed rejected them is hardly accurate, for one can

---

[8] Robert S. and Helen M. Lynd, _Middletown_ (New York: Harcourt, Brace and Company, 1929), pp. 315-56, _passim_; cf. _Middletown in Transition_ (New York: Harcourt, Brace and Company, 1937), p. 295.

[9] Richard L. Rapson, "The Religious Feelings of the American People, 1845-1935: A British View," _Church History_, XXXV (September, 1966), 324.

find informed apologists on both sides.[10] Furthermore, a Protestantism which had cultivated neither the intellectual ability nor the inclination to debate theological questions was just as conducive to uncritical acceptance as to outright rejection of these ideas.[11]

In any case, the Protestant churchmen who espoused the New Theology were inclined to make peace with the new science and criticism as well. They not only reformulated their views on God, man, the world, the Bible, and the future life to agree with modern thought but also insisted that the content of theology must never be regarded as fixed but always tentative and subject to further revision.

Within this growing body of theological "liberals" appeared two strains of thought. The "evangelical liberals," who dominated the early thinking of the movement, retained Jesus Christ as the primary source and starting point of Christian theology and preserved other concepts from orthodoxy such as divine sovereignty, sin, regeneration, and the Holy Spirit. "Modernistic liberals," on the other hand, who flourished in the scientifically-oriented post-World War I period, took modern knowledge and experi-

---

[10]Richard Hofstadter, Social Darwinism in American Thought (Revised ed.; Boston: Beacon Press, 1955), pp. 24-25, gives this impression. Yet he cites Charles Hodge, Princeton theologian, as a critic of Darwinism on p. 26. See also Robert Dick Wilson, Is the Higher Criticism Scholarly? (Philadelphia: Sunday School Times Company, 1922).

[11]Hudson, American Protestantism, p. 145.

ence as their starting point and tested all claims of revelation and tradition by them. The modernist professed to arrive at his acceptance of the Christian religion as a result of scientific investigation or social experience, and he assumed that anyone who followed these methods would likely reach a similar conclusion.[12]

Theological liberals exhibited several major emphases: (1) man's natural freedom and capacity for altruism; (2) ethical preaching and moral education as main tasks of the church; (3) fervent optimistic advocacy of evolutionary progress; (4) revelation as an evolutionary process, and religious experience as the seat of authority; and (5) movement away from the strict dualisms of orthodoxy, emphasizing the unity of man with nature and with God.[13] But none of these themes were dogmatically-held "doctrines." Liberalism, particularly of the modernistic variety, should rather be understood as a method of approaching and validating religion. Kirsopp Lake of Harvard University preferred to call himself an "experimentalist" on the ground that experiment is the basis of knowledge. Lake declared, "In the Western world the natural laboratories

---

[12]Lloyd J. Averill, American Theology in the Liberal Tradition (Philadelphia: Westminster Press, 1967), pp. 69-100.

[13]Sydney E. Ahlstrom, "Continental Influence on American Christian Thought Since World War I," Church History, XXVII (September, 1958), 259-60.

for religion are the Christian Churches."[14] Shailer Mathews of the University of Chicago Divinity School defined modernism as ". . . the use of the methods of modern science to find, state and use the permanent and central values of inherited orthodoxy in meeting the needs of a modern world." (Italics in original.)[15] Or, in the words of James H. Snowden of Western Theological Seminary, "Modernism is the principle and progressive process of continually unifying our growing experience in knowledge and life." (Italics in original.)[16]

Behind this experimental method lay the presupposition that change in religion is both inevitable and desirable. Mathews asserted that "Christians have never had a static system of philosophy or a finished theology. They have been moved by a spiritual loyalty to a succession of institutions and groups."[17] Echoing the same thought, Lake wrote, "A religion soon dies when it loses the power to assimilate new truth, and to adapt itself to new circumstances."[18] Snowden maintained, "If we have beliefs that

---

[14]Kirsopp Lake, The Religion of Yesterday and Tomorrow (London: Christophers, 1925), pp. 64, 66.

[15]Shailer Mathews, The Faith of Modernism (New York: The Macmillan Company, 1924), p. 23.

[16]James H. Snowden, Old Faith and New Knowledge (New York: Harper & Brothers Publishers, 1928), p. 22.

[17]Mathews, Faith of Modernism, p. 3.

[18]Lake, Religion of Yesterday and Tomorrow, p. 7.

never change, they are probably withered husks and are dead at the root,"[19] and Harry Emerson Fosdick, New York's popular modernist preacher, urged a modernization of Christian faith so that the younger generation would have "a type of Christianity that will not have to be unlearned."[20]

Still deeper imbedded in modernist thinking lay the assumption that a new source of authority in religion was needed. They believed that as a result of nineteenth-century scholarship the biblical record had become "completely discredited at every point where it can be reached."[21] But what authority should replace it as final? Authorities of varying degrees of compulsion were recognized--nature, man, Scripture, Christ, and God. But in the final analysis, in Snowden's words, "Reason is the supreme judge in the court of the mind. Only its decisions can determine what has authority to command our belief and obedience."[22] To most liberals, both evangelical and modernistic, reason was a broad term denoting not only formal logic but also intuition, conscience, and other components of man's inner being. The new seat of religious authority

---

[19]Snowden, Old Faith and New Knowledge, p. 4.

[20]Harry Emerson Fosdick, "What Christian Liberals are Driving At," The Ladies' Home Journal, XLII (January, 1925), 128.

[21]Lake, Religion of Yesterday and Tomorrow, p. 45; cf. Snowden, Old Faith and New Knowledge, pp. 90-108.

[22]Snowden, Old Faith and New Knowledge, pp. 40-41.

was the totality of personal human experience.[23] The following statement by Fosdick illustrates this assumption:

> Some of us began our religious life under the domination of ideas about the Bible, God, Christ, heaven, and hell, that were current half a century ago. *Then our minds grew up* to be citizens of the twentieth century. *Our experience with* prayer, forgiveness, faith, and spiritual renewal deepened and enlarged. We had to dispense with a smaller formulation and get a larger one to save our souls. They would have smothered if they could not have broken through into a larger air. (Italics mine.)[24]

These then were the theological presuppositions motivating the modernistic liberals of the twenties--an experimental approach to religion, corresponding to the methods of science; the inevitability and desirability of religious change; and, perhaps most significant, a shift in religious authority from the Bible to human experience. The distinctions between evangelical and modernistic liberals tended to blur in the twenties as controversy with the fundamentalists caused evangelical liberals to gravitate toward the more extreme modernist position.[25]

Just as the liberal movement achieved its distinctiveness only gradually, so also did fundamentalism. For the sake of accuracy it should be observed that the term,

---

[23] Averill, *Liberal Tradition*, pp. 84-85.

[24] Fosdick, "What Liberals are Driving At," p. 18.

[25] Robert T. Handy, "Fundamentalism and Modernism in Perspective," *Religion in Life*, XXIV (Summer, 1955), 392. Averill points out how Shailer Mathews shifted his position by 1924. *Liberal Tradition*, pp. 103-106.

"fundamentalism," was not used until 1920, even though the expression, "fundamentals of the faith," appeared with increasing frequency during the first two decades of the century. Some scholars, using hindsight, have imputed the term to its earlier nameless counterpart,[26] but I have preferred to limit its usage to the period when men referred to themselves or others as fundamentalists.

The predecessors of fundamentalism were all Protestant theological conservatives, who could fully agree with the creeds of the Reformation. But their emphases varied and at times required considerable accommodation in order to make possible a unified movement against modernism.

The most prominent of these forerunners were the millenarians. Drawing inspiration from John N. Darby and other British millennial teachers, they emphasized a premillennial return of Christ based upon a literal interpretation of Scriptural prophecy. In contrast to the many nineteenth-century American Protestants who expected continuous human progress under God to produce the millennium, these men believed world conditions were actually worsening and could be rectified only through the personal return of Jesus Christ.[27] Although they never controlled a Protes-

---

[26]E.g., Sandeen, Roots of Fundamentalism; Carroll Edwin Harrington, "The Fundamentalist Movement in America, 1870-1920" (Unpublished Ph.D. dissertation, University of California at Berkeley, 1959).

[27]The reasons for this movement's origins in the

tant denomination in the nineteenth century, the millenarians nevertheless came to exert considerable influence among Baptists and Presbyterians by 1890.[28] Through the proliferation of Bible and prophecy conferences after 1875, they not only promoted premillennial prophetic teaching but also stressed the importance of Bible study and the defense of a biblical theology.[29] This biblical emphasis, combined with the challenge of liberalism in theological seminaries, motivated several to found Bible institutes. The examples of Dwight L. Moody in Chicago and Adoniram J. Gordon in Boston prompted others to establish similar schools in Minneapolis, Los Angeles, Toronto, and Philadelphia.[30]

But the ultimate goal of the Bible Institute was not

---

midst of a nationalistic optimism are not clear. Sandeen traces its British counterpart to the French Revolution, but admits (Roots of Fundamentalism, pp. 57-58) that no existing explanation for millenarianism in America is adequate. Stow Persons suggests that millennialists differed from the majority not in social and economic status but simply in their rejection of the prevailing interpretation of the historical process. "Religion and Modernity, 1865-1914," in The Shaping of American Religion, Vol. I of Religion in American Life, ed. by James Ward Smith and A. Leland Jamison (4 vols.; Princeton, N.J.: Princeton University Press, 1961), pp. 399-401.

[28]Sandeen, Roots of Fundamentalism, chaps. 2-7. At times they also included Episcopalians, Congregationalists, Methodists, Adventists, Dutch Reformed, Lutherans, and others, but their generally Calvinist theological orientation tied them more closely to Baptists and Presbyterians. See pp. 152, 163-64.

[29]Ibid., pp. 144, 160. Note the rather comprehensive theological statement adopted at Niagara, pp. 273-77.

[30]Ibid., pp. 181-83.

sound doctrine but evangelization. The apparent inconsistency between evangelistic zeal and the prediction of a cataclysmic end to the present order has perplexed many an observer. Harrington, for example, concludes that millenarians swung between two "conflicting extremes," stressing passive millennial teaching during the period of progressive reforms and energetic revivalism during and after the First World War.[31] But the facts do not sustain this interpretation, for at any given time millenarians could be found emphasizing both facets of their faith. Their philosophy of evangelism and missions was simply this: "Sow the seed" of the gospel as broadly as possible, not to convert the world but to give people free access to it, and allow God to produce his desired results. Their belief in the imminent return of Christ added urgency to the work at hand, for if souls were to be saved, they must be saved quickly. Millenarians were therefore found in the forefront of evangelism and missions by the turn of the century.[32]

One further development within millenarianism deserves mention because it became a secondary feature of fundamentalism. This was the doctrine of the "victorious

---

[31] Harrington, "Fundamentalist Movement in America," pp. iii-v; 50-55.

[32] Sandeen, Roots of Fundamentalism, pp. 184-86; cf. I[saac] M. Haldeman, The Mission of the Church in the World (New York: Book Stall, 1917), p. 16.

Christian life," or the believer's ability to overcome temptation through the power of the Holy Spirit dwelling within him. Originating in the Keswick movement in England, it was introduced into the United States by speakers invited by Dwight Moody to his Northfield conferences and eventually incorporated into the teaching of many premillennial stalwarts.[33] Charles G. Trumbull, whose life was profoundly affected by this teaching, continually promoted this devotional emphasis in The Sunday School Times, of which he was editor.[34]

But millenarians were by no means the only forerunners of fundamentalism. Other conservative Protestants, alarmed by the erosion of biblical authority in liberal hands,[35] sought to clarify their doctrine of biblical inspiration. The proposition that the Bible was God's revelation to man had been believed by Christians for centuries, and the corollary that it was therefore inerrant in all its parts had also been accepted and defended prior to

---

[33]Sandeen, Roots of Fundamentalism, pp. 176-81.

[34]Charles G. Trumbull, "How I Came to Believe the Bible," The Sunday School Times, LXI (January 25, 1919), 37-38; "How the Victory Message is Sweeping On," ibid., LXI (April 5, 1919), 186-87; "Perils of the Victorious Life," ibid., LXI (October 11, 1919), 557-58; "The Tragedy of Christianity," ibid., LXII (November 6, 1920), 609.

[35]The terms, "conservative" and "liberal," are used in a theological sense in this study unless otherwise indicated.

the mid-nineteenth century.[36] But in the face of the new criticism Princeton theologians Charles Hodge, A. A. Hodge, and Benjamin B. Warfield forged a more precise statement of and apologetic for inspiration, based largely on external proofs. According to Sandeen, the Princeton men particularly emphasized the concepts that (1) inspiration extended to the words of Scripture, (2) the Scripture taught its own inerrancy, and (3) only the "original autographs" were inspired.[37]

The extent to which the Princeton formulation added anything distinctive to later fundamentalist theology can be debated, especially since its "distinctive emphases" were all asserted by Louis Gaussen of Geneva, Switzerland several decades earlier and were well known among millenarians.[38] Perhaps it is safest to say that the Princeton doctrine of inspiration added scholarly support to earlier statements, fortified conservative Protestants' faith in the Bible, and contributed a new line of argument for fundamentalists to use along with those from other sources.

Liberal advances and increasing secularization in

---

[36]Sandeen, Roots of Fundamentalism, pp. 111-14.

[37]Ibid., pp. 114-30.

[38]Louis Gaussen, Theopneusty, or, The Plenary Inspiration of the Holy Scriptures, trans. by Edward Norris Kirk (New York: John S. Taylor & Co., 1844), pp. 39, 44, 72-73, 345ff. Gaussen's work continued to be a popular defense of inspiration among fundamentalists, as Sandeen himself points out. Roots of Fundamentalism, pp. 204-5.

American life were also driving conservatives into defensive alliances that ultimately crossed denominational lines. One such venture was the American Bible League, later known as the Bible League of North America, founded in 1903. This organization's many branches sponsored local conferences on themes of current importance. It also published a periodical, first called The Bible Student and Teacher and later The Bible Champion, which drew its contributed articles from well-known conservative scholars. Though founded by nonmillenarians, the League gradually came to include millenarians, and an alliance was thus formed which was to continue throughout the controversies of the twenties.[39]

But the most impressive accomplishment of allied conservative forces before 1920 was the publication of The Fundamentals. Underwritten by California oil men Lyman and Milton Stewart and edited consecutively by Amzi C. Dixon, Louis Meyer, and Reuben A. Torrey, these twelve paperbound volumes included ninety articles written by sixty-four authors.[40] The Fundamentals were sent free to all English-speaking Protestant "pastors, evangelists, missionaries,

---

[39]Sandeen, Roots of Fundamentalism, pp. 201-3. In 1931 the name of the publication was again changed to Christian Faith and Life.

[40]The Fundamentals: A Testimony to the Truth (12 vols.; Chicago: Testimony Publishing Company, [1910-1915]). The Stewart brothers identified themselves only as "two Christian laymen."

theological professors, theological students, Y.M.C.A. secretaries, Y.W.C.A. secretaries, Sunday School superintendents, religious lay workers, and editors of religious publications" whose addresses could be obtained.[41] Nearly three million copies were eventually circulated, about two-thirds of them in the United States, one-sixth in Great Britain, and the remaining sixth in other parts of the world.[42] A later four-volume hardbound edition appeared in 1917.

The contributors to The Fundamentals included well-known conservatives from the United States, Canada, the British Isles, and Germany. The American authors, who comprised nearly two-thirds of the total, were predominantly Presbyterians and Baptists and came primarily from the Northeast. Over half came from the New York City, Philadelphia, Boston, and Chicago areas, and the South and West had only meager representation.[43]

An analysis of the subject matter of The Fundamentals illuminates the emphases of this movement soon to be known as fundamentalism. Although some of the articles are susceptible to more than one classification, the statistics in Table 1 show unmistakably what these editors considered to

---

[41] Ibid., XII, 6.

[42] Ibid., p. 4.

[43] See Sandeen's analysis of the authors, Roots of Fundamentalism, pp. 199-200, note.

be most "fundamental."[44]

TABLE 1

CONTENTS OF ARTICLES IN THE FUNDAMENTALS

Subject	Articles	% of Total Articles
The Bible	28	31.1
Jesus Christ	8	8.9
The Remedy for Sin	8	8.9
Evangelism and Missions	8	8.9
Modern Thought	7	7.8
False Religions and Cults	6	6.7
Sin and its Punishment	5	5.6
Apologetics	5	5.6
Devotional and Practical Christianity	4	4.4
Personal Testimonies	4	4.4
The Existence of God	2	2.2
The Holy Spirit	2	2.2
The Second Coming	2	2.2
The Church	1	1.1
Total:	90	100.0

The most striking, but hardly surprising, point was the overwhelming emphasis on the Bible. Nearly one-third of all the articles dealt with the Scriptures, focusing on inspiration and biblical criticism, and the vast majority of the rest presupposed the Bible as their authority. The themes of Jesus Christ, the remedy for sin, and evangelism were also prominent as the core of the Christian message and work, but even they were subordinated to the Bible, for

[44]The classification in Table 1 is my own, based on titles of articles and analysis of contents where titles were not sufficiently clear. Rudnick's analysis confirms these emphases. Rudnick, Fundamentalism and The Missouri Synod, pp. 40-41.

without an inspired revelation the Christian message was believed to lose its authority and evangelism was deemed unnecessary. The emphasis was thus determined by the need; the trustworthiness of Scripture was being attacked and these authors rose to its defense.

It is also instructive to observe what was not emphasized. In a publication edited by millenarians it is remarkable that only two selections dealt with the second coming of Christ, that only one of these was distinctly premillennial, and that even this one minimized eschatological differences among Christians.[45] Likewise, the one article on the church was sufficiently general to receive endorsement from all conservatives. Rudnick summarizes well the significance of the apportionment of subject matter:

> . . . *The Fundamentals* lived up to their title. Subject matter was restricted almost exclusively to the very basic items on which nearly all conservative Protestants could agree. . . . The conservatives called a truce on intramural conflicts so that they could unite against their common foe.[46]

The tone of the articles is also significant. Far from the anti-intellectual, vituperative harangues often attributed to fundamentalists, they were, with few excep-

---

[45]Harrington misses the mark badly when he maintains that after 1912 fundamentalists made the second coming their exclusive emphasis. "Fundamentalist Movement in America," pp. iii-iv, 81.

[46]Rudnick, *Fundamentalism and The Missouri Synod*, p. 45.

tions, sober arguments designed to appeal to the mind as well as the heart, written by reputable educators and clergymen. Much of their material was unquestionably controversial, but, as Andrew K. Rule has pointed out, "Certainly the writers were neither ignorant nor hostile towards real contemporary scholarship."[47]

In these ways the forces of fundamentalism were drawn together. Millenarians zealous for Bible study, evangelism, and personal devotion became comrades in arms with other conservative Protestants equally committed to an inspired and authoritative Scripture. Their doctrinal differences temporarily appeared insignificant in comparison to the chasm which separated them from their modernist opponents. Together they declared war on secularism in American life and the theological ideas to which they attributed it.

A portrait of American Protestantism at the end of World War I must then include at least three groups: the liberals, leaning increasingly toward the extreme modernist position; the conservatives, soon to be called fundamentalists, becoming ever more vocal and active in their opposi-

---

[47]Andrew K. Rule, "Liberalism," Twentieth Century Encyclopedia of Religious Knowledge (2 vols.; Grand Rapids, Mich.: Baker Book House, 1955), II, 663; cf. Paul A. Carter, "The Fundamentalist Defense of the Faith" in Change and Continuity in Twentieth-Century America: The 1920's, ed. by John Braeman, Robert H. Bremner, and David Brody (Columbus, Ohio: Ohio State University Press, 1968), p. 206.

tion to liberalism; and a somewhat neutral group between them, minimizing doctrinal issues in order to maintain peace within ecclesiastical organizations.[48] Against this backdrop we are able to observe the fundamentalism of the twenties in a clearer light.

The name, "fundamentalist," was coined in 1920 by Curtis Lee Laws, editor of the Baptist publication, The Watchman-Examiner. Laws wrote:

> We here and now move that a new word be adopted to describe the men among us who insist that the landmarks shall not be removed. "Conservatives" is too closely allied with reactionary forces in all walks of life. "Premillennialists" is too closely allied with a single doctrine and not sufficiently inclusive. "Landmarkers" has a historical disadvantage and connotes a particular group of radical conservatives. We suggest that those who still cling to the great fundamentals and who mean to do battle royal for the fundamentals shall be called "Fundamentalists." By that name the editor of The Watchman-Examiner is willing to be called. It will be understood therefore when he uses the word it will be in compliment and not in disparagement.[49]

Laws' definition focuses on two characteristics of a fundamentalist: (1) he still clings to the "great fundamentals," and (2) he does "battle royal" for them. Many of

---

[48]Kirsopp Lake recognized these three groups as fundamentalists, experimentalists, and institutionalists. "The Real Divisions in Modern Christianity," The Atlantic Monthly, CXXXV (June, 1925), 755-61. Although controversy induced many Protestants to take sides (see Handy, "Fundamentalism and Modernism," p. 392), the Lynd "Middletown" study would seem to confirm Cole's observation that most laymen continued in a "middle-of-the-road" position. Fundamentalism, p. 321.

[49]Curtis Lee Laws, "Convention Side Lights," The Watchman-Examiner, VIII (July 1, 1920), 834-35.

Laws' colleagues echoed the same theme in their constant use of the biblical phrase, " . . . earnestly contend for the faith which was once delivered unto the saints" (Jude 3).

But what were these "fundamentals" which must be defended? Contrary to widespread opinion, no single "fundamentalist creed" was ever drawn up to embody the doctrines common to all fundamentalists, and the several statements of faith which appeared varied in inclusiveness.[50] This lack of unanimity may lead some to conclude with Cole or Le Roy Moore that the war in the churches revolved about church politics rather than theology.[51] But such a superficial judgment overlooks the fundamentalists' distinction between major and minor differences in theology. Like their predecessors they maintained a set of basic orthodox assumptions which, while putting an impassable gulf between them and the modernists, produced unity of conviction and purpose among themselves.

At times these assumptions were unspecified, for they were taken for granted. J. C. O'Hair, for example, saw no need to spell out the obvious. "By 'Fundamentalism' we

---

[50]Of ten statements of faith chosen from the literature of the period five of them had five points, two had seven, and three had nine. Only two agreed exactly.

[51]Cole, Fundamentalism, pp. 321-24; Le Roy Moore, Jr., "Another Look at Fundamentalism: A Response to Ernest R. Sandeen," Church History, XXXVII (June, 1968), 201.

simply mean that we are old fashioned orthodox Christians and we believe the Bible;--that's all."[52] J. Gresham Machen, who feared that a new name would for many imply a strange new sect, asserted, " . . . we are conscious simply of maintaining the historic Christian faith and moving in the central current of Christian life."[53] William L. Pettingill offered a similar generalization: "Far from being new, Fundamentalism is just oldfashioned Christianity, and to be a Fundamentalist is to be in the 'goodly company of the apostles.'"[54]

But when stated more precisely, fundamentalist theology always had an inspired, inerrant Bible at its core as the final authority. In the words of Joseph Kyle, the Bible is " . . . the fundamental of fundamentals, the great foundation principle, the great corner-stone which is to sheath the whole system of Christian truth which we pro-

---

[52]J. C. O'Hair, "Why I am a Fundamentalist," Moody Bible Institute Monthly (hereinafter referred to as Moody Monthly), XXVI (August, 1927), 576.

[53]J. Gresham Machen, "What Fundamentalism Stands For," The Bible Champion, XXXI (October, 1925), 489.

[54]William L. Pettingill, "Very Much Alive," Serving and Waiting, XII (June, 1922), 57. Even unsympathetic outsiders recognized substance in these claims to historic orthodoxy. See Lake, "Divisions in Christianity," p. 757; Rollin Lynde Hartt, "Deep Conflict Divides Protestantism," New York Times, December 16, 1923, X, 5; "The Case of the Fundamentalists," The Nation, CXVII (December 26, 1923), 729.

fess."[55] Walter Lippmann, though no friend to fundamentalism, caught the significance of this doctrine in an imaginary dialogue between a fundamentalist and a modernist:

> Fundamentalist: . . . For me the hope of salvation depends upon the authority of the Scriptures.
> Modernist: The account of creation in Genesis has nothing to do with the promise of salvation.
> Fundamentalist: You are quite wrong. It would make no difference if the Bible had said that the world was created in seven million years rather than in seven days or that man was descended from an ape. I could believe that as readily as I believe what I now believe. The important question is not what the Bible says about creation, but that the Bible says it. If the Bible is wrong about creation, how am I to know that it is not also wrong about salvation . . . ?[56]

Thus the Bible was the crux of the controversy, as both fundamentalists and modernists recognized. "It is not a controversy between conservatives and 'liberals,' nor between old fashioned traditionalists and 'modernists,'" declared David J. Burrell, pastor of New York's Marble Collegiate Church, "but between believers in Christ who accept God's Word as authoritative, and rationalists who hold that our 'inner consciousness' is the Court of Last Appeal . . . "[57] Unitarian Albert C. Dieffenbach, editor of The Christian Register, agreed: "The question, the only question, . . . in this matter is this: Is the Bible the

---

[55]Joseph Kyle, "The Fundamental of Fundamentals," Serving and Waiting, VIII (April, 1919), 473.

[56]Lippmann, American Inquisitors, pp. 50-51.

[57]David James Burrell, "Why and Where we Differ," The Bible Champion, XXXII (June-July, 1926), 301.

inerrant Word of God or is it a record of spiritual experience and thought . . . "[58] The wording of the issue might vary, but the issue remained, "What is the status of the Bible?"

Accepting the proposition of an inerrant and authoritative Bible, fundamentalists also accepted more specific doctrines taught in the Scriptures. They believed in the existence of a personal, transcendent God and the reality of the supernatural, whether manifested in creation, miracles, bodily resurrection, or spiritual regeneration.[59] They emphasized the uniqueness of Jesus Christ as displayed in his virgin birth, perfect life, atoning death, physical resurrection, and promised return. They also stressed, as both Puritans and nineteenth-century evangelicals had done, the necessity of conversion to transform the individual from a sinner into a child of God. This last point was not always emphasized in the controversies of the twenties, but was nevertheless basic in the fundamentalists' approach to social issues, setting them apart from the liberal "social gospel" and its emphasis on environmental improvement.

---

[58]Quoted by Leon Tucker, "The Shipwreck of Faith," The Wonderful Word, XIV (May, 1922), 365.

[59]The contrast between fundamentalists' and modernists' attitudes toward the supernatural is epitomized in their respective answers to the question, "Does prayer affect the weather?" See "Does Prayer Change the Weather?" The Christian Century, XLVII (September 10, 1930), 1084-86.

Whatever their differences, fundamentalists all agreed on these theological assumptions. Eldred C. Vanderlaan observed in 1925:

> Baptists and Presbyterians stand side by side. . . . the Episcopal bishops and the tent evangelists find themselves together. Scholarly conservatives of Princeton Theological Seminary align themselves with men from Bible Institutes whose audacious charting of future events they regard as folly.[60]

But even though they seemed to be strange bedfellows to an outsider, their cooperation was simple evidence of the unifying power of common convictions when the "great matters" of the Christian faith were threatened.

At this point we must clarify the place of premillennial eschatology in fundamentalism, since many have assumed that it was essential to the movement.[61] It should be noted, first, that premillennialism was widespread among fundamentalists and that the largest fundamentalist organization, the World's Christian Fundamentals Association (WCFA), included it as an article of faith. A majority of the Bible institutes also were premillennial.[62] Yet it

---

[60] Eldred C. Vanderlaan (ed.), Fundamentalism versus Modernism (New York: H. W. Wilson Company, 1925), p. 13.

[61] Rudnick, Fundamentalism and The Missouri Synod, p. 54, restricts his definition to those of this persuasion. Apparently it was a perennial question in the twenties as well, for clarifications are frequent.

[62] "World's Christian Fundamentals Association," The Christian Fundamentalist, I (July, 1927), 4; David R. Breed, "Bible Institutes of the United States," The Biblical Review, XII (July, 1927), 374.

must be remembered that these did not comprise the whole of fundamentalism and that even they relegated this doctrine to a secondary position in the interests of unity.

William B. Riley, executive secretary of the WCFA, reminded his readers that the issue with modernism was not the millennial one but the more "fundamental questions" regarding the Bible and Christ. While he defended the premillennial article of faith he emphasized that his organization utilized conference speakers who dissented from it.[63] James M. Gray, president of Moody Bible Institute, also regularly included nonmillenarian speakers in conferences sponsored by his school, and seriously doubted that the doctrine of the second coming would ever become a crucial dividing line between Protestants.[64] A Moody Monthly reader who inquired whether premillennialism was fundamental to apostolic Christianity was told, " . . . we do not regard as unorthodox those who may have a different view, providing they sincerely subscribe to . . . the Apostles' Creed."[65] Thus millenarians continued, as in the past, to

---

[63]W[illiam] B. Riley, "Millennialism and Modernism--A Challenge," Christian Fundamentals in School and Church, VI (October-December, 1923), 14; "What is Fundamentalism?" The Christian Fundamentalist, I (August, 1927), 6. Also note his endorsement of amillennial Westminster Seminary, ibid., III (January, 1930), 502-3.

[64]"Moody's Great Work for the Common Faith," The Essentialist, IV (October, 1928), 93-94; [James M. Gray], "No 'New Denomination,'" Moody Monthly, XXI (April, 1921), 347.

[65]Moody Monthly, XXXIII (July, 1933), 504.

welcome the contributions of others in the struggle with modernism.

The same willingness to minimize eschatological differences is evident among fundamentalists on the other side. The editor of The Bible Champion, for example, refused to discuss the millennial issue because of his magazine's wide evangelical constituency.[66] Frank M. Goodchild stated that many fundamentalists in the Northern Baptist Convention did not even know one another's views on Christ's return because they had never discussed them.[67] David James Burrell, addressing a New York prophecy conference in 1918, admitted his uncertainty about millennial questions but declared his unity with premillennialists on the basis of their mutual biblical faith.[68] Princeton professor J. Gresham Machen, who frankly labeled premillennialism as an error, welcomed millenarians' cooperation in the struggle against what to him was a far greater error, and criticized those who "coldly stand aside" because of the "obvious imperfections" of other Christians.[69] Presby-

---

[66]Jay Benson Hamilton, "Pre and Postmillenarism [sic]," The Bible Champion, XXVI (January, 1920), 21.

[67]Frank M. Goodchild, "The Spirit and Purpose of the Fundamentalists," The Watchman-Examiner, X (March 2, 1922), 268.

[68]David James Burrell, "Signs of the Times," in Christ and Glory, ed. by Arno Clemens Gaebelein (New York: Publication Office "Our Hope," n.d.), pp. 67, 74.

[69]J. Gresham Machen, Christianity and Liberalism

terian Clarence Edward Macartney and Methodist Harold Paul Sloan similarly welcomed millenarians as allies while disavowing agreement with their prophetic interpretations.[70]

Such an alliance, forged out of necessity, was obviously fragile and could be shattered when either partner no longer recognized its usefulness. Indeed, this actually happened in the thirties when fundamentalists despaired of recapturing the major denominations and withdrew to form new groups. The pugilistic spirit fostered by the frustrating war with modernism often remained, venting itself upon erstwhile allies. But to call The Fundamentals (1910-1915) "the last flowering of a millenarian-conservative alliance," as Sandeen does,[71] is hardly accurate, for that alliance continued, despite occasional cracks, for another fifteen years, and the controversies of the twenties focused on historic Protestant essentials rather than premillennialism.

Fundamentalism, then, rested upon an orthodox Chris-

(Grand Rapids, Mich.: Wm. B. Eerdmans Publishing Company, 1946), pp. 49-50; "The Claims of Love," in God Transcendent and Other Selected Sermons, ed. by Ned B. Stonehouse (Grand Rapids, Mich.: Wm. B. Eerdmans Publishing Company, 1949), p. 69.

[70]Clarence Edward Macartney, "The Crux of the Present Controversy," The Sunday School Times, LXV (April 21, 1923), 247; Harold Paul Sloan, Historic Christianity and the New Theology (Louisville, Ky.: Pentecostal Publishing Company, 1922), p. [6].

[71]Sandeen, Roots of Fundamentalism, p. 207.

tian theology with special emphasis on the Scriptures. But this theology itself did not make one a fundamentalist, for, as Vanderlaan observed, some men held the old doctrines without exhibiting a "belligerent attitude" as fundamentalists did.[72] The second distinguishing feature of fundamentalism was its militancy--its determination to "do battle royal" for the faith.

Because it often took the negative form of denouncing error, this militancy exposed fundamentalists to the charge of hatred. This they denied, asserting that it was not lack of love but devotion to truth that motivated them. No amount of love, argued Leander S. Keyser, could heal a doctrinal schism of such magnitude. "Evangelical Christians feel no rancor toward the liberalists; they love them. . . . Sharp rebuke does not mean hostility; it means earnestness of conviction."[73] Machen, too, saw militancy as a matter of Christian consistency and faithfulness:

> If these views of ours are wrong, they should be refuted; but it is unreasonable to ask us to hold these views and then act as though we did not hold them. . . . God has placed us in the world as witnesses, and we cannot . . . allow our witness to become untrue.[74]

Militancy was also felt necessary because the present

---

[72]Vanderlaan, Fundamentalism versus Modernism, p. 1.

[73]Leander S. Keyser, "Can there be Union through Love?" The Bible Champion, XXXIII (March, 1927), 134.

[74]Machen, "What Fundamentalism Stands For," p. 492; cf. Christianity and Liberalism, p. 174.

situation was urgent and even grave. While evangelicals had no doubts as to the final victory of God's truth, said A. Z. Conrad, they were deeply concerned about the effects of the present apostasy on children and youth. "We have no right to cry, 'Peace, Peace' while thousands of immortal souls are imperiled."[75] W. B. Riley asserted that fundamentalism refused to be a "blind leader of the blind," standing mute while a "false science" pushed society over the "precipice of ruin." It was, claimed Riley, "a movement in defense of children and future civilization."[76]

But militancy has its hazards, and in spite of noble motives it often bred self-righteousness and personal animosities. Fundamentalists were not insensitive to these dangers, as their own admissions and reminders testify. In a moment of self-criticism, W. B. Riley conceded:

> If I were in the great secret fraternity of my fellow fundamentalists and were frankly confessing our faults, I should be compelled to say that too many of us are Pharisees . . . we too often create the impression that . . . our opinions are well-nigh infallible, and our abilities superb, if not supreme; and the very truth we seek to defend suffers.[77]

The periodic rebukes and reminders issuing from fundamen-

---

[75]A[rcturus] Z. Conrad, "Are Evangelicals Afraid?" The Bible Champion, XXXI (July, 1925), 352.

[76]W. B. Riley, "The Old vs. the New Faith, or Why Fundamentalism?" The Christian Fundamentalist, IV (June, 1931), 455.

[77]W. B. Riley, The Bible of the Expositor and the Evangelist (40 vols.; Cleveland: Union Gospel Press, 1926-1938), New Testament, VIII, 62-63.

talist ranks--reminders that spiritual warfare could not be won with carnal weapons, that love was a "forgotten fundamental" and its lack was a heresy, that respect for one's adversary was essential to success, and that energy expended upon denunciation could be put to better use[78]--were evidence that this had become a perennial fundamentalist problem.

Often overlooked, however, was the positive militancy which went beyond condemning the enemy and promoted the constructive work of evangelization and biblical instruction. Fundamentalist publications abounded in news of foreign and home missions, Bible institutes, evangelistic teams, Bible distribution, and religious radio stations. They contained expositions of biblical books and doctrines, illustrative and devotional materials for pastors, and detailed lesson plans for Sunday school teachers. These emphases evidence a sense of need among fundamentalists not only to denounce error but also to lay a foundation for the faith of posterity.

The fundamentalists of the twenties, then, were in a sense the heirs of nineteenth-century evangelical Protes-

---

[78]See, e.g., "A Heresy of the Orthodox," The Bible Champion, XXVIII (June-July, 1922), 328-30; Keith L. Brooks, "The Forgotten Fundamental," Moody Monthly, XXIV (March, 1924), 340-41; A. C. Gaebelein, "The Conflict and How to War," Our Hope, XXX (February, 1924), 459-62; [Melvin Grove Kyle], Editorial, Bibliotheca Sacra, LXXXII (January, 1925), 5-6; William P. White, "Love and Humility," The King's Business, XXII (December, 1931), 531-32.

tantism in the Baptist and Presbyterian traditions, often with a premillennial prophetic emphasis blended in. They focused their energies on preserving what they considered to be the basic concepts of Christian orthodoxy: a personal and transcendent God, the reality of the supernatural, a unique Christ, and a transforming rebirth based on faith in his atoning work. And essential to these doctrines was the recognition of the Bible as God's inerrant revelation to man and the ultimate authority for faith and life.

But they were militants as well as doctrinal purists, responding to a crisis in American religion. By exposing heterodoxy, propagating biblical teaching, and evangelizing the uncommitted, they hoped to reclaim individuals and institutions from modernist, evolutionist, and secular influences. Both doctrinal purity and militant method were inherent in fundamentalism.[79] One fundamentalist tied these elements together in a concise definition of the movement:

> Positively, a call back to the faith once for all delivered; negatively, an earnest protest against . . . modern skepticism and denial; historically, a new movement occasioned by the widespread defection in Christian belief and consequent practice.[80]

---

[79]Here I concur essentially with Carter's analysis--that fundamentalists were simply defending what they honestly believed gave meaning to life, the orthodox faith. "Fundamentalist Defense," p. 212.

[80]N. S. McPherson, "Why I Am a Fundamentalist," Moody

One important practical question remains, however: How does one decide who, among American Protestant leaders, fit the description above? Many of them, of course, pose no problem, for they called themselves fundamentalists or identified with groups which bore the label. But others, who just as vigorously opposed modernism, avoided and even disliked the name. Machen, as noted before, feared its implication of a "strange new sect," and, according to his biographer, he also disliked fundamentalism's "meagre skeletal creeds" and some of his contemporaries' methods.[81] Melvin Grove Kyle avoided the term because of its "Pharisaical sound" and its abuse by the modernists.[82] A. Z. Conrad preferred to call himself a "Progressive Evangelical,"[83] while Donald Grey Barnhouse used the term "Bible Christian."[84]

Should we therefore exclude these and other such opponents of modernism from our study? I do not think so, for several reasons. First, they were as thoroughly

---

Monthly, XXXI (January, 1931), 254.

[81]Ned B. Stonehouse, J. Gresham Machen: A Biographical Memoir (Grand Rapids, Mich.: Wm. B. Eerdmans Publishing Company, 1954), pp. 40, 336-38.

[82][Melvin G. Kyle], Editorials, Bibliotheca Sacra, LXXXII (January, 1925), 5-6; LXXXV (April, 1928), 127.

[83]A. Z. Conrad, Jesus Christ at the Crossroads (New York: Fleming H. Revell Company, 1924), p. 9.

[84]Donald Grey Barnhouse, "History of Fundamentalism," Revelation, I (October, 1931), 334.

involved in the crusade against modernism as those who called themselves "fundamentalists." Many times they supported the same ventures, shared the same conference platforms, and contributed to the same religious periodicals. Even while Machen expressed distaste for the fundamentalist label he expressed his unity with those who used it: "I have little time to be attacking my brethren who stand with me in defense of the Word of God. I must continue to support an unpopular cause."[85] He further declared that ". . . if the disjunction is between 'Fundamentalism' and 'Modernism,' then I am willing to call myself a Fundamentalist of the most pronounced type."[86] Kyle, who found labels disagreeable, also accepted his classification somewhat philosophically: "Those who are fond of classifying everybody would, I suppose, unhesitatingly set me down as a Fundamentalist, seeing that for fifteen years I have been Archeological Editor of the Sunday School Times."[87] Clearly, then, such men were not mere fundamentalist sympathizers. With or without the label, they were active participants in the crusade.

Secondly, to exclude such persons on semantic grounds

---

[85]Quoted by Stonehouse, J. Gresham Machen, pp. 337-38.

[86]Letter, J. G. Machen to F. E. Robinson, June 25, 1927, reproduced in Stonehouse, J. Gresham Machen, pp. 426-29.

[87]Melvin G. Kyle, "Some Fundamentals," Bibliotheca Sacra, LXXXV (July, 1928), 298.

would be to invest a term with an importance not even recognized by its most ardent supporters. Curtis Lee Laws, who coined the term, declared, "The name of the movement is a mere incident and is relatively unimportant. The movement itself will never die."[88] In similar vein, James M. Gray asserted that "'Fundamentalism' as a slogan may go, but that which gives it reason can never go. It is the Rock of Ages that remains forever."[89] The essence of fundamentalism, then, was the content, not the name.

Thirdly, the deep involvement of such men identified them with the movement in the eyes of the public. Journalist William G. Shepherd, for example, called David James Burrell "as sound a representative of the fundamentalist school as I have encountered,"[90] even though Burrell did not, in writing at least, employ the term. Rollin Lynde Hartt called Princeton Seminary a "Fundamentalist stronghold" because of Machen's influence,[91] and Vanderlaan, as previously noted, included "scholarly conservatives" of

---

[88] [Curtis Lee Laws], "Fundamentalism Is Very Much Alive," The Watchman-Examiner, IX (July 28, 1921), 941.

[89] [James M. Gray], "The Breakup of Protestantism," Moody Monthly, XXVII (June, 1927), 472; cf. "Bishop Manning's Sermon," ibid., XXIV (April, 1924), 400.

[90] William G. Shepherd, Great Preachers As Seen By a Journalist (New York: Fleming H. Revell Company, 1924), p. 12.

[91] Hartt, "Deep Conflict Divides Protestantism," p. 5.

Princeton among fundamentalists.[92] Such statements, of course, must be used with caution, but they are sometimes interesting confirmations of other more solid evidence.

In this study, then, I have included as fundamentalists persons who (1) identified themselves as such, or (2) embraced the movement's theology and militancy without using the term. If these criteria appear to allow undue latitude, let it be remembered that the crusade against modernism never was highly organized or well disciplined, and it permitted precisely the kind of individualism indicated above. I have, conversely, excluded theological conservatives and even fundamentalist sympathizers who watched the action from a distance.[93]

Fundamentalism can be adequately understood only in its historical and theological context. It was conceived and born in an atmosphere of change in American Protestantism, when complacency and theological erosion were secularizing the churches, when environmental improvement, rather than personal conversion, was being proposed to remedy the human condition, and when new scientific and literary the-

---

[92]Vanderlaan, Fundamentalism versus Modernism, p. 13.

[93]This would exclude most Lutherans, Disciples of Christ, Southern Presbyterians, and even Southern Baptists. Members of these groups occasionally expressed support, but often exhibited an Olympian attitude toward their quarreling brethren. Probably the major reason for their aloofness was the fact that modernism was not a serious threat in their own denominations.

ories were shifting religious authority from the Bible to human experience. The millenarian-conservative alliance which became fundamentalism suppressed its internal conflicts and rose to the defense of the "fundamentals." The essence of fundamentalism was a militant defense of Protestant orthodoxy, with special emphasis on the inerrancy of the Bible, in the face of serious aberrations from that profession by many American Protestants.

But we can identify fundamentalism even more precisely if we consider its denominational and geographical scope. From one standpoint, fundamentalism tended to minimize existing denominations because its common denominator was theological rather than institutional. "Who are my brethren?" asked William B. Riley. "Baptists? Not necessarily and in thousands of instances, NO! My Brethren are those who believe in a personal God, in an inspired Book, and in a redeeming Christ."[94] It is therefore not surprising to find the World's Christian Fundamentals Association or some of the Bible institutes assuming functions of ecclesiastical organizations, to see a man like Arno C. Gaebelein severing his Methodist ties,[95] or to discover new denominational groupings springing up during the thirties

---

[94]W. B. Riley, "What is Fundamentalism?" <u>The Christian Fundamentalist</u>, I (July, 1927), 14.

[95]A. C. Gaebelein, "The Only Way," <u>Our Hope</u>, XXX (August, 1923), 76-78.

and forties.[96]

But most fundamentalist spokesmen of the twenties, even the most militant, were still tied to existing Protestant groups, which they sought to restore to a pristine faith, and they counseled their supporters to follow their example. J. Frank Norris advised a pastor considering separation from the Northern Baptist Convention, "By all means stay in,"[97] and as late as 1931 William B. Riley rebuked those who were leaving their denominations because of war-weariness.[98] Fundamentalists, rather, expected the modernists to leave, for they were the polluters of the sanctuary. Let doubters believe and preach what they like, declared Clarence Edward Macartney, but let them do it outside the churches. To withdraw church membership from a defector from Christ, argued Harold Paul Sloan, was not persecution but simply fair dealing.[99]

---

[96] For the later developments in fundamentalism, see Louis Gasper, _The Fundamentalist Movement_ (The Hague: Mouton & Co., 1963).

[97] Letter, J. Frank Norris to T. W. Callaway, November 5, 1927, Southern Baptist Convention, Archives, John Franklyn Norris Papers.

[98] W. B. Riley, "The Come-Outers," _The Christian Fundamentalist_, V (August, 1931), 46-51. Rudnick is inaccurate in claiming that Riley "repeatedly" recommended separation, _Fundamentalism and the Missouri Synod_, p. 21.

[99] Clarence Edward Macartney, "Believers and Doubters," _The Ladies' Home Journal_, XLI (May, 1924), 24, 200-3; Harold Paul Sloan, _The Christ of the Ages_ (Garden City, N.Y.: Doubleday, Doran & Company, Inc., 1928), p. 167.

The crusade for orthodoxy within the denominations struck a responsive note among persons of many Protestant groups. A series of sermons on fundamental doctrines by Reuben A. Torrey, for example, brought requests for reprints from Episcopalian, Presbyterian, Methodist, and Baptist ministers.[100] An even broader spectrum was represented on the editorial staff of The Bible Champion, which in 1923 included Presbyterians, Methodists, Episcopalians, Lutherans, Congregationalists, Brethren, Baptists, Dutch Reformed, and United Evangelicals.[101] The evening school of Moody Bible Institute in 1920 enrolled men from 157 Chicago churches of fourteen denominations and women from 134 Chicago churches of twenty-four denominations.[102]

This denominational breadth is further illustrated by a biographical analysis of forty prominent fundamentalist leaders, who represented fourteen church bodies in comparison to seven for the same number of prominent modernists (see Table 2).[103] Over half of them, however, were either

---

[100]R[euben] A. Torrey, The Fundamental Doctrines of the Christian Faith (New York: George H. Doran Company, 1918), p. v.

[101]Frank J. Boyer, "Our Church Connections," The Bible Champion, XXIX (August-September, 1923), 403.

[102]William L. Pettingill, "Bible Schools Crowded," Serving and Waiting, X (November, 1920), 403-4.

[103]See Appendixes A and B for biographical sketches. While the choice of subjects for such a study must be somewhat subjective, I have tried to include the most widely recognized ecclesiastical and educational leaders on both

TABLE 2

CHURCH AFFILIATIONS OF 40 PROMINENT FUNDAMENTALISTS AND 40 PROMINENT MODERNISTS COMPARED

Church Body	Fundamentalists		Modernists	
	No.	%	No.	%
Baptist (Northern)	10	25.0	10	25.0
Baptist (Southern)	1	2.5		
Baptist (Canadian)	1	2.5		
Church of England	1	2.5	1	2.5
Congregational	3	7.5	7	17.5
Disciples of Christ			2	5.0
Lutheran (United)	1	2.5		
Mennonite	1	2.5		
Methodist Episcopal (North)	2	5.0	4	10.0
Methodist Episcopal (South)	1	2.5		
Mission Covenant	1	2.5		
Presbyterian (United)	1	2.5		
Presbyterian (U.S.A.)	12	30.0	8	20.0
Protestant Episcopal			4	10.0
Reformed Episcopal	1	2.5		
Seventh-Day Adventist	1	2.5		
Independent or Interdenominational	3	7.5	1	2.5
Unknown			3	7.5

Northern Baptists or Northern Presbyterians, as were also forty-five percent of their modernist opponents, a concentration indicating the two denominations in which the hottest battles were fought. The relative lack of fundamen-

---

sides. There may be some question as to whether all the modernists fit the precise definition of that term offered earlier in this study. But inasmuch as the meanings of "liberal" and "modernist" tended to blur in the twenties, I have included men who either identified themselves as modernists or opposed fundamentalist theology from a pronounced liberal viewpoint.

talist leadership among Congregationalists and Methodists, on the other hand, and the total absence of it from the Protestant Episcopal Church and the Disciples of Christ reflect the absence of serious fundamentalist challenges in those bodies.

While fundamentalist leadership thus represented many Protestant groups, especially those of non-liturgical and evangelical traditions, this representation was unevenly distributed. Apparently those bodies whose forms of polity had permitted the growth of modernist influence in their organization also offered substantial hope for fundamentalists to restore conservative control. This was especially true among Baptists and Presbyterians because the dual heritage of Calvinism and millenarianism among them had laid a foundation for orthodoxy that was not easily dislodged.

Fundamentalism's geographical scope has been frequently discussed but often imperfectly understood. Even during the twenties its critics made conflicting analyses. The persistent rural-Southern-Midwestern image most likely originated with the anti-evolution crusade. Commenting on the Scopes trial, Dean William Inge of St. Paul's Cathedral in London asserted that fundamentalists were chiefly farmers of old English stock.[104] Another British observer reported that the "attack on science" came from Southern

---

[104]Quoted in "A Dean's Fund of Misinformation," The Bible Champion, XXIV (February, 1928), 73-74.

Baptists and Methodists and rural Presbyterians and Lutherans in the West.[105] John Dewey in 1922 and H. Richard Niebuhr in 1931 both offered similar interpretations.[106]

Yet other observers found that fundamentalism was more than opposition to evolution. The Nation, for example, reported that the 1923 Presbyterian General Assembly, while rejecting William Jennings Bryan as moderator, nevertheless reaffirmed all the orthodox doctrines at the insistence of an Eastern group, the Philadelphia Presbytery.[107] Indeed, even the war on evolution was found to be more widespread than some had supposed. One writer concluded that anti-evolution sentiment was "the normal American condition," even in such "formerly progressive regions" as Oregon, Minnesota, and California.[108] Another declared that ninety percent of the population was fundamentalist on the evolution issue, either actively or by its silence.[109]

---

[105]Quoted in "Notes and Comments," ibid., XXXV (February, 1929), 66.

[106]John Dewey, "The American Intellectual Frontier," The New Republic, XXX (May 10, 1922), 303-5; H. Richard Niebuhr, "Fundamentalism," Encyclopaedia of the Social Sciences (15 vols.; New York: Macmillan Company, 1931), VI 526-27.

[107]"The Orthodoxy of Democracy," The Nation, CXVI (June 6, 1923), 645.

[108]Miriam Allen De Ford, "The War Against Evolution," ibid., CXX (May 20, 1925), 565.

[109]Albert C. Dieffenbach, as quoted in "Organized Religious Groups Form Political Bloc in Country, Is Charge of Publicist," The Christian Fundamentalist, I (November,

Even allowing for some exaggeration here, one finds many lines of evidence that fundamentalism in the twenties was, indeed, a nationwide phenomenon, and that it even exerted an international influence in other English-speaking countries. Its greatest strength lay neither in the South nor in the Midwest, broadly defined, but in the Middle Atlantic and East North Central states, with considerable influence along the Pacific coast as well. A large percentage of its leaders lived not in rural areas but in the nation's largest metropolitan centers.

A comparison of the birthplaces of fundamentalist and modernist leaders (see Table 3 and Figure 1) reveals that the fundamentalists came from a broader geographical area (18 states, 3 foreign countries) than the modernists (11 states, 3 foreign countries). But half of them were born in the Middle Atlantic and East North Central states, and the percentage of those born in the Southern regions was no more than that of those born abroad. The western two-thirds of the country contributed only ten percent to this group.

The birthplaces of prominent modernists were even more restricted, for three-fourths of them were born in the New England, Middle Atlantic, and East North Central states. New York, Massachusetts, and Ohio accounted for

---

1927), 6.

more than half of them. While a few came from the mid-western regions, none were born in the Southeast or the West. So the ecclesiastical protagonists on both sides were largely Easterners, and although the fundamentalists represented a broader area, even a majority of them were born in the Northeast.

TABLE 3

BIRTHPLACES OF 40 PROMINENT FUNDAMENTALISTS AND 40 PROMINENT MODERNISTS COMPARED

State or Country	Fundamentalists		Modernists	
	No.	%	No.	%
Alabama	1	2.5		
California	1	2.5		
Colorado	1	2.5		
Connecticut	1	2.5		
Georgia	2	5.0		
Illinois	1	2.5		
Indiana	4	10.0		
Iowa			1	2.5
Kansas	1	2.5		
Maine	1	2.5	2	5.0
Maryland	1	2.5		
Massachusetts			7	17.5
Minnesota	1	2.5	1	2.5
Missouri			1	2.5
New Jersey	2	5.0	1	2.5
New York	2	5.0	9	22.5
North Carolina	1	2.5		
Ohio	5	12.5	6	15.0
Pennsylvania	5	12.5	4	10.0
Texas			1	2.5
Virginia	2	5.0		
Wisconsin	1	2.5	1	2.5
Canada	2	5.0	2	5.0
England	3	7.5	3	7.5
Germany	2	5.0		
Scotland			1	2.5

BIRTHPLACES OF 40 PROMINENT FUNDAMENTALISTS
AND 40 PROMINENT MODERNISTS COMPARED
BY REGION°

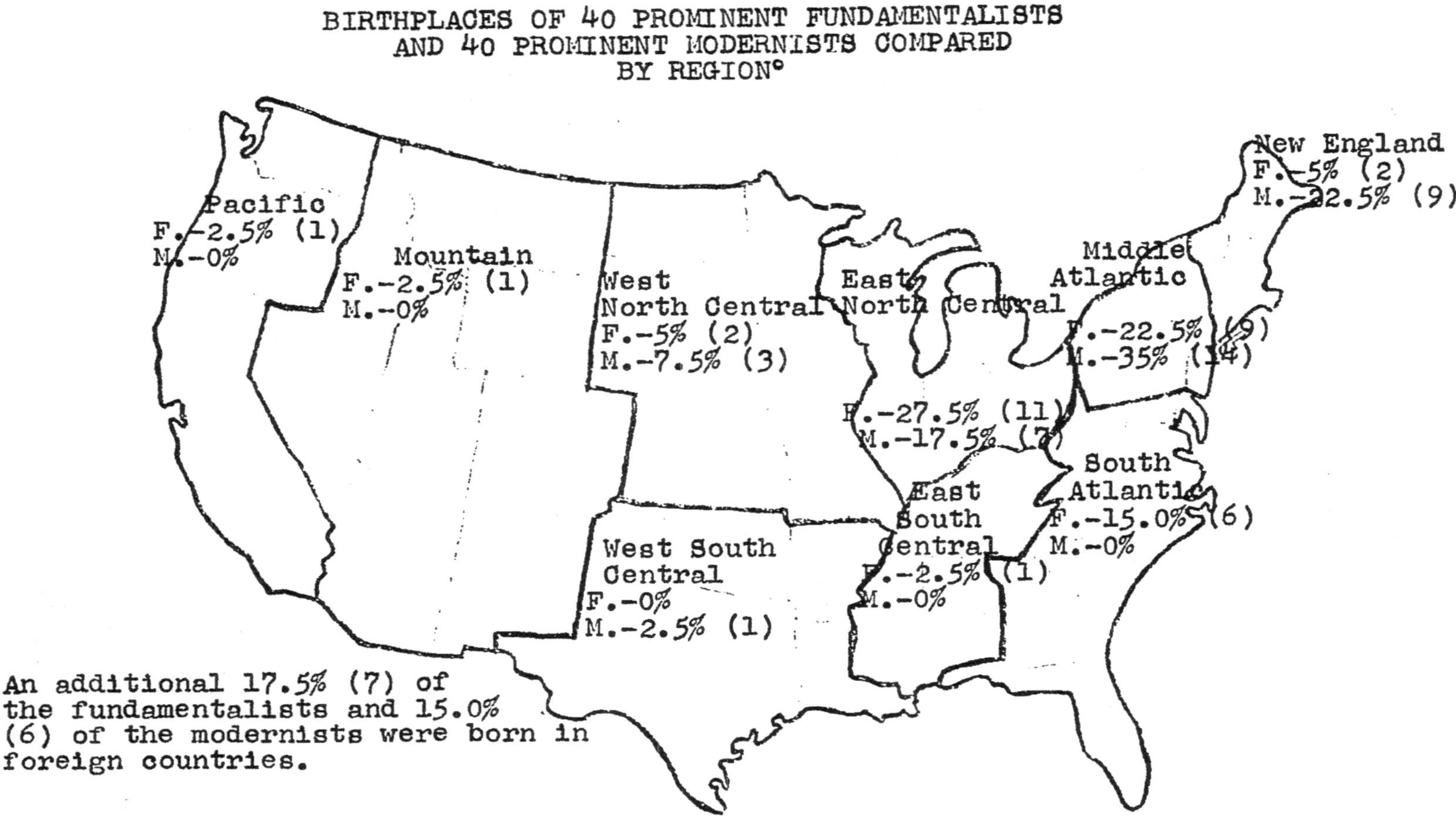

° An additional 17.5% (7) of the fundamentalists and 15.0% (6) of the modernists were born in foreign countries.

FIGURE 1

This concentration becomes even more evident when one compares the places of residence of the same fundamentalist and modernist leaders in 1920 (see Table 4 and Figure 2).

TABLE 4

1920 PLACES OF RESIDENCE OF 40 PROMINENT FUNDAMENTALISTS AND 40 PROMINENT MODERNISTS COMPARED

State or Country	Fundamentalists		Modernists	
	No.	%	No.	%
California	3	7.5	1	2.5
Connecticut			3	7.5
Illinois	2	5.0	8	20.0
Indiana	1	2.5		
Maryland	1	2.5		
Massachusetts	2	5.0	5	12.5
Michigan			1	2.5
Minnesota	1	2.5		
New Jersey	3	7.5		
New York	9	22.5	18	45.0
Ohio	2	5.0		
Pennsylvania	7	17.5	2	5.0
Rhode Island			1	2.5
Texas	1	2.5		
Vermont			1	2.5
Washington	2	5.0		
Canada	2	5.0		
Itinerant Ministry	4	10.0		

By that time the forty selected fundamentalists were working chiefly in twelve states, although a few were in Canada or engaged in itinerant ministry. The percentage of those in the Northeast sections now reached sixty-five percent, and the only other concentration of leadership was in the Far West. A majority lived in the metropolitan areas of

1920 PLACES OF RESIDENCE OF 40 PROMINENT FUNDAMENTALISTS AND 40 PROMINENT MODERNISTS COMPARED BY REGION°

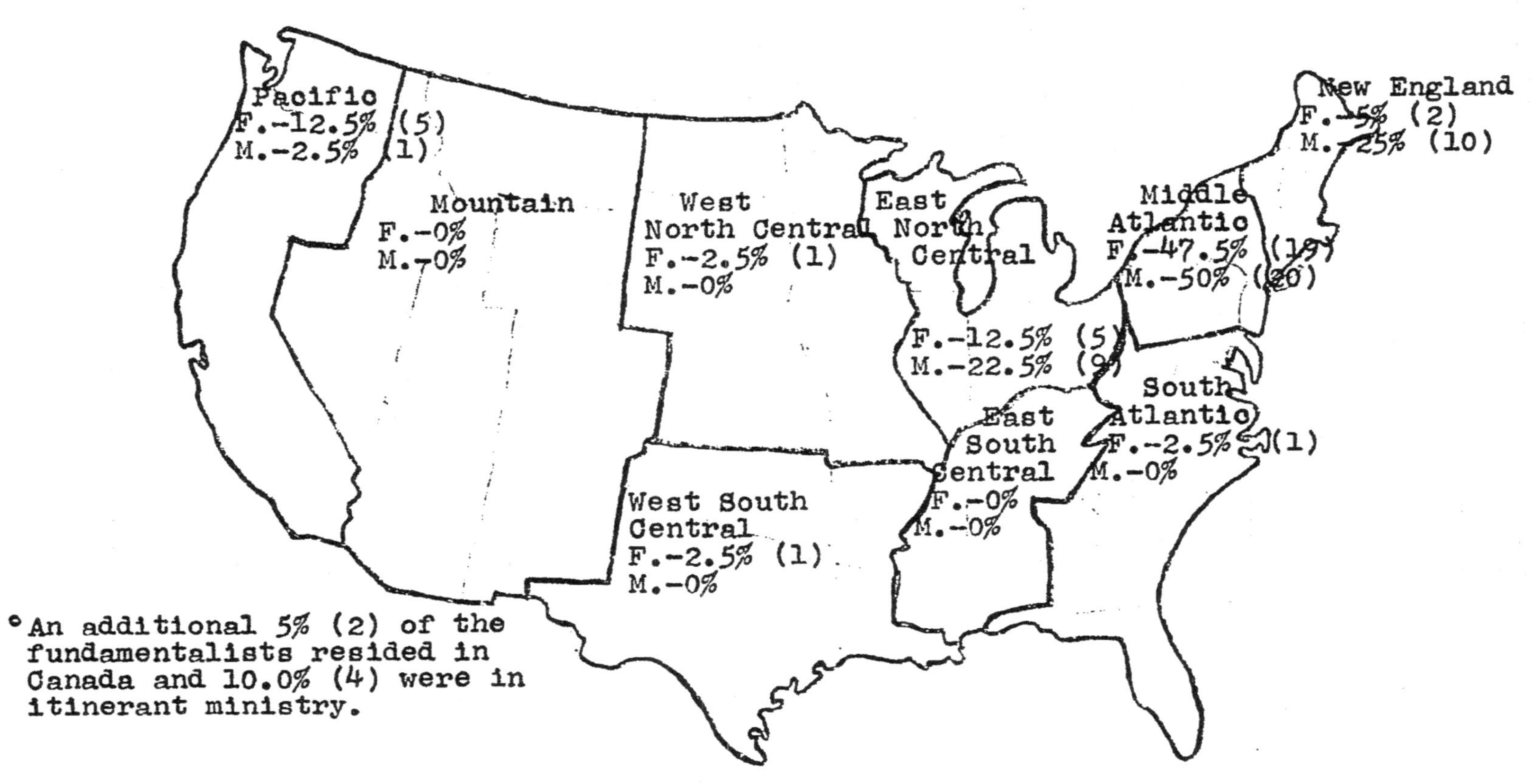

° An additional 5% (2) of the fundamentalists resided in Canada and 10.0% (4) were in itinerant ministry.

FIGURE 2

New York, Philadelphia, Boston, Chicago, and Los Angeles.[110]

At the same time the concentration of selected modernists in the Northeast had become almost total, for eight of the nine states in which they lived were in the New England, Middle Atlantic, and East North Central regions. More than three-fourths of them now resided in the New York, Philadelphia, Boston, Chicago, and Los Angeles areas, where many were professors in universities and divinity schools.[111]

In both birthplace and 1920 residence the fundamentalist leaders represented a broader geographical area than their modernist counterparts. Nevertheless, their heaviest concentration in both cases was in the North, east of the Mississippi, the same area in which modernism displayed its greatest strength.

Fundamentalism's geographical sphere of influence can also be ascertained statistically by determining the residences of the students who attended its schools. Only fragmentary student information is available from Moody Bible Institute, the largest and best known Bible insti-

---

[110]Nine (22.5%) lived in New York, six (15.0%) in Philadelphia, and two (5.0%) each in Boston, Chicago, and Los Angeles--a total of 52.5 percent.

[111]Seventeen (42.5%) lived in New York, seven (17.5%) in Chicago, five (12.5%) in Boston, and one (2.5%) each in Philadelphia and Los Angeles.

tute. A report in the fall of 1920 stated that its 835 day students represented nearly all the states and more than twenty foreign countries.[112] Which states were most heavily represented is uncertain, but scattered graduate lists of the early twenties reveal that they were almost certainly not Southern states.[113]

We can be more specific about students enrolling in the Evangelical Theological College of Dallas, Texas (since 1936 known as Dallas Theological Seminary). This interdenominational divinity school, founded in 1924 by Lewis Sperry Chafer and other premillennial fundamentalists of Presbyterian background, is of particular geographical interest because of its Southern location. One might expect to find many Southern students enrolled there.

But an analysis of its first eight entering classes reveals that from the beginning this seminary's influence crossed local and regional lines. The 118 students in these early classes came from twenty-five states and seven foreign countries (see Table 5 and Figure 3).[114] While

---

[112]Pettingill, "Bible Schools Crowded," pp. 403-4.

[113]Research by Moody Librarian Richard Schock shows that in six of nine classes graduated from Moody between August, 1920 and April, 1923 only 7.8 percent of the 370 graduates came from Southern states, while 11.4 percent came from foreign countries. The other three graduate lists were not available. Percentages computed from data in letter, Richard Schock to Robert E. Wenger, March 29, 1972.

[114]Statistics compiled from student lists in <u>Evangel-</u>

TABLE 5

HOME STATES OF ENTERING STUDENTS AT THE EVANGELICAL THEOLOGICAL COLLEGE, 1924–1931

State or Country	'24	'25	'26	'27	'28	'29	'30	'31	Total	%
Penn.	2	2	2		3	1	2	2	14	11.9
Ill.			1			4	4	3	12	10.2
Cal.	1	2	2	2		2		1	10	8.5
Tex.	2	1	1	2	1		2	1	10	8.5
Ohio		1	1		2		1	2	7	5.9
N.J.				2	2	1	1		6	5.1
Wash.	2		1			1		2	6	5.1
Iowa				1			1	1	3	2.5
Mich.	1					1		1	3	2.5
Mo.			2					1	3	2.5
Nebr.			1					2	3	2.5
N.Y.				1		1	1		3	2.5
Tenn.					2		1		3	2.5
Wis.								3	3	2.5
Ala.			1		1				2	1.7
N. Mex.					1	1			2	1.7
Okla.		1					1		2	1.7
Va.				1			1		2	1.7
Fla.						1			1	.8
Idaho						1			1	.8
Ind.		1							1	.8
Kan.								1	1	.8
Miss.							1		1	.8
N.C.		1							1	.8
Ore.					1				1	.8
Can.	1	1		3	2		2		9	7.6
N.Ire.				1	1				2	1.7
Scot.							1	1	2	1.7
Bulg.						1			1	.8
Eng.							1		1	.8
Holland								1	1	.8
Austral.							1		1	.8
Total	9	10	12	13	16	15	21	22	118	

ENTERING STUDENTS AT THE EVANGELICAL THEOLOGICAL COLLEGE, 1924-1931 BY REGION°

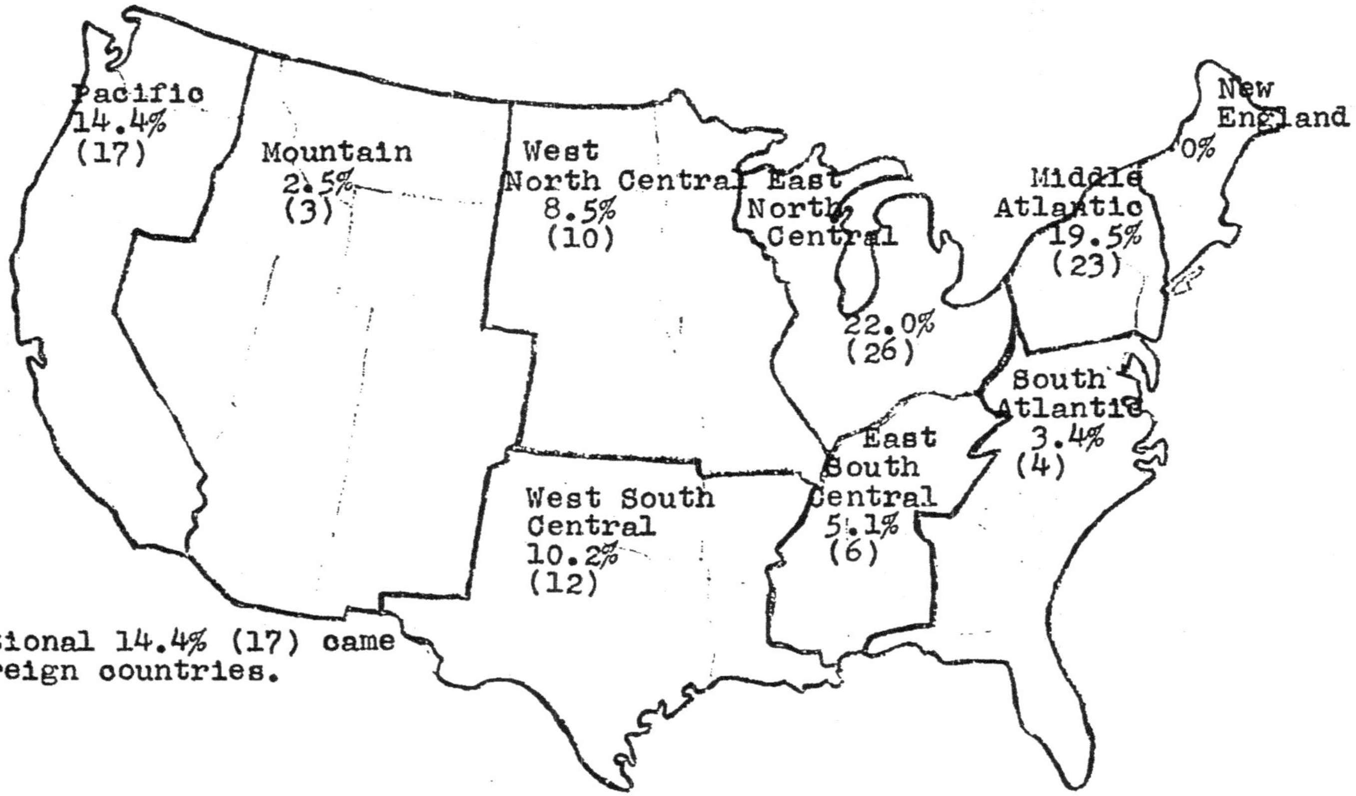

° An additional 14.4% (17) came from foreign countries.

FIGURE 3

New Englanders were conspicuously absent, the East North Central and Middle Atlantic regions together contributed over forty percent of the students and the Pacific states were also strongly represented. Among the rest of the states only Texas contributed a considerable number of students, and the South outside Texas was rather poorly represented.

Hints of the same broad participation combined with a Northeastern dominance are found in two early Bible conferences, although specific information in these is limited. The Philadelphia Prophetic Conference of 1918, a precursor to later fundamentalist gatherings, drew an estimated ten thousand persons from thirty-six states and six foreign countries.[115] The Conference on Christian Fundamentals, held the following year in the same city, registered fewer delegates (6,000) but a slightly broader geographical representation of forty-two states and seven foreign countries.[116] Charles G. Trumbull's chance remark, however, that at least one thousand came from "beyond the bounds of Pennsylvania" would indicate that the great majority were

---

ical Theological College Bulletin, 1926-1931.

[115] William L. Pettingill, "The Philadelphia Prophetic Conference," Serving and Waiting, VIII (July, 1918), 86-87.

[116] World Conference on Christian Fundamentals, God Hath Spoken (Philadelphia: Bible Conference Committee, 1919), p. 8.

from Pennsylvania itself.[117]

Pennsylvania also ranked first among states contributing subscribers to The Bible Champion in 1923. The published list of twenty-six states in order of their number of subscribers, while incomplete, is still instructive. It includes one of six New England states, all three Middle Atlantic states, five of eight South Atlantic states, all five East North Central states, two of four East South Central states, six of seven West North Central states, one of four West South Central states, one of eight Mountain states, and two of three Pacific states. But the order of their inclusion is also significant, for the first seven--Pennsylvania, New York, California, Ohio, Illinois, Massachusetts, and New Jersey--are all (with the possible exception of Massachusetts) in regions previously shown to have strong fundamentalist leadership.[118]

Lay geographical representation can also be measured by the number of financial contributions made to fundamentalist enterprises by residents of various states. Although such information is rarely accessible, one Bible study magazine, The Wonderful Word, listed the initials and addresses of donors to its missions projects from 1919

---

[117] [Charles G. Trumbull], "A World Conference Affirming the Faith," The Sunday School Times, LXI (June 14, 1919), 325-26, 339.

[118] The Bible Champion, XXIX (May, 1923), 249.

through 1926, making it possible to calculate the number and percentage of donations from each state. I have therefore analyzed one general missionary fund which received 291 donations during this time (see Table 6 and Figure 4). These gifts originated in thirty-one states and four foreign countries, indicating a rather broad base of support. But again the greatest percentage came from persons living in the Middle Atlantic, East North Central, and Pacific regions.

It remains to be determined how this geographical distribution of fundamentalism compared with the national distribution patterns of total population and church membership. Some indication can be obtained by comparing the rank of the ten most populous states (both in total population and church membership) with their rank in _The Bible Champion's_ list of states supplying subscribers (see Table 7). It will be observed that the standing of most of these states in the subscribers they contributed corresponded closely to their ranks in the other two categories, indicating that fundamentalism's distribution largely followed the national pattern. California, however, contributed a disproportionately high number of subscribers, while Michigan and Texas contributed fewer than might be expected of them with their total and religious populations.

A broader, and perhaps more accurate, comparison can be obtained by comparing the regional distribution of

TABLE 6

ORIGINS OF 291 DONATIONS TO THE WONDERFUL WORD GENERAL MISSIONARY FUND, 1919-1926

State or Country	No. of Gifts	% of Total
Pennsylvania	45	15.5
California	41	14.1
New York	38	13.1
Illinois	32	11.0
Minnesota	24	8.2
Indiana	11	3.8
Michigan	10	3.4
Ohio	9	3.1
Missouri	8	2.7
New Jersey	8	2.7
Washington	6	2.1
Colorado	5	1.7
Massachusetts	5	1.7
Texas	5	1.7
Iowa	3	1.0
Kansas	3	1.0
Florida	2	.7
Kentucky	2	.7
Maryland	2	.7
Montana	2	.7
North Carolina	2	.7
Arizona	1	.3
Arkansas	1	.3
Connecticut	1	.3
District of Columbia	1	.3
New Hampshire	1	.3
North Dakota	1	.3
Oklahoma	1	.3
Oregon	1	.3
South Carolina	1	.3
Wisconsin	1	.3
Canada	14	4.8
England	2	.7
China	1	.3
Ireland	1	.3

ORIGINS OF 291 DONATIONS TO THE WONDERFUL WORD GENERAL MISSIONARY FUND, 1919-1926 BY REGION°

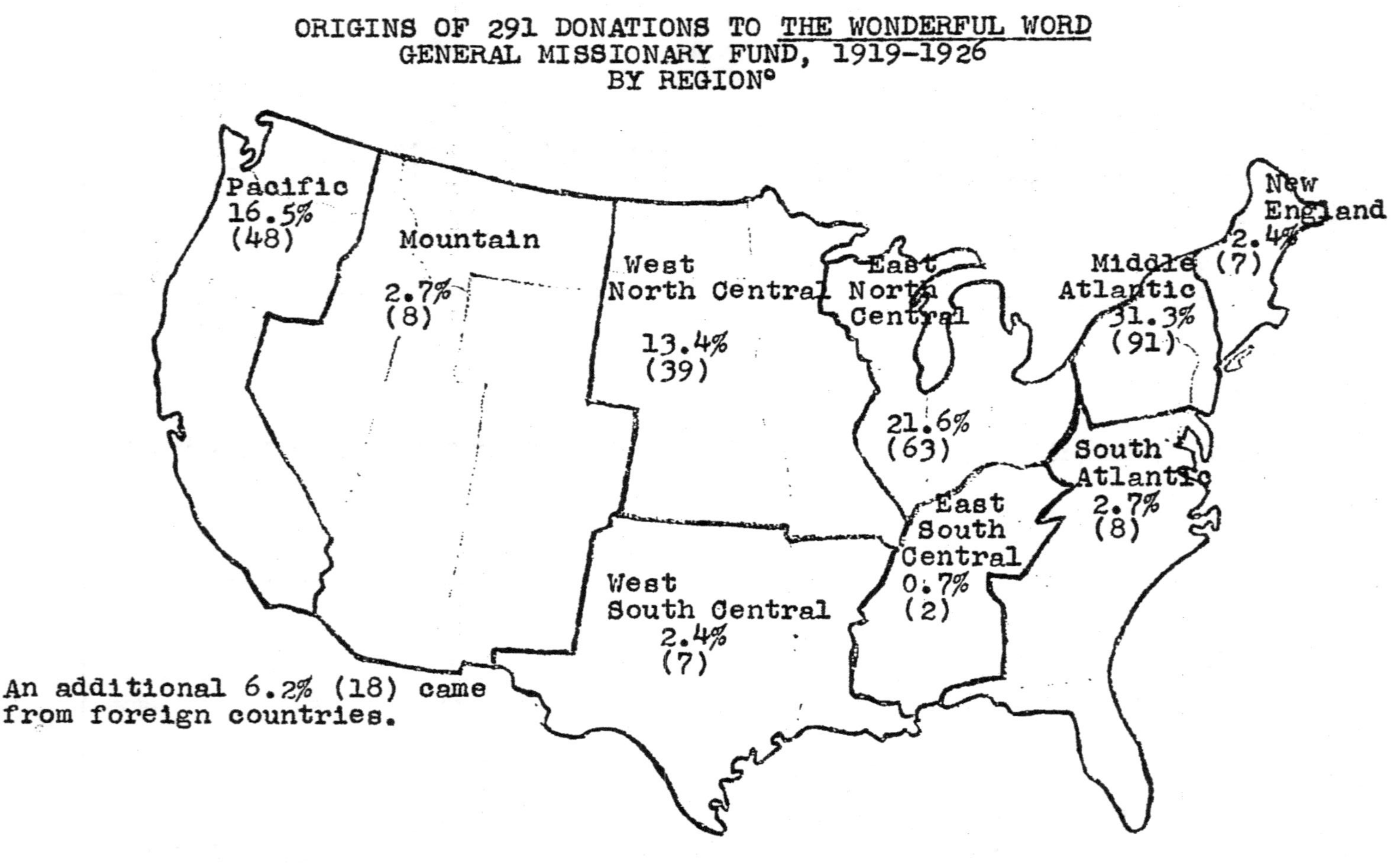

°An additional 6.2% (18) came from foreign countries.

FIGURE 4

American population and church membership with the regional statistics of fundamentalism previously cited in this study (see Table 8). Although some of the percentages vary widely between fundamentalist clergy and laity, a general pattern nevertheless emerges. Fundamentalism was weaker than might be expected in New England and the South, corresponded roughly to national distribution trends in the Middle Atlantic, East North Central, West North Central, and Mountain regions, and drew a disproportionate share of support from the Far West.

TABLE 7

RANK OF 10 STATES OF HIGHEST POPULATION AND CHURCH MEMBERSHIP COMPARED WITH THEIR RANK IN NUMBER OF SUBSCRIBERS TO THE BIBLE CHAMPION

State	Rank in Population, 1920[a]	Rank in Church Membership, 1926[a]	Rank in No. of Subscribers to Bible Champion, 1923
New York	1	1	2
Pennsylvania	2	2	1
Illinois	3	3	5
Ohio	4	4	4
Texas	5	6	23
Michigan	6	8	15
California	7	10	3
Massachusetts	8	5	6
New Jersey	9	7	7
Missouri	10	9	11

[a]Source: U.S. Department of Commerce, Bureau of the Census, Religious Bodies: 1926 (Washington: U.S. Government Printing Office), Vol. I, Summary and Detailed Tables, p. 32.

TABLE 8

DISTRIBUTION OF FUNDAMENTALISTS COMPARED WITH DISTRIBUTION OF AMERICAN POPULATION AND CHURCH MEMBERSHIP

Region	% of U.S. Population, 1920[a]	% of U.S. Church Members, 1926[b]	% of 40 Prominent Fundamentalists, 1920	% of Entering Students at Evangelical Theol. Coll., 1924–1931	% of Donations to *Wonderful Word* Gen. Miss. Fund, 1919–1926
New England	7.0	8.4	5.0	0.0	2.4
Middle Atlantic	21.1	25.6	47.5	19.5	31.3
East North Central	20.3	19.9	12.5	22.0	21.6
West North Central	11.9	10.7	2.5	8.5	13.4
South Atlantic	13.2	12.8	2.5	3.4	2.7
East South Central	8.4	7.9	0.0	5.1	0.7
West South Central	9.7	8.3	2.5	10.2	2.4
Mountain	3.2	2.7	0.0	2.5	2.7
Pacific	5.3	3.9	12.5	14.4	16.5
Itinerant			10.0		
Outside U.S.			5.0	14.4	6.2

[a]Calculated from: U.S. Department of Commerce, Bureau of the Census, *Population: 1920* (Washington: U.S. Government Printing Office), Vol. II, *General Report and Analytical Tables*, p. 31.

[b]Calculated from: U.S. Department of Commerce, Bureau of the Census, *Religious Bodies: 1926* (Washington: U.S. Government Printing Office), Vol. I, *Summary and Detailed Tables*, p. 136.

From the foregoing evidence several facts about the geography of fundamentalism emerge. First, the geographical patterns were similar for both leadership and laity, although lay participation was understandably more broadly based. Secondly, fundamentalism drew support and exerted influence in all sections of the United States and in several foreign countries. Thirdly, its greatest numerical strength lay east of the Mississippi River and north of the Mason-Dixon line, especially in the Middle Atlantic and East North Central regions. This is understandable because this area contained a high percentage of the nation's population and church membership and because modernism posed a strong threat there. Pennsylvania was, from many indications, a particularly influential center of fundamentalism. Fourthly, another sphere of strength lay in the Pacific region, especially California, proportionately more influential than anywhere else in the country. Fifthly, while the West North Central area displayed some fundamentalist strength, the Southern and Mountain states were among the weakest supporters of the movement. Sparse population accounts for this weakness in the Mountain region, while in the South it was due to the lack of a liberal challenge to theological orthodoxy. Perhaps fundamentalism's relative weakness in New England, on the other hand, was caused by the widespread dominance of modernism there. Finally, although the rural-urban distribution of fundamentalists cannot be accurately determined, enough evidence is available to challenge their characterization as "direct heirs" of the Populists. At best such a thesis is a gross oversimplification.[119]

Fundamentalism's character as a militant theological protest movement can account for its denominational and geographical scope. It flourished where (1) a theology with a strong biblical emphasis recently existed, where (2) that theology was now being seriously threatened, and where (3) considerable hope for its restoration still remained. Modernism was to some degree affecting all of American Protestantism, so fundamentalism appeared in most major Protestant denominations. But because modernism was making its strongest bids for power in the Presbyterian Church in the U.S.A. and the Northern Baptist Convention in the postwar years, fundamentalism appeared in its most vigorous form in those bodies. It had a fair chance of success there because they formerly held a strong emphasis on biblical doctrine. Geographically, fundamentalism became a nation-wide phenomenon because modernism potentially affected the whole country. But because modernism had become entrenched in the churches, divinity schools, and universities in the urban centers of the Northeast and Far

---

[119] Harrington, "Fundamentalist Movement in America," pp. 169-70. See Paul Carter's critique of this theory in "Fundamentalist Defense," pp. 202-6.

West, fundamentalism displayed its greatest strength in roughly the same areas.

New England Congregationalism, from which a number of prominent modernists sprang, was fairly immune to fundamentalism because an earlier liberalizing trend had by this time taken it out of the conservative camp. On the other hand, the conservative Presbyterians, Baptists and Disciples of the South were weak in fundamentalism because they had as yet experienced no serious modernist challenge. Conservative theology could exist by itself, but fundamentalism could survive only in the presence of an opponent, for fundamentalism was the offspring of conflict.

CHAPTER III

"THE FAITH" AND THE INTELLECT

Many scholars believe fundamentalism and scholarship should not be mentioned in the same context except as opposites. Sydney Ahlstrom, for example, limits the movement strictly to

> . . . those large areas of America's church-membership which . . . became almost totally estranged from the on-going intellectual enterprise of the Atlantic community during the nineteenth century. (Without this estrangement and ignorance and its attendant hostility, there is no "Fundamentalism" by my definition of the word.)[1]

Ahlstrom excludes from fundamentalism anyone who "speaks to the issues, is well-informed, and is in communication with those from whom he dissents."[2] Furniss also speaks of a "complete misunderstanding" of evolution and modernism by "innumerable fundamentalist leaders," based on "prejudice and ignorance."[3]

The label of ignorance was stamped upon fundamental-

---

[1]Sydney E. Ahlstrom, "Continental Influence on American Christian Thought Since World War I," Church History, XXVII (September, 1958), 257.

[2]*Ibid.*, p. 271, note 3.

[3]Norman F. Furniss, The Fundamentalist Controversy, 1918-1931 (New Haven: Yale University Press, 1954), pp. 19-20.

ists by their contemporaries, to whom it seemed incredible that anyone should any longer oppose the evolutionary hypothesis or the "assured results" of biblical criticism. Machen was essentially correct when he predicted that reopening the question of the validity of orthodoxy would lead liberals to say, "The phenomenon is interesting as a curious example of arrested development, but it is nothing more,"[4] for scientists, liberal churchmen, and eventually most of the academic community came to share this opinion. T. V. Smith attributed William Jennings Bryan's "aversion to change" to his "reluctance to endure the pain of thinking,"[5] while Howard Chandler Robbins accused fundamentalists of "profound and perfect obscurantism."[6] Four of seven prize-winning definitions of a "fundamentalist" in the December, 1926 issue of The Forum displayed contempt for the movement's intellectual stature.[7] By 1928 Melvin Grove Kyle observed with distress that fundamentalists were being contrasted with the "intelligent class."[8] Contempo-

---

[4] J. Gresham Machen, Christianity and Liberalism (Grand Rapids, Mich.: Wm. B. Eerdmans Publishing Company, 1946), p. 9.

[5] T. V. Smith, "Bases of Bryanism," The Scientific Monthly, XVI (May, 1923), 509.

[6] Howard Chandler Robbins, "'Fundamentalism' and 'Modernism,'" The Forum, LXXI (June, 1924), 652-53.

[7] "What Is a Fundamentalist?" ibid., LXXVI (December, 1926), 861-63.

[8] [Melvin Grove Kyle], Editorial, Bibliotheca Sacra,

rary and later critics did, to be sure, pay passing tribute to such a scholar as J. Gresham Machen, but only as an exception to the general rule.[9] They assumed the norm to be located closer to the Georgia assemblyman who declared:

> Read the Bible. It teaches you how to act. Read the hymnbook. It contains the finest poetry ever written. Read the almanac. It shows you how to figure out what the weather will be. There isn't another book that is necessary for anyone to read, and therefore I am opposed to all libraries.[10]

Machen was, indeed, exceptional, and the one looking for his antithesis within fundamentalism can find many examples. One could cite the Oregon evangelist with a Ph.D. after his name who wrote to J. Frank Norris, "I was so glad to meete you once agen . . . ,"[11] or the Canadian engineer who wrote articles to refute not Darwin and evolution but Copernicous and the sphericity of the earth.[12] One could point out the following unscholarly tactics of Reuben A. Torrey as he attempted to discredit contemporary

---

LXXXV (April, 1928), 127.

[9]See Walter Lippmann's tribute to Machen as "a scholar and a gentleman" in _A Preface to Morals_ (New York: Macmillan Company, 1929), pp. 32-33.

[10]Quoted by Richard Hofstadter in _Anti-Intellectualism in American Life_ (New York: Alfred A. Knopf, 1963), p. 125.

[11]Letter, Elwood J. Bulgin to J. Frank Norris, April 18, 1929, Archives, Southern Baptist Convention, John Franklyn Norris Papers.

[12]Arthur V. White, "Science and Religion," _The Wonderful Word_, XX (November, 1927), 20-25.

theology:

> God says something in this Book; Prof. So and So says it is not so, and the Rev. Dr. Bighead, D.D., Ph.D., LL.D., Litt.D., F.R.G.S., A.S.S., says it cannot be so; but as God says so, you and I . . . will believe it in spite of all the A.S.S.E.S. in the world.[13]

The demagoguery of J. Frank Norris and the sensationalism of John Roach Straton are matters of record, and Darrow's humiliation of William Jennings Bryan at Dayton is well known. Moreover, the heat of battle sometimes induced otherwise intelligent men to substitute eloquence for logic, overstatement for fact, and literary quantity for quality.

Yet with these facts at hand only a fraction of the story is told, and a generalization would be premature. A final judgment on fundamentalist scholarship must keep in view several additional facts. First, as a protest movement fundamentalism attracted persons of varying intellectual abilities from diverse educational backgrounds and addressed itself to the average church member, which helps to account for its ambiguous intellectual legacy. Secondly, fundamentalists held theologically-based assumptions about reason and science which went far toward explaining their opposition to certain features of modern learning. Thirdly, fundamentalists, granted their assumptions, held a more logical system of thought than their opponents and

---

[13] R. A. Torrey, The Importance and Value of Proper Bible Study (New York: Fleming H. Revell Company, 1921), p. 45.

were quick to exploit modernist inconsistencies. It is to these matters that attention must now be given if we would understand fundamentalism's relationship to modern scholarship.

The measurement of intellectual stature and scholarship is ideally based on several criteria, including educational experience, breadth of knowledge, original and critical thinking, logical consistency, comprehension of alternate views, and fairness of presentation. Taken alone, education is an inadequate yardstick because it excludes well-informed but self-taught thinkers and may include those who have long abandoned the rigorous canons of scholarship. Nevertheless, it is an appropriate starting point for considering fundamentalists' intellectual qualifications.

Comparing the education of forty prominent fundamentalists with that of forty prominent modernists (see Table 9), one finds that the modernists held a clear-cut advantage. Practically all the modernists (97.5%) had undertaken some graduate study, and twelve (30.0%) had earned doctor's degrees. They had attended forty-six graduate schools and seminaries, including some of the most prestigious of their day, fifteen of which were in Europe (see Appendix D). Union Theological Seminary of New York and the University of Berlin apparently exerted a strong educational influence over this group, since at least one-fourth of them attended each of these schools. The high level of the modernists' education is reflected in their occupations (see Table 10), for over half of them held full-time teaching positions in seminaries and universities, while a number of others taught part-time or spent a part of their careers as professors.[14]

TABLE 9

EDUCATIONAL EXPERIENCE OF 40 PROMINENT FUNDAMENTALISTS AND 40 PROMINENT MODERNISTS COMPARED

Amount of Education	Fundamentalists		Modernists	
	No.	%	No.	%
Earned doctor's degree	5	12.5	12	30.0
Master's degree and seminary graduation	9	22.5	13	32.5
Master's degree	2	5.0	3	7.5
Seminary graduation	6	15.0	8	20.0
Some seminary or graduate work	6	15.0	3	7.5
Bachelor's degree	2	5.0		
Some undergraduate work	5	12.5	1	2.5
No college education	3	7.5		
Not known	2	5.0		

Fundamentalist leadership represented a broader educational spectrum. It included well-educated men, to be sure, for seventy percent of those selected had received graduate training in thirty-one institutions, including six

[14]This confirms Winthrop Hudson's contention that modernism was "the product of the academic concerns of professors in colleges and theological seminaries." American Protestantism (Chicago: University of Chicago Press, 1961), pp. 143-44.

TABLE 10

OCCUPATIONS OF 40 PROMINENT FUNDAMENTALISTS AND 40 PROMINENT MODERNISTS COMPARED

Occupation	Fundamentalists		Modernists	
	No.	%	No.	%
Pastor	18	45.0	17	42.5
Educator	11	27.5	22	55.0
Editor	5	12.5	1	2.5
Evangelist or Bible Lecturer	6	15.0		

European universities (see Appendix C). Five (12.5%) held earned doctor's degrees. But there were those with less education, and at least three (7.5%) had not been to college at all. Fundamentalist occupations (Table 10) also reflect an evangelistic rather than a critical approach to religion. While modernist and fundamentalist pastors were almost identical in number, only half as many fundamentalists were full-time educators, and the rest were engaged in evangelism, popular lectures, and editorial work. This should not be interpreted as a neglect of education, for a number of men not listed as educators devoted considerable time to teaching also.[15] But it does confirm a point yet

[15] The occupational classification of fundamentalists is difficult because they engaged in many activities simultaneously. I have attempted in Table 10 to classify them by their _primary_ occupations. But in addition to the eleven listed as educators, nine others taught part-time. Of these twenty, eight worked in seminaries, six in Bible institutes, three in colleges, and three in both seminaries and Bible institutes.

to be developed, that to fundamentalists the cultivation of the mind must always be accompanied by a growth in faith and godliness. It also suggests that their appeal was more often directed toward the pew than toward the classroom.

With its variety in personnel, its appeal to the average church member, and its opposition to the current trend in theological scholarship, fundamentalism was bound to have its intellectual stature questioned. When this occurred, fundamentalists would sometimes borrow the prestige of outstanding conservative scholars, some of whom were not fundamentalists. Challenging the claim that scholarship was all on the side of the Bible's critics, one writer argued:

> When one examines the books of men like Orr, Cave, Girdlestone, Green, Wace, Wilson, Machen, Faulkner, Raven and Robertson, and notes how much acquaintance with science, philosophy, archeology, theology, etc., they display, and particularly with the books of the radical critics themselves, one is . . . puzzled to know how the liberalists can . . . claim a monopoly of . . . "scholarship" . . .[16]

Another reminded those who were leaving orthodoxy in order to avoid committing "intellectual suicide" that such biblical scholars as Orr, Denney, Seeberg, Zahn, Faulkner, and Bettex were still orthodox.[17]

---

[16] "The Question of Scholarship," The Bible Champion, XXVIII (November, 1922), 448.

[17] Harold Paul Sloan, Historic Christianity and the New Theology (Louisville, Ky.: Pentecostal Publishing Company, 1922), pp. 18-19.

But in addition fundamentalism could justly claim several outstanding scholars of it, own. Highly respected by both sides in the controversy was Princeton professor J. Gresham Machen, whose critique of modernism, Christianity and Liberalism, drew these comments from Walter Lippmann:

> It is an admirable book. For its acumen, for its saliency, and for its wit this cool and stringent defense of orthodox Protestantism is, I think, the best popular argument produced by either side . . . We shall do well to listen to Dr. Machen.[18]

The book to which Lippmann referred was only one of several closely reasoned works Machen wrote during the twenties, and in addition to his apologetical books, he produced a grammar of New Testament Greek.

Machen's zeal for scholarship was surpassed only by his zeal for the Christian faith, and he never doubted that the two could be reconciled. He criticized those who sidestepped intellectual difficulties by separating science and religion into distinct realms. He preferred, rather, to meet problems between the two head-on, keeping to "the high, rough, intellectualistic road of a sound epistemology."[19] Ironically, the same high regard for scholarship made him excessively cautious about discussing publicly the

---

[18] Lippmann, Preface to Morals, p. 32.

[19] J. Gresham Machen, "The Relation of Religion to Science and Philosophy," The Princeton Theological Review, XXIV (January, 1926), 38-66.

theory of evolution, for he refused to pose as an authority on biology or geology.[20]

Of equal brilliance was Machen's Princeton colleague, Robert Dick Wilson, whose knowledge of forty-five languages and dialects enabled him to study exhaustively the Old Testament and related Oriental literature. Wilson followed this course because he believed the controversies over the Bible must be decided not on the basis of subjective personal opinion but of objective proven fact. His research convinced him that no one knew enough to assail the truthfulness of the Old Testament.[21] He declared:

> When a man says to me, "I don't believe the Old Testament" . . . he makes no impression upon me. When he points out something there that he doesn't believe, he makes no impression on me. But if he comes to me and says, "I've got the evidence here to show that the Old Testament is wrong at this or that point"--then that's where my work begins! I'm ready for him![22]

One is also impressed with the consistent, painstaking scholarship of Melvin Grove Kyle, archeologist, professor, and president of Xenia Theological Seminary. Kyle earned international recognition for his explorations at

---

[20]Ned B. Stonehouse, J. Gresham Machen: A Biographical Memoir (Grand Rapids, Mich.: Wm. B. Eerdmans Publishing Company, 1954), pp. 401-2.

[21]Robert Dick Wilson, Is the Higher Criticism Scholarly? (Philadelphia: Sunday School Times Company, 1922), pp. 5-10.

[22]Ibid., pp. 10-11; cf. Wilson's "Scientific Biblical Criticism," The Princeton Theological Review, XVII (April, 1919), 190-240; and XVII (July, 1919), 401-56.

Sodom and Gomorrah in 1924 and at Kirjathi Sepher from 1926 to 1928, as well as for his numerous literary contributions on archeology. He served as revising editor for the conservative International Standard Bible Encyclopedia in 1929.[23]

Also worthy of mention is Harold Paul Sloan, Methodist pastor, lecturer, and writer from Haddonfield, New Jersey, whose lucid, logically-reasoned apologies and critiques of modernism were a credit to fundamentalist literature. His colleague, Lutheran professor Leander S. Keyser, displayed in his books and articles a broad acquaintance with literature on both sides of the religious controversy and always approached an opponent with moderation and respect.[24]

Indeed, as one examines much of the fundamentalists' literature, he is impressed with the relative absence of the inflammatory, emotional content he has been conditioned to expect. Not all authors stood on the level of Machen, Wilson, or Kyle, but their logically-reasoned expositions of doctrine and critiques of modernism, as well as their

---

[23]Kyle's scholarly approach is illustrated by "A New Solution of the Pentateuchal Problem," Bibliotheca Sacra, LXXV (January, 1918), 31-69; and LXXV (April, 1918), 195-212.

[24]One of Sloan's outstanding works is The Christ of the Ages (Garden City, N.Y.: Doubleday, Doran & Company, Inc., 1928). Keyser's fairness toward opponents is evident from his review of The Virgin Birth--Fact or Fiction? in The Bible Champion, XXX (October, 1924), 540.

moderately worded editorials, evidence the fact that the rational approach employed in The Fundamentals had not been abandoned in a decade of controversy.

Some works, as previously noted, did not meet these standards, and no one was more aware of that fact than the more scholarly fundamentalists themselves. "One seldom gains anything by belittling his enemies," wrote Melvin Grove Kyle as he criticized one such book.[25] Kyle also revealed that many of those who agreed with William Jennings Bryan's views on evolution were often disappointed with his method and illustrations.[26]

Critics naturally seized upon these less scholarly aspects of fundamentalism and, with Walter Lippmann, branded the movement as "bizarre," or repugnant to "the best brains and the good sense of the modern community."[27] But it is a gross exaggeration to charge fundamentalists in general with violent rhetoric because they felt "rationalism and modernism could no longer be answered in debate,"[28] for reasoned defenses of orthodoxy continued to dominate their literature throughout the period.

---

[25][Melvin Grove Kyle], Editorial, Bibliotheca Sacra, LXXXII (January, 1925), 6.

[26]Melvin Grove Kyle, "A Review of The Earth Speaks to Bryan," Bibliotheca Sacra, LXXXII (October, 1925), 516-18.

[27]Lippmann, Preface to Morals, p. 31.

[28]Hofstadter, Anti-Intellectualism, p. 123.

Neither can most fundamentalists be called "wilfully ignorant" of modern thought.[29] R. A. Torrey testified that during his student days at Yale he reveled in philosophy, especially that of Hegel, and that one of his "chief joys" through the years was to continue his studies in philosophy, science, history, literature, and languages.[30] James M. Gray advised a graduate of Moody Bible Institute contemplating pastoral work to enrich his ministry by reading current newspapers, books, and magazines. He especially recommended biography, not only of Christian ministers, but of scientists, artists, statesmen, travelers, and writers as well.[31]

Fundamentalists as diverse as J. Gresham Machen and J. Frank Norris emphasized the value of reading. Objecting to a clause in the Vestal Copyright Bill of 1926 which he felt would discourage and retard the importation of foreign books, Machen asserted that its passage would be "an unparalleled calamity to the literary and educational develop-

---

[29]Kirsopp Lake, The Religion of Yesterday and Tomorrow (London: Christophers, 1925), p. 69.

[30]R. A. Torrey, "God--His Relations to Man in Creation and in Regeneration," in God Hath Spoken (Philadelphia: Bible Conference Committee, 1919), p. 142; Bible Study, p. 25.

[31]Letter, James M. Gray to a Moody Bible Institute graduate, reproduced in William M. Runyan, Dr. Gray at Moody Bible Institute (New York: Oxford University Press, 1935), pp. 180-81.

ment of our country."[32] Norris, for his part, encouraged "the education of the masses" by urging the construction of a new library in Fort Worth.[33]

Defending his practice of requiring his students to master technical terms, Leander S. Keyser asked,

> How can you understand the learned books . . . if you are not versed in the nomenclature that scholars use? And how can you keep up with the progress of the times, if you do not read scholarly literature?[34]

And, said Keyser, this included reading modernist literature, " . . . for the only way to be solidly grounded in the true faith is to know both sides of the question."[35] Charles G. Trumbull, too, believed that reading the opposite viewpoint could not only strengthen one's convictions but provide ammunition to be used against the modernist.[36] In many cases, then, fundamentalists may have read their opponents' books only to refute them and to confirm their own beliefs. But at least they knew what they were saying.

---

[32] J. Gresham Machen, Letter in New York Herald Tribune, April 19, 1926, p. 12.

[33] Letter, J. Frank Norris to Public Works Administration, Fort Worth, Texas, November 16, 1933, Archives, Southern Baptist Convention, John Franklyn Norris Papers.

[34] Leander S. Keyser, A Reasonable Faith (New York: Fleming H. Revell Company, 1933), p. 187.

[35] Leander S. Keyser, "Reviews of Recent Books," The Bible Champion, XXX (October, 1924), 540.

[36] [Charles G. Trumbull], "Should Christians Have Modernist Books?" The Sunday School Times, LXXII (June 28, 1930), 386.

The educational and intellectual qualifications of prominent fundamentalists varied considerably, and, unfortunately for their cause, the outrages against scholarly standards were more widely publicized than the intellectual assets. A fair evaluation compels recognition that in education, in reasoned presentation of their case, and in awareness of current scholarship, a number of fundamentalist leaders stood on as high a scholarly plane as their opponents.

An accurate portrayal of fundamentalism's relationship to scholarship must also keep in view its theologically-based assumptions concerning faith and reason. The fundamentalist-modernist controversy was, to a large extent, a struggle between faith and reason, as Robert T. Handy has pointed out,[37] but it must be understood that neither side monopolized either one of these two commodities. Modernists, who venerated the scientific method, found it necessary to base many of their conclusions on faith, while fundamentalists, using faith as their starting point, called on reason to support them.[38]

Because fundamentalists refused to accept evolution

---

[37] Robert T. Handy, "Fundamentalism and Modernism in Perspective," <u>Religion in Life</u>, XXIV (Summer, 1955), 393.

[38] This combination is illustrated in the titles of two previously-quoted works, Shailer Mathews' <u>The Faith of Modernism</u> (modernist) and Leander S. Keyser's <u>A Reasonable Faith</u> (fundamentalist).

or the higher critical views they were often accused of rejecting reason entirely and, as one writer put it, "following a lapsed tradition, accepting what our fathers honoured and loved simply because they were our fathers." But the author maintained that fundamentalists differed from modernists not because of ignorance or traditionalism but "for reasons valid to our own conscience and intelligence."[39] These reasons should be explored.

Fundamentalists recognized a legitimate function for reason which did not conflict with faith, and they disavowed the charge of obscurantism. "No really healthy Christian mind can advocate obscurantism," declared Dyson Hague of Toronto. "The obscurantist who opposed the investigation of scholarship and would throttle the investigators, has not the spirit of Christ."[40] Alva J. McClain asserted that "Faith is indeed _supra_-rational, but never _anti_-rational. It is a great pity that the word 'rational' should have been so often surrendered to the enemy."[41] A. Z. Conrad reminded his readers that emotionalism was not true religion, and that Christianity would lose much of its

---

[39] "Do Evangelicals Think?" _The Bible Champion_, XXXII (January, 1926), 35-36.

[40] _The Fundamentals: A Testimony to the Truth_ (12 vols.; Chicago: Testimony Publishing Company, [1910-1915]), I, 115.

[41] Alva J. McClain, "Christian Faith--Its Nature, Object, and Intelligible Medium," _Bibliotheca Sacra_, XC (April, 1933), 157.

vitality and virtue if divested of intelligence. Intelligence, said Conrad, was essential to proper interpretation of Scripture, evangelism, church organization, philanthropy, prayer, worship, and ethics.[42] Machen, in his attempt to show the consistency of faith and reason, went so far as to assert "the primacy of the intellect."[43]

But fundamentalists were also careful to point out the limitations of the intellect. Harold Paul Sloan cautioned that the intellect was not the total man:

> Truth does not belong to the intellect alone. . . . Truth is a personal value. It belongs to men and can only be pursued with all the faculties of our beings. The conscience and the heart are as important in the pursuit of truth as is the intellect.[44]

Others pointed out that reason is by its nature subordinate to special revelation from God. George W. McPherson, for example, argued that since reason could not originate a supernatural religion like Christianity it must therefore be "subordinated to that which it could never discover or create," though it was a legitimate aid in interpreting Christianity.[45] McClain also contended that "sense-

---

[42] A. Z. Conrad, "Putting Intelligence into Religion," The Bible Champion, XXXV (January, 1929), 4-5.

[43] J. Gresham Machen, What Is Faith? (New York: Macmillan Company, 1925), p. 26.

[44] Harold Paul Sloan, "America's School System and Can a University be Christian?" Christian Faith and Life, XXXVII (January, 1931), 4.

[45] George W. McPherson, "What is Modernism and What is Fundamentalism," The Bible Champion, XXX (April, 1924),

experience, historical investigation and the powers of reason . . . are only channels . . . not original sources of faith's existence and authority."[46] James M. Gray told seniors at Moody Bible Institute that while learning and Christian faith both were essential to the complete man, faith was primary: "Higher scholarship is a branch, but you have the root. Remember that 'the fear of the Lord is the chief part of knowledge.'"[47]

Fundamentalists also repeatedly asserted that it was regeneration, not reason, that produced a Christian. A believing scholar and an unbelieving scholar could not attribute their respective spiritual conditions to their education, argued Leander S. Keyser, but only to the fact that one was spiritually reborn and the other was not.[48] Mark A. Matthews, observing that the most scientific criminals were the most highly educated, cited this fact as proof that education "can not change the human heart."[49] Gerald B. Winrod summed it up thus: "The educated person must come in humility, the same way the most uneducated

---

223.

[46]McClain, "Christian Faith," p. 158.

[47]James M. Gray, "Scholarship and Evangelical Christianity," Moody Monthly, XXIX (October, 1928), 53-55.

[48]Keyser, A Reasonable Faith, p. 57.

[49]Mark A. Matthews, Gospel Sword Thrusts (New York: Fleming H. Revell Company, 1924), pp. 107-8.

individual must come. There is no established connection between a college diploma and a clean heart."[50]

While the exercise of the intellect was considered important in the understanding, defense, and promotion of one's faith, that faith itself was not the product of reasoning. To be "wise unto salvation" was the result of believing the biblical message, and this required only a minimal education. R. A. Torrey claimed to know uncultured, almost illiterate persons who "knew more of the wisdom that really counts, the wisdom that spells salvation, in five minutes, than . . . learned professors knew in their whole lifetime."[51] Even the cultured, scholarly Machen affirmed that when God gave men a glimpse of himself in the Scriptures, it was "Not only to the wise and the mighty . . . but to plain people whom wise men despise."[52]

This insight from Scriptural revelation and divine guidance always took precedence over unassisted human scholarship, according to the fundamentalists. David R. Breed argued that because scholarship had never discovered any great spiritual truth it was incapable of discrediting

---

[50] Gerald B. Winrod, Christ Within (3d ed.; Wichita, Kans.: Defender Publishers, 1929), p. 40.

[51] Torrey, Bible Study, pp. 18-19.

[52] J. Gresham Machen, "God Transcendent," in God Transcendent and Other Selected Sermons, ed. by Ned B. Stonehouse (Grand Rapids, Mich.: Wm. B. Eerdmans Publishing Company, 1949), p. 22.

revealed truth, except to those who had never embraced it. No process of reasoning could negate the reality of that truth in the experience of the believer.[53] The Christian should therefore test all scholarship by the combined standard of Scripture and spiritual experience. To accept a view that contradicted one's spiritual judgment simply because it was prompted by a "scholar," wrote Dyson Hague, was "to abdicate his franchise as a Christian and his birthright as a man."[54] W. H. Griffith Thomas considered it "infinitely better to trust the average intellect with spiritual experience than the greatest intellect without it,"[55] for the unaided human mind was not qualified to comprehend divine truth.

It was precisely here that fundamentalists found fault with much of modern scholarship. It had not only ceased to build on the Bible, the divinely-revealed foundation of true knowledge; it was trying to hack that foundation to pieces. Intoxicated with "mind worship," to use Bryan's term, it was trusting unverified human speculations which, if followed to their conclusions, would foster a

---

[53]David R. Breed, "The Limitations of Scholarship," _The King's Business_, XVI (May, 1925), 203.

[54]_Fundamentals_, I, 115.

[55]W. H. Griffith Thomas, "How Can the Saints Preserve the Faith?" _The Sunday School Times_, LXIII (November 19, 1921), 651. Cf. Leon Tucker, "Where Is John Brown's Soul?" _The Wonderful Word_, XV (December, 1922), 102.

disastrous moral irresponsibility.[56] Repelled by what they considered to be the ultimate arrogance of unenlightened reason, fundamentalists were scarcely willing to call it scholarship. "We are not afraid of scholarship," declared W. H. Griffith Thomas. "The only thing we have a right to be afraid of is that which denies God and the supernatural."[57] To him, clearly, antisupernaturalism and scholarship were in two different classes.

This revulsion on occasion led fundamentalists to overstate the importance of faith or to undervalue reason. Bryan dogmatically asserted, "When reform starts in this country, it starts with the masses. Reforms do not come out of the brains of scholars."[58] Leon Tucker, while recognizing the marvelous results of human thought, expressed the opinion that "The age does not need great thinkers, it has too many; it needs great believers."[59] George Boddis

---

[56] William Jennings Bryan, "'All,'" Christian Standard, LVII (July 15, 1922), 3-5; "Hon. William Jennings Bryan Addresses the Moody Bible Institute," The Wonderful Word, XIII (August, 1921), 505-9; Henry Frey Lutz, "Evolution and Scholarship: The Limitations of Scholarship," The Bible Champion, XXXII (May, 1926), 273-77.

[57] W. H. Griffith Thomas, "The German Attitude to the Bible," Bibliotheca Sacra, LXXVI (April, 1919), 173. Cf. Frank M. Goodchild, "The Spirit and Purpose of the Fundamentalists," The Watchman-Examiner, X (March 2, 1922), 268-69.

[58] "Hon. William Jennings Bryan Addresses the Moody Bible Institute," p. 509.

[59] Leon Tucker, "'A Thinking Age,'" The Wonderful Word, XX (November, 1927), 4.

declared that, while he valued scholarship, he was "more in favor of piety and zeal in the Master's cause."[60] Even educator James M. Gray leaned in this direction when observing that nearly half of all Protestant ministers were not college or seminary graduates. "While the Christian faith has no fear of scholarship and is greatly indebted to it," said Gray, "yet its faithful propagation does not require it, and has sometimes been hindered by it."[61] These statements all evidence a reaction against what was considered an overemphasis on the powers of the mind. While those who made them probably did not intend to minimize all scholarship, one wonders how they affected lay listeners and readers.

While modernists recognized reason as "master of the house," fundamentalists saw it only as a steward, always responsible to God's previously-revealed authority and subject to censure when it overstepped its limits. Spiritual truth, although reasonable to the believer, had to be embraced initially by faith before reason could interpret and apply it. David Breed declared, "It is not scholarship which renders one competent to decide whether a doctrine is

---

[60]George Boddis, "Our Scrap Book," Serving and Waiting, XVIII (August, 1928), 120.

[61][James M. Gray], "The Church and Its Ministry," Moody Monthly, XXXI (October, 1930), 52.

from God or not, but honest devotion to the will of God."[62] The modernist denial of revealed truth brought a vigorous protest and, in some cases, an underrating of the intellect which modernists had emphasized. W. B. Riley bluntly but accurately defined the limits of reason which fundamentalists recognized:

> I believe in education, but not in an anti-Christian one! I believe in science, but not in an anti-Scriptural one! I believe in the college, but not if it deny my Christ! I believe in the theological seminary, but not if it oppose spirituality.[63]

Fundamentalists not only questioned the sufficiency of the intellect in an age of reason; they rejected a leading scientific theory in a day when science was revered for its achievements. This stand often brought the reaction typified by a reader of The Sunday School Times: "Your stupid attitude toward science has decided us to drop The Sunday School Times. We do not belong to that ignorant class to whom you cater."[64] Since their vigorous campaign against the teaching of evolution earned fundamentalists the reputation of obscurantism and medievalism, it is important to examine the basis for their attitudes toward scientific study.

---

[62] Breed, "Limitations of Scholarship," p. 235.

[63] W. B. Riley, The Bible of the Expositor and the Evangelist (40 vols.; Cleveland: Union Gospel Press, 1926-1938), New Testament, XVII, 244.

[64] [Charles G. Trumbull], "'That Ignorant Class,'" The Sunday School Times, LXVII (January 31, 1925), 58.

Many observers interpreted their anti-evolution stand as evidence of a general anti-scientific spirit. Clifford Kirkpatrick wrote:

> If they want to strangle science, the goose that has laid them many a golden egg, it is their affair, although other beneficiaries have equal right to struggle to keep so valuable a bird alive.[65]

But fundamentalists almost unanimously disavowed any opposition to science. John Horsch accused modernists of repeating this charge only because it was useful to them in the present controversy.[66] Leander Keyser claimed that not one of the thousands of conservative Christians he knew opposed true science.[67] "I would not be so foolish as to belittle true science," wrote Gerald Winrod. "We need science. The scientific method . . . has revolutionized things in the last half century. Marvellous are the accomplishments of true science."[68] Mark A. Matthews, in a particularly strong statement, advocated removing children from parents who opposed public health measures in order to

---

[65]Clifford Kirkpatrick, Religion in Human Affairs (New York: John Wiley & Sons, Inc., 1929), p. 405.

[66]John Horsch, The Failure of Modernism: A Reply to Harry Emerson Fosdick (Chicago: Bible Institute Colportage Association, 1925), pp. 22, 27-28.

[67]Leander S. Keyser, "Some Samples of Illogical Thinking," The Bible Champion, XXIX (October, 1923), 470.

[68]Gerald Winrod, Science, Christ and the Bible (New York: Fleming H. Revell Company, 1929), p. 34.

give them "the advantage of every discovery of science."[69]

Indeed, scientific study was regarded as a means of uncovering new facets of God's truth. W. B. Riley declared, "We venerate science as much as we do the Scriptures because we believe in the common authorship of both,"[70] and David S. Kennedy expressed the opinion that "the preacher who does not believe that the Christianity of the apostles will harmonize with the ultimate science . . . is poorly qualified for his task."[71] The narratives of Scripture could be harmonized with scientific facts, they maintained, by recognizing the biblical authors' use of figurative language and nonscientific vocabulary. Alva J. McClain set forth a proposition with which practically all fundamentalists could agree: "The Bible, although not written primarily to teach science, is nevertheless, when correctly interpreted, in harmony with all the established facts of science."[72]

But they did not regard evolution as "true science"

---

[69]Matthews, Gospel Sword Thrusts, pp. 81-83.

[70]W. B. Riley, "The Old vs. The New Faith, Or Why Fundamentalism?" The Christian Fundamentalist, IV (June, 1931), 454.

[71][David S. Kennedy], "Preaching in the Modern World," The Presbyterian, LXXXIX (November 27, 1919), 7; cf. A. Z. Conrad, "Are Evangelicals Afraid?" The Bible Champion, XXXI (July, 1925), 351.

[72]Alva J. McClain, "The Bible and Science," Serving and Waiting, XV (May, 1925), 23. Cf. Horsch, Failure of Modernism, p. 23.

for at least two reasons. First, fundamentalists considered it to be irreconcilable with the Genesis narrative and the biblical view of God and man. Having chosen the Bible as the basis of their world-view, they believed any reasonably literal interpretation of it ruled out evolution. The Bible pictured man as the masterpiece of an intelligent creator; evolution portrayed him as the chance product of natural forces. The Bible taught the uniqueness of man among created things; evolution taught his common ancestry with other forms of life. The Bible saw humanity as morally responsible to its creator; evolution left doubts as to both the existence and the proper object of moral responsibility. The Bible traced the human condition from perfection to depravity; evolution implied to many an opposite process. Charles G. Trumbull, who claimed to rejoice in the benefits of science to the human race, therefore drew the line when scientists "usurped the place of God" and rejected his word.[73] George Boddis also warned of dangerous tendencies in the evolutionary theory when he asserted that "From its inception it has been antagonistic to the Christian religion" and that "most evolutionists are still agnostics or atheists." Even the theistic evolutionist, Boddis claimed, made concessions which changed the

[73]Trumbull, "'That Ignorant Class,'" p. 58.

entire character of Christianity.[74] Evolution thus was unthinkable because it could not be harmonized with God's revealed truth.

Evolutionary theory would eventually produce social as well as theological aberrations, claimed the fundamentalists. David S. Kennedy feared that it would destroy morality, and John Roach Straton discerned, even then, in the Franks murder and other violence of 1924, the logical outcome of "the survival of the fittest." Gerald B. Winrod maintained that if the teaching of evolution continued unchecked the moral erosion it caused would destroy civilization itself.[75]

But were such theological and moral considerations legitimate reasons for rejecting the findings of scientific research? By letting their theology determine their science, were not fundamentalists in the same category as the churchmen who, for theological reasons, rejected the findings of Galileo? It was relatively easy, after all, to proclaim the harmony of Scripture with "true science" when one could arbitrarily exclude from that term all that contradicted the Bible. But fundamentalists claimed that this

---

[74]George Boddis, "Evolution versus Facts," _Serving and Waiting_, XIII (May, 1923), 29.

[75][David S. Kennedy], "The Error of Evolution," _The Presbyterian_, XCI (May 12, 1921), 3, 6; _New York Times_, September 15, 1924, p. 16; Winrod, _Christ Within_, pp. 111-12. Cf. James M. Gray, "Modernism a Foe to Good Government," _Moody Monthly_, XXIV (July, 1924), 546-47.

misrepresented their position, for they had a second reason for rejecting evolution--the fact that evolution was an unproved theory. If scientific evidence was not available to support it, or if the evidence adduced was capable of proving something else, why should they be called unscholarly for repudiating evolution?

James M. Gray combined both lines of reasoning as he wrote to Leander S. Keyser:

> As a Christian believer, my strongest reason for rejecting such a theory is that it contradicts the Bible which I regard as an inspired revelation of a personal God who declares the very opposite. And in saying this, I am not at all afraid of the charge of obscurantism, because that evolution is merely a hypothesis, a theory, a guess, is witnessed to by scientific men themselves.
>
> However, when it comes to pure logic . . . a universe created out of nothing and set going by a Creator and Ruler, is a belief not a whit less satisfactory than that of a universe uncreated, or self-created, and set going by its own natural laws.[76]

From a logical standpoint, then, the choice was reduced to two hypotheses, each of them beyond the realm of absolute empirical proof. The conflict was not between science and faith, declared Harold Paul Sloan, but between two faiths--Christ and the supernatural on one side, and evolution and the antisupernatural on the other.[77]

Yet, because evolution was usually taught as a science rather than a philosophy, fundamentalists felt they

---

[76]Letter, James M. Gray to Leander S. Keyser, reproduced in Runyan, Dr. Gray, p. 95.

[77]Sloan, Historic Christianity, p. 203.

had a legitimate right to question its scientific credibility. As George Boddis contended, "Surely . . . we have the right to demand that they should prove their assertions or cease to dogmatize where science is silent."[78] This did not imply a repression of scientific research or discussion, for, as Edwin Deacon asserted, "We have nothing to fear from the freest possible discussion, or the most thorough investigations." But it did mean that the anti-evolution case should not be thrown out of court while the evolutionist was still searching for proof.[79] Even W. B. Riley, the most vigorous anti-evolution crusader, disclaimed any intention of stifling the scientific spirit. Riley wrote:

> They can go on searching for bones as much as they like. . . . What we are demanding is that the philosophy wait until the bones are discovered and the facts are forthcoming . . .[80]

Meanwhile, fundamentalist critics set out to exhibit the scientific vulnerability of the theory and to suggest alternate interpretations of evolutionary "proofs."[81] They

---

[78]Boddis, "Evolution versus Facts," p. 31.

[79]Edwin Deacon, "Taxed, but not Represented," The Bible Champion, XXXIV (May, 1928), 277-78.

[80]W. B. Riley, "The Defense of Fundamentalism in the Matter of Evolution," The Christian Fundamentalist, I (November, 1927), 11.

[81]See, e.g., Boddis, "Evolution versus Facts," pp. 30-37; Philip Mauro, Evolution at the Bar (New York: George H. Doran Company, 1922); George McCready Price, "The Fossils as Age-Markers in Geology," The Princeton Theologi-

also insisted that it be taught strictly as a hypothesis to students mature enough to evaluate it. Several proposed that it be taught in advanced university classes, and one writer suggested that it be discussed in relation to Greek philosophy, which it closely resembled.[82]

Evolution was in no way essential to the teaching of science, the fundamentalists insisted, for it was not really scientific. The question of origins was beyond the reach of the scientific method, and was therefore in the realm of philosophy or religion. So they viewed their anti-evolution crusade as a struggle not with science, but with a rival religion which had its own explanation of origins, evaluation of man, philosophy of history, and faith for the future.[83]

But even while fundamentalists claimed to respect "true science," they warned their generation that even this was inadequate and irrelevant in some areas of life. Even in the realm of physical knowledge new questions and problems were arising for which the inductive method had no

---

cal Review, XX (October, 1922), 585-615; and "Modern Botany and the Theory of Organic Evolution," ibid., XXIII (January, 1925), 51-65.

[82]W. Bell Dawson, "The Teaching of Evolution," The Christian Fundamentalist, III (January, 1930), 497; Winrod, Christ Within, p. 118; [James M. Gray], "Evolution in Our Schools," Moody Monthly, XXX (March, 1930), 328.

[83]See Leander S. Keyser, "Shall We Teach Science or Speculation?" The Presbyterian, XCVII (April 7, 1927), 7-8.

answers. What, then, could it do for man's spiritual welfare? "When the issue is spiritual life and death," declared A. Z. Conrad, "we well know that science is absolutely speechless."[84]

In view of these limitations, fundamentalists felt that scientists might well assume a more humble posture, and that they especially ought not make pontifical pronouncements on spiritual matters. Herbert W. Magoun warned them not to be oversure of their judgment of biblical narratives, for many of the "contradictions" were merely misunderstandings. Magoun concluded:

> Scientific books are proverbially short-lived. Other books die sooner or later. One and only one lives, and that is the Bible, which the critics would have us believe is just like all the rest. Is it?[85]

The fundamentalist viewed science as he viewed reason upon which it rested. It held no fears for the Christian as long as it confined itself to its proper task--the study and use of observable data. It could even strengthen his faith by demonstrating the harmony of divine truth. But when it attempted to philosophize on the basis of a shaky hypothesis it ceased to be "true science" and exposed

---

[84]A. Z. Conrad, Jesus Christ at the Crossroads (New York: Fleming H. Revell Company, 1924), p. 110; cf. Sloan, The Christ of the Ages, p. 7; Philip Mauro, "Enlarging the Area of Human Ignorance," The Bible Champion, XXXV (August, 1929), 398-99; Machen, Christianity and Liberalism, pp. 9-10.

[85]Herbert W. Magoun, "Do We Really Try to Understand?" The Biblical Review, XVI (January, 1931), 76.

itself to well-deserved censure. It was the standard of a spiritually disciplined science, rather than a wholesale rejection of science, that underlay the fundamentalist hostility to evolution.

Whatever one may think of the theological assumptions of fundamentalists, he is compelled to recognize that they built on them a coherent system of thought and action. Choosing as their starting point the "propositional truth" of a verbally-inspired Bible, they believed a consistent Christian faith must accept it in its entirety. Any retreat in religion, be it intellectual or institutional, must logically lead to another, and they were therefore determined not to take that first backward step. They also believed that those who no longer could embrace biblical fundamentals should voluntarily dissociate themselves from the Christian community.

The modernists saw religion in an entirely different light. They believed the essence of Christianity was not in its theology but in its ideals operating in the individual and the community, and the church should be broad enough to accommodate the dissenter as well as the orthodox believer.[86] Yet even modernists doubted that both concepts of Christianity could long live peaceably under one roof, and they joined the fundamentalists in predicting that one

---

[86]Shailer Mathews, The Faith of Modernism (New York: Macmillan Company, 1924), pp. 18-19, 178-79.

must displace the other or Christianity must split.[87]

While the fundamentalist view of the faith was narrower, it was, given its theological assumptions, also the more logical, and its advocates constantly reminded the modernists of their inconsistencies. One could not borrow Christian ideals while denying the historical facts of Christianity, argued Clarence E. Macartney.

> Christianity cannot be ethically divine and historically false. The man who is preaching the so-called ideals of the Christian faith and at the same time ignoring, or evading, or denying its facts, is indulging in a sort of theological legerdemain, which, if followed and adopted by others, could have no other result but complete denial of Christianity, ideals, facts, hopes, and all.[88]

Neither could one logically accept Jesus as a moral guide and deny his claims, declared J. Gresham Machen. That was nothing but "investing our pride in human goodness with the borrowed trappings of Christianity's emotional appeal."[89] By borrowing Christian morality while rejecting its theological foundations, said John Horsch, modernism was paving the way for the eventual breakdown of morality itself.[90]

---

[87] "Fundamentalism and Modernism--and God," The Christian Century, XLI (March 20, 1924), 359; cf. "Modernist--Modernism," The Bible Champion, XXVIII (May, 1922), 274-75.

[88] Clarence E. Macartney, Twelve Great Questions About Christ (New York: Fleming H. Revell Company, 1923), p. 69; cf. Machen, Christianity and Liberalism, p. 6.

[89] Machen, What Is Faith?, p. 39.

[90] John Horsch, Modern Religious Liberalism (Scottdale, Pa.: Fundamental Truth Depot, 1920), p. 130.

This eclectic approach to Christianity and the lack of a defined theology indicated to fundamentalists a lack of intellectual rigor. Alva McClain puzzled over this "vogue of vagueness" in view of the fact that the scientific method venerated by modernists demanded exactness in terms, formulas, definitions, and statements, and Leander Keyser termed "anemic" any religion that had no certain data and could not be schematized and supported by rational processes.[91] Machen declared that the church was perishing through the lack of thinking as men refused to come to grips with its logical alternatives. He characterized typical university students not as original thinkers but as sheep who followed their professors, repeating the same stock phrases with little comprehension of their meaning. Yet they imagined that they were "bold, bad, independent young men" because they abused what everyone else was abusing, the Christian religion. The only truly independent thinkers, asserted Machen, were the believers in historic Christianity.[92]

Fundamentalist critics therefore discounted modernist

---

[91] Alva J. McClain, "Current Tendencies Which Limit Faith and Life," The Biblical Review, XVI (January, 1931), 35-36; Keyser, A Reasonable Faith, p. 183.

[92] J. Gresham Machen, "Christianity and Culture," in What Is Christianity?, ed. by Ned B. Stonehouse (Grand Rapids, Mich.: Wm. B. Eerdmans Publishing Company, 1951), p. 168; What Is Faith?, p. 17; cf. W. B. Riley, "Will Princeton Be Lost to Presbyterianism?" The Christian Fundamentalist, I (July, 1927), 27.

claims to superior scholarship. Such claims were signs of intellectual adolescence, not maturity, contended Harold Paul Sloan, for "No man who can demonstrate his position by scientific certainties ever hangs it upon a claim of intellectual superiority."[93] W. E. Scofield complained of the dogmatic assertions and mere listing of scholarly support one encountered when criticizing evolutionary philosophy. He demanded, "We want the difficulties grappled with and overcome. There they have stood for more than fifty years, and not one of them has been fairly met."[94] Keyser concluded that biblical critics were not answering the arguments of their conservative opponents either because they did not know or did not care what they were writing. "If they do not know, it is a reflection of their scholarship; if they do not care, it is a question of ethics. On which horn of the dilemma will they hang themselves?"[95]

The issue of intellectual honesty loomed large for the fundamentalists. Not only did they believe the modernists were avoiding direct confrontation with the problems but also that they were using the prestige of the churches

---

[93] Sloan, The Christ of the Ages, p. 51; Historic Christianity, p. 13; cf. A. Z. Conrad, Jesus Christ at the Crossroads, pp. 106-7.

[94] W. E. Scofield, "Is the Modern Mind Really Modern?" The Bible Champion, XXIX (April, 1923), 234-35.

[95] Leander S. Keyser, "Do the Destructive Critics Read the Conservative Scholars?" The Sunday School Times, LXV (January 6, 1923), 2.

and the terminology of Christianity to gain a hearing for their heresies.[96] Modernism was not Christianity, they argued, and had no right to be paraded as such. It was built on a human foundation, it denied the reality of the supernatural, and even its system of ethics was little more than "baptized paganism." It was but a dead scion which men had unsuccessfully attempted to graft onto Protestantism.[97]

In effect, the fundamentalist was saying to his opponent, "I have, for reasons valid to me, taken the Bible as my basis for theology and conduct. I will therefore defend its integrity at every point and at all costs. Furthermore, historic Protestantism supports me, and it is you who are out of step. If you wish to teach a new religion, be honest enough to call it that and bid the church farewell." And the modernist, for all his irritation with "antiquated creeds," still bore the burden of proving the fundamentalist's logic wrong.

To generalize about the intellectual stature of fundamentalism in the twenties is difficult, for just as its spokesmen represented a broad denominational and geographi-

---

[96] J. Gresham Machen, "The Modern Use of the Bible," The Princeton Theological Review, XXIII (January, 1925), pp. 80-81; Horsch, Failure of Modernism, pp. 26-27.

[97] Machen, Christianity and Liberalism, pp. 6-7, 79; Horsch, Liberalism, pp. 9-17; "Modernist--Modernism," pp. 274-75; Macartney, Twelve Great Questions, p. 193.

cal base, so they also varied widely in their abilities, education, and methods. But when seen in the light of their theological assumptions, they present a more reputable profile than many scholars have depicted. Broadly speaking, their education was not as extensive as that of the modernists, but it was still respectable and they could count several scholars of national repute among their number. While their literature contained its share of sensational, illogical, and prejudiced material, this was more than offset by reasoned critiques of their opponents and presentations of their own case. Their appeal, however, was more often directed to the average reader or listener than to the scholar.

The fundamentalist recognized reason as an essential element in religion, but he believed spiritual life and understanding began with faith. An uneducated believer, aided by written revelation and divine guidance, could enjoy a spiritual wisdom denied the unregenerate intellectual. He did not despise the intellect, however. He merely challenged what he considered to be its illicit present use and sought to make it accountable again to its divine author.

In the same way he praised science as a means of enriching human life and displaying the harmony of God's creation. But he excluded evolution from "true science" because it contradicted the biblical view of God and man and because its hypothetical nature gave it the character of a philosophy rather than a science. He also pointed out that all science, being limited to the natural sphere, was incapable of meeting spiritual needs.

Both reason and scientific study had legitimate roles to play, but always under the discipline of divine truth in the Bible. And upon this assumption of biblical primacy the fundamentalist built a coherent system of thought and program of action. While it may be true that some fundamentalists could not endure "the pain of thinking," in the final analysis it was not ignorance, misunderstanding, or an anti-intellectual approach to life that kept fundamentalists from embracing some features of contemporary scholarship. It was rather a tenacious personal commitment to a theology they believed was eternal. To compromise God's changeless message with current human hypotheses was simply out of the question.

CHAPTER IV

"THE FAITH" AND THE NATION

World War I was an unsettling experience for almost all Americans. Idealists of all political shades had been swept into the crusade to make the world safe for democracy, and gave undivided allegiance to President Wilson's war programs. But when the fighting ended and they gradually became aware of how impossible their chosen task was, many Americans came to look upon their European involvement as a gigantic mistake. Idealism was conspicuously absent from European politics as embittered and suspicious nations sought revenge for their losses. It was also rapidly diminishing in the United States as the Senate rejected the Versailles treaty and the people settled into the rut of "normalcy."

As the progressive ideals of prewar America were discarded for moneymaking and standardized mediocrity, disillusionment seized many erstwhile progressives and young radicals. This despair with American life manifested itself in the aimless life of the "lost generation" in Greenwich Village and the Left Bank of the Seine, the cynical blasts of Henry L. Mencken in the *American Mercury*, and the defeatist thread running through much of American literature.

Conservatives had much reason to be disillusioned, too, for the orderly America they had known and optimistically promoted before the war was fragmentizing before their eyes. Private and public morals seemed to have taken a vacation; family life appeared to be disintegrating; pursuit of wealth and pleasure were crowding out the more intangible values; crime was on the rise and foreign-bred anarchism seemed to be stalking the land. They were being awakened from the nineteenth-century dream of inevitable American progress, and were chagrined at what they saw.[1]

Fundamentalism is often portrayed as a conspicuous example of this postwar disillusionment. Its adherents, as they are usually sketched, saw the America they once knew rapidly disappearing and, being psychologically incapable of adapting to the strange new world, they either struck out vehemently against its innovations or retreated to the security of the Bible and its comforting theology. Moreover, the residue of their hatred for all things German during the war is often blamed for their militancy against modernist theology in the years that followed.[2] In short,

---

[1]Henry F. May, The End of American Innocence (New York: Alfred A. Knopf, 1959), pp. 393-98; John D. Hicks, Republican Ascendancy, 1921-1933 (New York: Harper & Row, Publishers, 1960), pp. 179-86.

[2]John Higham, Strangers in the Land: Patterns of

they are viewed as simple patriots whose loyalty to a bygone America forbade them to make peace with the changed postwar America.

There are elements of truth in this portrait but the emphases are wrong. The typical fundamentalist was, for example, strongly patriotic, with the same idealized conception of American history and sense of national mission that had characterized his countrymen since independence. But his patriotism was never a simple "my country right or wrong," for he believed that America could continue to receive divine blessings only as she submitted to God's authority as revealed in the Bible.

The fundamentalist also agreed with many other Americans that a national turning point, or crisis, was at hand. He viewed the growing secularism apprehensively and especially cast a suspicious eye on the amoral, state-controlled educational system. But to call this disillusionment is hardly accurate, for the recent war had shown him America's potential for good if she were only turned in the right direction again, and he set about to change the present drift with considerable zest and optimism. Fur-

---

American Nativism, 1860-1925 (New Brunswick, N.J.: Rutgers University Press, 1955), p. 293; Robert Moats Miller, American Protestantism and Social Issues, 1919-1939 (Chapel Hill, N.C.: University of North Carolina Press, 1958), p. 155; Milton L. Rudnick, Fundamentalism and The Missouri Synod (St. Louis: Concordia Publishing House, 1966), pp. 19-20.

thermore, the dreary aftermath of the war brought no surprises to him. It only seemed to confirm the inadequacies of humanism and convince him further that his cause was right.

The typical fundamentalist, moreover, supported the war against Germany wholeheartedly and warned America not to espouse the rationalist theology that had developed there. But he rarely expressed hostility toward Germans as a people. He limited his censure to the theological theories he believed responsible for their downfall.

Finally, the fundamentalist did not develop his theology in response to his patriotism, the war, the secularization of American life, or as a psychological escape from a new era. Instead, he applied the theology he already believed to all the national and international issues the war and its aftermath produced. His theology, in other words, was more often the cause than the result of his thinking on the issues of his times.

"I cannot draw any line between Christianity and patriotism," wrote George F. Pentecost in 1918. "I cannot understand any man's Christianity who is not a loyal patriot."[3] While this strong statement must be understood in its World War I context, many fundamentalists of the twenties would have endorsed it without serious modifica-

---

[3]George F. Pentecost, "The Church and the War," The Presbyterian, LXXXVIII (January 3, 1918), 11.

tion. The relative emphases on Christianity and patriotism differed with individuals, but both values were clearly in their thinking, and the February, July, and November issues of many of their magazines could usually be counted on for some patriotic emphasis.

In a few cases this nationalism was expressed with a racially-tinged, flag-waving zeal reminiscent of Josiah Strong and Theodore Roosevelt. A pair of articles by George Boddis in July, 1928 argued that God had as definitely directed American history as he had that of ancient Israel, and that the United States would determine the future destiny of world civilization.[4] Boddis maintained that God oversaw the circumstances of the country's discovery and development, chose its inhabitants, and prepared them spiritually for their role. He aided them in the Revolution, led them to adopt the Constitution, preserved their Union while abolishing slavery, provided natural resources, and gave them a beneficent influence over other peoples.[5] Boddis also predicted the expansion of American influence. "Living nations always expand: when they cease to grow they begin to decay. That part of the American continent now dominated by the Anglo-Saxon race may some

---

[4]George Boddis, "The Hand of God in American History," The Bible Champion, XXXIV (July, 1928), 370-77; "The Influence of the United States on History," Serving and Waiting, XVIII (July, 1928), 76-79.

[5]Boddis, "Hand of God," pp. 370-77, passim.

day absorb the rest." The Anglo-Saxon people, who allegedly had the combined desirable characteristics of the Jews, Greeks, and Romans, still had a "great work" to perform, and the United States was destined for the leading role.[6]

A. William Lewis echoed the same theme in a rather unique interpretation of Jesus' statement that he would remove the kingdom of God from Israel and give it to "a nation bringing forth the fruits thereof" (Matt. 21:43). Lewis declared dogmatically, "This is the Anglo-Saxon nation," and supported his assertion with the observation that English-speaking peoples had been the most prominent participants in world evangelization.[7]

While few were ready to exalt Anglo-Saxondom to this extent, many spoke in tones of reverence of American heroes and institutions. "What nation of earth ever knew a line of rulers more remarkable or more righteous?" asked W. B. Riley. "The exception has so seldom occurred as to merely emphasize the rule."[8] A. Z. Conrad took sharp exception to the current debunking tendency of American historians, and

---

[6]Boddis, "Influence of the United States," pp. 78-79.

[7]A. William Lewis, "The Keystone," The Bible Champion, XXXIV (December, 1928), 681; cf. David James Burrell, "Our Christian Land," The Bible Champion, XXXII (February, 1926), 64-66.

[8]W. B. Riley, The Bible of the Expositor and the Evangelist (40 vols.; Cleveland: Union Gospel Press, 1926-1938), Old Testament, III, 170.

declared that the accomplishments of American political leaders should not be subordinated to their faults. On the other hand, he saw no harm in idealizing a man like George Washington.[9] John Roach Straton thought it perfectly consistent to include in the same sermon an appeal "for the old faith upon which the best of our Anglo-Saxon civilization is founded" and "a tribute to the glorious flag of our country."[10] Cortland Myers deplored the decline of "real patriotism and deathless love for the Republic" and advocated a return to the old-fashioned, noisy Fourth of July. But more important to him was the return of the Bible to the schools. He concluded:

> By God's grace, we must make this ideal for every citizen under the best flag which the breezes wave, and the sunlight kisses, and the round world respects,--"The Bible and flag, now and forever, one and inseparable."[11]

Fundamentalists were convinced that at heart America was a Christian nation, both a recipient and a channel of divine blessing. David S. Kennedy recounted its physical, intellectual, spiritual, and moral blessings and found proof of its Christian pedigree in its political philoso-

---

[9] A. Z. Conrad, "Neutralizing the Poison of Muckraking Malcontents," The Bible Champion, XXXVI (August, 1930), 397-99.

[10] John Roach Straton, The Gardens of Life (New York: George H. Doran Company, 1921), p. 17.

[11] Cortland Myers, "The Crime of Our Godless Schools," The King's Business, XV (May, 1924), 270, 273.

phy, its respect for the Bible and sabbath, and its leadership in temperance reform.[12] Curtis Lee Laws rejoiced in 1918 that Americans in the World War had no cause for shame, and nearly a decade later Charles G. Trumbull made reference to the higher moral tone existing in America than in Europe.[13] These idealized conceptions of their country's history and purpose make it clear that fundamentalists had by no means escaped the "cultural captivity" into which other Protestants had fallen. In their thinking the Christian and American traditions were inextricably woven together.

But to occupy such a position of divine favor placed Americans on a precarious pinnacle, and fundamentalists therefore urged that moral vigilance replace complacency and boasting. C. H. Buchanan warned,

> Do we not believe Americans are the greatest people in all the world, that God has made us out of a little finer clay than any other people in the world? It does not require a prophet to proclaim that "pride foreruns a downfall."[14]

---

[12] David S. Kennedy, "Thanksgiving Day: Its History and Meaning," The Bible Champion, XXXIV (November, 1928), 585-86; cf. Riley, Bible of the Expositor, Old Testament, XI, 122-23.

[13] [Curtis Lee Laws], "The Flag Without a Stain," The Watchman-Examiner, VI (December 5, 1918), 1489-90; [Charles G. Trumbull], "America's Peril," The Sunday School Times, LXX (January 14, 1928), 13.

[14] C. H. Buchanan, "An Inventory of the National Trend," Christian Faith and Life, XXXVII (November, 1931), 588.

The need for moral vigilance was especially emphasized during the World War. David Kennedy reminded his readers, "There is no more patriotic duty at the present time than the support of the Church,"[15] and George Pentecost asserted in similar words, "The Church is the soul of the nation. If that soul weakens or dies, the nation will die." (Italics in original.)[16] But even after the conflict ended, they cautioned again that the nation could ill afford complacency. Kennedy declared:

> America is narrowed to a choice. She must restore the Bible to its historic place . . . and thus through daily life and thought revive and build up her moral life and faith, or else she must collapse and fail the world in this crucial age.[17]

Even George Boddis, for all his jingoistic tone, warned that without proper spiritual undergirding the United States could wield a harmful influence over the world. The ideal patriot, he maintained, must exhibit more than national pride, for that, taken alone, is only "refined selfishness." Instead, he must try to make his country the best on earth so that "the world may be uplifted and blessed by our efforts and example." His love of country must not produce in him a pharisaism toward others or a

---

[15][David S. Kennedy], "An Indispensable Aid to Victory," The Presbyterian, LXXXVIII (January 24, 1918), 7.

[16]Pentecost, "Church and War," p. 11.

[17][David S. Kennedy], "The American Crisis," The Presbyterian, XC (January 8, 1920), 3.

blindness to national faults, but rather a desire to eliminate such evils through an application of biblical principles.[18]

The Christian and the church were thus expected to display patriotism by upholding the spiritual and moral tone of the nation. The church must be "patriotically Christian," said Mark Matthews, by teaching loyalty to God, obedience to government, and personal and civic righteousness. He urged Christians to show their national interest by fulfilling their political responsibilities, but more especially by exemplifying justice and righteousness in their personal conduct.[19] W. B. Riley counseled his members to counteract the trend toward commercialism, which he considered one of America's gravest dangers, by turning from the "mad race for prosperity" to a genuine concern for the physical and spiritual needs of others.[20] J. Gresham Machen, while not especially vocal on the subject of patriotism, nevertheless set a personal example of the Christian citizen intensely interested in public issues, speaking, writing, and even testifying in Washington on matters he

---

[18]George Boddis, "Ideal Christian Patriotism," Serving and Waiting, XVII (July, 1927), 60-61; "Influence of the United States," p. 79.

[19]Mark A. Matthews, Building the Church (New York: American Tract Society, 1940), pp. 71-72.

[20]Riley, Bible of the Expositor, New Testament, IX, 163-79.

considered essential to individual liberty and the quality of American life.[21]

There was nothing particularly unusual about viewing the United States as a providentially-guided nation with a divinely-given mission, for Russel B. Nye and others have traced these strands of thinking from colonial times to the present.[22] But the fundamentalist version was far more biblically-oriented than the nationalism of most Americans. The God who oversaw the nation was not the impersonal Creator of Jefferson or the benevolent and humanistic Father of their liberal contemporaries, but the sovereign God of Scripture who held nations and individuals accountable for their actions, punishing the self-willed and rewarding the faithful. The national mission also was more rigidly defined. It included not only the exhibition and promulgation of political liberty, but also the propagation of the Christian gospel and the display of the Christian morality

---

[21]See, e.g., J. Gresham Machen, Christianity and Liberalism (Grand Rapids, Mich.: Wm. B. Eerdmans Company, 1946), pp. 9-16, passim; "The Necessity of the Christian School," in What Is Christianity? ed. by Ned B. Stonehouse (Grand Rapids, Mich.: Wm. B. Eerdmans Publishing Company, 1951), pp. 288ff.; "The New Education Bill," Congressional Digest, V (May, 1926), 157-59; New York Times, November 18, 1924, p. 24; The New York Herald Tribune, December 10, 1924, p. 26; December 7, 1925, p. 14.

[22]Russel B. Nye, This Almost Chosen People (East Lansing, Mich.: Michigan State University Press, 1966), pp. 43-103; 164-207; cf. Ralph Henry Gabriel, The Course of American Democratic Thought (2d ed.; New York: Ronald Press Company, 1956), pp. 26-39; 367-404.

upon which that political system was allegedly founded. In brief, fundamentalists assumed that America was essentially Christian, and therefore held the nation to the same biblical standard they had adopted as their own.

But as they observed American life in the twenties they had to admit that the nation was not living up to this standard. Jasper C. Massee confessed in 1926 to "a great fear" that evil influences were undermining American social institutions, and urged his audience to meet the challenge, "not alone as Christians, but as citizens who fear God."[23] National shortcomings were numerous. Personal morality was slipping, with literature, the stage, and movies giving it an additional downward push. The family was endangered by divorce, birth control, and "companionate marriage." The pursuit of pleasure, the cult of science, and an insatiable commercialism had come to rival the Christian faith for the devotion of Americans. Government scandals, a rising crime rate, and lax law enforcement seemed to signal the disappearance of ethical principles.

As fundamentalists attempted to sort out causes for these disturbing developments they most often pointed to a faulty educational system, whose secularism, evolutionary emphasis, and standardization were weakening the nation's moral fiber. Education had become one-sided, claimed

---

[23]J[asper] C. Massee, Sunday Night Talks (Chicago: Bible Institute Colportage Ass'n., 1926), p. 78.

Charles G. Trumbull, emphasizing efficiency apart from morality or religion. While he insisted he was a believer in both education and efficiency, Trumbull thought "those great fundamentals that make for sound citizenship and clean living" were too often neglected.[24] A. Z. Conrad flatly pronounced American education "godless," and Mark Fakkema warned that if the current secularistic drift was a gauge of national life it was a cause for alarm.[25]

For some, educational standardization caused as much alarm as secularism. J. Gresham Machen forcefully criticized this trend as inimical to academic excellence and personal liberty. He challenged Phi Beta Kappa's resolution to forbid the formation of chapters in schools which did not allow academic freedom. In the name of free speech, Machen asserted, it was really advocating "an extremely narrow form of intolerance," for it thus ruled out all schools that maintained a certain point of view. He also testified against the creation of a federal department of education, contending that such control would be "the worst fate into which any country can fall." Machen

---

[24]Charles G. Trumbull, "Christian Business Efficiency," The Sunday School Times, LXVII (October 10, 1925), 628; "The Breakdown of Modern Education," ibid., LXV (October 20, 1923), 617.

[25]A. Z. Conrad, "Putting Religion into Intelligence," The Bible Champion, XXXV (February, 1929), 58; Mark Fakkema, "Our Educational Dilemma," The Sunday School Times, LXIX (August 6, 1927), 463-64.

declared that an educational "mess" in the name of liberty would be better than the intellectual and spiritual death standardization would bring.[26]

In spite of these disturbing educational trends most fundamentalists preferred to believe that the majority of Americans did not favor them. Instead, they attributed them to a small, influential minority of intellectuals who valued neither American institutions nor Christian morals. Cortland Myers asked:

> Why should a comparatively small branch of the nominal Christian church and a few Jews and foreigners be permitted to commit this offense against the original Americans and the much larger class of citizens? . . . I have no enmity toward a certain branch of the Christian church. I have no hatred for the Jews. I have only love for the foreigner, but there is not a square foot of ground in these United States for . . . a man who places dynamite underneath the foundations of the Republic.[27]

The influence of this minority, they believed, was

---

[26] J. Gresham Machen, Letter in New York Times, September 18, 1925, p. 22; What Is Faith? (New York: Macmillan Company, 1925), p. 17; Christianity and Liberalism, p. 176; "New Education Bill," pp. 157-58. Other fundamentalists also opposed federal control of education. See, e.g., the resolution of the WCFA in 1924, "Resolutions and Reports," Christian Fundamentals in School and Church, VI (July-September, 1924), 16; [Melvin Grove Kyle], Editorial, Bibliotheca Sacra, LXXXVI (January, 1929), 6. David S. Kennedy, however, favored federal control. "Romanists Oppose Educational Bill," The Presbyterian, XCI (June 16, 1921), 6.

[27] Myers, "Our Godless Schools," p. 270; cf. Gerald B. Winrod, Christ Within (3d ed.; Wichita, Kans.: Defender Publishers, 1929), p. 118; [David S. Kennedy], "Imperiling Our Heritage," The Presbyterian, LXXXVIII (May 16, 1918), 1; "Making Socialists Out of College Students," Our Hope, XXVIII (August, 1921), 105.

best exemplified by the teaching of evolution in public schools, a practice which weakened students' faith and morals and foisted on Christian taxpayers a theory that contradicted their own beliefs. The anti-evolution crusades for which fundamentalists became famous were motivated by the patriotic desire to free Christian America from noxious educational influence that could destroy the faith of the next generation.[28]

But for some the removal of a harmful influence was not sufficient. They believed that since the Bible played a prominent role in the founding and preservation of the republic it should be restored to a prominent place in American schools. Such a step, said J. C. Massee, was essential to national well-being:

> It is with the fact of God that all schools and school teachers should begin. . . . Any teacher denying or ignoring this fact is a traitor to good government. He has removed the only source of a conscious moral responsibility.[29]

Those who followed this line of reasoning believed the nineteenth-century working relationship between the state

---

[28]The anti-evolution movement will be treated more fully in a later chapter.

[29]J. C. Massee, The Ten Greatest Chapters in the Bible (Nashville, Tenn.: Sunday School Board of the Southern Baptist Convention, 1924), p. 13; cf. Sunday Night Talks, pp. 76-77; Myers, "Our Godless Schools," pp. 270-71; [David S. Kennedy], "The Evolution Skirmish in Kentucky," The Presbyterian, XCII (March 23, 1922), 6-7; [James M. Gray], "Bible in the Schools," Moody Monthly, XXVI (January, 1926), 213.

and evangelical Christianity could and should be restored.

Others, however, more realistically saw that American religious life had become too complex for that, and that any attempt at cooperation between evangelicals and the state would break down the constitutional wall of separation. These contented themselves with the argument that the state which would not allow its schools to teach religion should not allow them to teach irreligion, either.[30] To fill the growing vacuum in religious instruction they advocated the establishment of private Christian schools or the improvement and promotion of Sunday schools.[31]

But whether by public or private means, all fundamentalists agreed that the Bible must be returned to a place of major influence in national life. America's problems were being caused by increasing theological defection, and that defection began with the degradation of the Scriptures.[32] If the nation would only return to its founda-

---

[30]Leander S. Keyser, "Let us Stick to Facts," The Bible Champion, XXXIII (June-July, 1927), 310; cf. George McCready Price, "Shall the taxpayers Support Darwin?" The Bible Champion, XXX (April, 1924), 210; John Roach Straton in New York Times, March 25, 1925, p. 13. Machen opposed Bible reading in public schools (What Is Christianity? p. 299), and likely also opposed anti-evolution legislation, if one can speculate on the basis of his passion for individual freedom. See Christianity and Liberalism, p. 11.

[31]Fakkema, "Our Educational Dilemma," pp. 463-64; Clarence H. Benson, A Popular History of Christian Education (Chicago: Moody Press, 1943), pp. 344, 347-51.

[32]Milton Rudnick has pointed out correctly that fun-

tion, its strength and usefulness could continue. If it would not, however, the consequences were just as certain. T. C. Horton warned:

> If the Bible goes, our country is gone. . . . We are rich and prosperous. We stand in the forefront of the nations of the world. Our rise has been rapid. But if we fail in this time of testing; if we are indifferent to our country's peril; if we close our eyes to the stratagem of the enemy--we will awake--too late!--to find ourselves headed toward the Bolshevistic hell.[33]

The fundamentalists were patriots concerned about their country. But they were not blind patriots who feared evil in every change that occurred. Their concerns were narrowed to changes that contradicted the biblical faith for which they stood--a faith they believed decisive in America's rise and essential to her survival. Christian America was backsliding and therefore headed for trouble, but her restoration was still possible. Fundamentalists accepted this challenge with militant zeal.

Fundamentalist fervor for Christian nationalism can be adequately understood, however, only by taking into account the impressions left by World War I. This conflict increased the determination to revive America's faith in several ways. First, it confirmed the conviction that the

---

damentalists were so thoroughly theologically oriented that they blamed secularism on theological defection alone and sometimes failed to recognize other causes. Rudnick, Fundamentalism and The Missouri Synod, pp. 16-17.

[33]T. C. Horton, "A Royal Rally," The Bible Champion, XXXVI (June, 1930), 286.

United States, when divinely directed, could be a decisive force for the good of humanity. Secondly, it demonstrated to fundamentalists that modernist theology, consistently followed, could produce only the moral ruin they observed in Germany. Thirdly, for premillennialists at least, the war portended the near return of Christ, adding urgency to their mission.

Woodrow Wilson and other national leaders, combining the theme of the church militant with the secular religion of democracy, gave World War I the aura of a religious crusade.[34] With few exceptions fundamentalists also had seen the war effort as a national mission. America was fighting on the side of "light and righteousness" against "the powers of darkness and evil."[35] As their countrymen mobilized for war, fundamentalists had sought to place the struggle in biblical perspective. William L. Pettingill argued that waging war was sometimes necessary for governments to fulfill their God-given task of maintaining justice, and in such a "righteous war" the Christian was obligated to give his government full support.[36] James M. Gray agreed that

---

[34] William E. Leuchtenburg, The Perils of Prosperity, 1914-32 (Chicago: University of Chicago Press, 1958), p. 46; cf. Nye, This Almost Chosen People, pp. 176, 200.

[35] [David S. Kennedy], "This War a Crusade," The Presbyterian, LXXXVIII (October 31, 1918), 7; [A. C. Gaebelein], "An Answered Question," Our Hope, XXV (July, 1918), 48; Massee, Ten Greatest Chapters, pp. 36-37.

[36] William L. Pettingill, "Should a Christian Go to

declaring war was sometimes a national duty, and this was particularly true of the present conflict. "If it is not the clear duty of this nation to do its part to save humanity from this scourge," wrote Gray, "then it is difficult to see what duty in the case of any nation means."[37]

The cause was righteous, and perhaps a sovereign and omniscient God had even prepared America for this hour of the world's need. W. B. Riley speculated:

> It is just possible, you know, that when God made America the refuge for the oppressed of the Old World, and pushed the savage back to give the Puritan a new standing ground, that He was only determining a new Canaan in which to build a light, the shining of which would be seen afar and the warmth and radiance of which should yet keep the world from freezing by infidelity, and from dying from increasing darkness.[38]

Riley especially discerned God's guidance in the leadership of President Wilson, whose "mistakes were few, while his counsels had about them the aroma and clear hints of a higher source."[39] A. C. Gaebelein saw the same divine power displayed on the battlefield:

> We speak now of the masterly strategy of Marshal Foch, the brilliant leadership of Generals Haig, Petain and others, including our own General Pershing, and our noble army with its truly wonderful achievements. But let us never forget what is behind it all. It is God

---

War?" Serving and Waiting, VII (June, 1917), 54-55.

[37]James M. Gray, "What the Bible Teaches About War," The Christian Workers Magazine, XVII (July, 1917), 858.

[38]W. B. Riley, Bible of the Expositor, Old Testament, III, 179.

[39]Ibid., p. 170.

in His government of justice and righteousness who has, through these agencies, displayed His power.[40]

Not all fundamentalists had so positively identified national war policy with the purposes of God, however. Philip Mauro condemned all war as contrary to Christ's teachings and warned that Christians serving in the military were implicating themselves in its atrocities.[41] Only a strong patriotism and love of liberty swayed J. Gresham Machen from an initial pro-German attitude, and although he voluntarily served with the YMCA overseas, he regarded compulsory military service as an unwarranted infringement on personal freedom.[42] Others like Mennonite John Horsch doubtless refused to participate on grounds of conscience. But most fundamentalists seem to have shared the zeal of the 1918 International Sunday School Convention, which featured patriotic songs and closed with a patriotic rally.[43] In this spirit Mark Matthews had predicted that Americans would return from their victory to "build America on a foundation of absolute equity, democracy, and righteous-

---

[40][A. C. Gaebelein], "Divine Justice Displayed," Our Hope, XXV (January, 1919), 396.

[41]Philip Mauro, Shall We Smite With the Sword? (Boston: Scripture Truth Depot, n.d.).

[42]Stonehouse, J. Gresham Machen, pp. 243-51.

[43][Charles G. Trumbull], "The Sunday School's Peril From the War," The Sunday School Times, LX (July 27, 1918), 413-14.

ness."[44]

Such was the promise of patriotic and religious idealism. But fundamentalists were not as naive about the country's future as Matthews' statement seems to indicate. The saloon was on its way out, but as the war drew to a close other problems loomed ahead. George Davis proposed a national day of humiliation and prayer to call attention to sabbath desecration, divorce, and other evils, and shortly after the armistice James M. Gray convened a "Conference on World Evangelism and Vital Christianity After the War" to head off errors fostered by the war itself, notably the idea that good deeds or physical sacrifice on the battlefield could atone for sin or win God's favor.[45]

Modernist theology, with its evolutionary and higher critical emphases, also was continuing to invade American Protestantism. Observing how many German things had been banned during the war, A. C. Gaebelein expressed surprise that "the worst German thing under the sun," the higher criticism, had escaped censure.[46] To Gaebelein and his

---

[44]Mark A. Matthews, "The Morale of America in the War," The Presbyterian, LXXXVIII (August 8, 1918), 10; cf. W. B. Riley, Bible of the Expositor, New Testament, IX, 133-48.

[45]George T. B. Davis, "When Will the War End?" The Sunday School Times, LX (April 20, 1918), 219; [Charles G. Trumbull], "And Now for Vital Christianity," The Sunday School Times, LXI (February 22, 1919), 101-2.

[46][A. C. Gaebelein], "The Worst Has Been Spared," Our Hope, XXIV (March, 1918), 587-88.

fundamentalist colleagues it was inconceivable that alert Americans should continue to admire "German-made" theology. The war had demonstrated America's potential usefulness in the hand of God, but to worship the impotent gods of one's fallen enemy seemed to them the shortest route to national suicide.

World War I, therefore, was to fundamentalists a global exhibition of a nation's spiritual bankruptcy when it substituted human speculations for divine truth. A. C. Dixon found in Germany's example the ultimate logic of evolutionary theory, which, he said, "has fostered autocratic class distinctions and is no friend to the democracy which stands for the protection of the weak against the oppression of the strong." He reasoned that "If the strong and fit have the scientific right to destroy the weak and unfit . . . Germany should not be criticized."[47] W. H. Griffith Thomas argued that Germany's alleged atrocities proved that biblical scholarship without spiritual insight was morally useless,[48] while John Horsch used the war as

---

[47]A. C. Dixon, "The Menace of Evolution," The Bible Champion, XXIX (January, 1923), 29; cf. William B. Riley, "The Last Days; the Last War and the Last King," in Christ and Glory, ed. by Arno C. Gaebelein (New York: Publication Office "Our Hope," n.d.), p. 168.

[48]W. H. Griffith Thomas, "German Moral Abnormality," Bibliotheca Sacra, LXXVI (January, 1919), 84-104; cf. Albert L. Berry, "The Trail of the German Critics," The Presbyterian, LXXXVIII (February 28, 1918), 9-10; W. W. Moore, "The Lesson of Prussia's Moral Shipwreck," Our Hope, XXV (September, 1918), 179-82.

evidence of the shallowness of liberal evolutionary optimism.[49] Numerous others emphasized the faith-robbing character of German theology, usually adding a pointed warning that America was not immune from Germany's fate.[50]

Many have taken such warnings as evidences of hatred bred by the war fever--hatred which persisted and was directed toward other "devils" after the conflict ended. Rudnick asserts, for example, that "The hatred originally cultivated against the 'Hun' was warmed over in the hearts of Fundamentalists and directed against the liberal."[51] Undoubtedly in some cases this was true, but to apply this characteristic to the whole movement is to ignore much evidence to the contrary. In fact, if Leuchtenburg's description of wartime intolerance is reasonably accurate,[52] fundamentalists were no more chauvinistic, and in many cases less so, than their fellow citizens.

They had been subjected to the same barrage of propaganda and emotional pressure as others, and these had taken

---

[49] John Horsch, Modern Religious Liberalism (Scottdale, Pa.: Fundamental Truth Depot, 1920), pp. 280-84.

[50] See, e.g., William L. Pettingill, "Germany's Lapse Into Barbarism," Serving and Waiting, VII (December, 1917), 281; A. C. Gaebelein, "The Pre-eminence of the Lord Jesus Christ," in Christ and Glory, p. 12.

[51] Milton L. Rudnick, Fundamentalism and The Missouri Synod (St. Louis: Concordia Publishing House, 1966), p. 83.

[52] Leuchtenburg, Perils of Prosperity, pp. 44-45.

a toll. The editorials of German-born Arno C. Gaebelein may serve as an interesting study in modification. In 1914, while placing the largest share of blame for the war on Germany, he also implicated Serbia, Russia, and France. During the same year he denied atrocity reports from both sides, but when criticized for this by British and Canadian subscribers he adopted a policy of silence on the war's details. When the United States finally aligned itself with the Allies he spoke out again with a considerably changed perspective. Now he praised Serbia for its "heroism" during the early months of the war, and he had a simple answer concerning responsibility: "The question, 'Who started this horrible world-conflict?' has been positively answered. The entire responsibility rests upon the Kaiser and his Prussian outfit."[53]

But Gaebelein's comments were mild when compared with those of Jay Benson Hamilton, who until his death in 1920 edited *The Bible Champion*. In his rabid editorials Hamilton called neutrals and German sympathizers "copperheads" and invited them to leave the country if they did not know the difference between "The Hymn of Hate" and "The Star-Spangled Banner." He labeled a religious leader who urged

---

[53][A. C. Gaebelein], "Who is Responsible," *Our Hope*, XXI (October, 1914), 198; "Charges of Atrocities Unfounded," *ibid.*, XXI (November, 1914), 301; "Serbia's Destruction," *ibid.*, XXIV (May, 1918), 688-89; "An Answered Question," *ibid.*, XXV (July, 1918), 47-48.

tolerance for German language and culture "a kaiser in embryo" and expressed hope that he could label every "Hun school" where "German science and theology" were taught.[54]

A similar spirit was evident in the impassioned remarks of Cortland Myers, who asserted in 1918 that "hidden traitorism" ought to be "hunted down to the last single man or woman, and just as quickly as possible." He especially detested "foreign innovation or immigration into our religious world," and concluded on this emotional pitch:

> I hate this traitorous stuff. Yes, I hate it! I have seen too much of it. . . . I see it damning our theological seminaries. I hate it! I hate it! I hate the new theology as I hate hell, from which it came![55]

But Hamilton and Myers were rare exceptions, and such anti-German outbursts were often challenged by other fundamentalist leaders. Leander Keyser, for example, took issue with Hamilton's editorials. Keyser tactfully suggested that the editor either lacked information or was blinded by prejudices. Assuring Hamilton that he was "pro-American to the core," with ancestors who fought in the Revolution, the War of 1812, and the Civil War, he nevertheless insisted

---

[54]Jay Benson Hamilton, "Hun Hymn of Hate," The Bible Champion, XXIV (January-February, 1918), 41; "What Shall We Do With the Copperhead?" ibid., XXIV (March-April, 1918), 59-62; "A Kaiser in Embryo," ibid., XXIV (December, 1918), 502-3; "Ban Hun Propaganda," ibid., XXV (January, 1919), 43-44.

[55]Cortland Myers, "War on German Theology," in Light on Prophecy: The Proceedings and Addresses at the Philadelphia Prophetic Conference, May 28-30, 1918 (New York: Christian Herald, 1918), pp. 180-82.

that true patriotism demanded fairness. He pointed out that modernism could be traced to France and England as well as Germany, that Germany had produced a consistent stream of evangelical scholars, and that much in American secularism was totally unrelated to German thought. Keyser urged that evangelical truth be promoted, not by "heat, passion, and wrathful epithets," but by "prayer, faith, strict regard for the truth, and invincible argument."[56]

One of the most balanced treatments of the World War came from the pen of James M. Gray in 1917. Although Gray believed the war was necessary and urged Christian citizens to give their support, he cautioned that "The 'Hymn of Hate' must not be sung by those who praise the grace of God." With a tolerance that Paul Carter terms "exceedingly rare,"[57] Gray exhorted German and American Christians to let their common love for "the Author of their spiritual birth" transcend loyalties to their respective fatherlands, not praying for the victory of their troops but for God's will to be done. Gray himself hoped to bring to America after the war a German pastor friend who was presently min-

---

[56]Leander S. Keyser, "Let us be Just and Fair," The Bible Champion, XXVI (February, 1920), 51-54; XXVI (March, 1920), 108-10; cf. A. C. Dixon, "Menace of Evolution," p. 30.

[57]Paul A. Carter, "The Fundamentalist Defense of the Faith," in Change and Continuity in Twentieth-Century America, The 1920's, ed. by John Braeman, Robert H. Bremner, and David Brody (Columbus, Ohio: Ohio State University Press, 1968), pp. 195-96.

istering to German troops.[58] Instead of blaming others for the conflict, he insisted, Americans should profit from its divinely-intended lessons, for God may have been using Germany to scourge other nations for their sins. Gray declared:

> Belgium, whose sorrows we deplore, is reaping what she sowed in the atrocities of the Congo. Bleeding France . . . is paying the penalty of her atheism. Russia is receiving of the Lord's hand for her persecution of the Jew, and Turkey for her treatment of the Armenian. Great Britain has been mocking God as a Christian nation while fostering, for commercial gain, the rank heathenism of India. And the United States? Is there any nation . . . more proud, more worldly-minded, more self-contained, more needing a humbling at the hand of God in the experiences of a distressing war?[59]

Numerous other fundamentalists expressed similar sentiments more briefly. A. C. Gaebelein, while showing little pity for Prussian militarists, deplored the lynchings and other indignities suffered by suspected German sympathizers, and he was disappointed by the lack of forgiveness evident at the peace conference. He assured his readers that "the Lord will be mindful of His people in Germany, who are just as beloved to Him as those . . . in other nations."[60] J. Gresham Machen also was disturbed by Ameri-

---

[58]Gray, "What the Bible Teaches About War," p. 861.

[59]*Ibid.*, p. 858. Note a similar emphasis by Luther T. Townsend, who accused the United States of "commercial greed and other unsanctified ambitions," making millions while Europe was at war. "Germany, God's Battle Axe," *The Bible Champion*, XXIV (March-April, 1918), 63-68.

[60][A. C. Gaebelein], "A Just Word and Rebuke," *Our Hope*, XXV (October, 1918), 241-42; "The Justice of the

can vindictiveness and deplored the high reparations imposed on Germany. To him the peace treaty looked like "an old-fashioned land-grab."[61]

Watching the feverish war preparations in 1917, Leon Tucker called for sanity, prayerfulness, and love. In words that anticipated those of Gray he urged Christians to rise above national loyalties and display their spiritual unity.[62] At the height of the war Curtis Lee Laws condemned the injustices done to German-Americans as "un-American, un-democratic and un-Christian." He was appalled at the glorification of hatred of "the Hun," and complained that "The profane maledictions that otherwise would fill us with horror are all right when hurled from Christian lips at the Kaiser." He advised, "Let us do more, and swear less."[63]

Undoubtedly it was hatred already present in the

Peace Treaty," _ibid._, XXVI (October, 1919), 228-29; "The Hope of Young Germany," _ibid._, XXIX (April, 1923), 604-5.

[61]Stonehouse, _J. Gresham Machen_, p. 299.

[62]W. Leon Tucker, "Poor Peace Prospects," _The Wonderful Word_, IX (March, 1917), 246-47; "A Bond or a Break?" _ibid._, IX (May, 1917), 338-40; "Human Hate," _ibid._, X (November, 1917), 55-56.

[63][Curtis Lee Laws], "Hysteria Concerning Disloyalty," _The Watchman-Examiner_, VI (April 18, 1918), 493; "Patriotism and Profanity," _ibid._, VI (October 10, 1918), 1281. See also [David S. Kennedy], "Fairness Toward the German People," _The Presbyterian_, LXXXVIII (June 20, 1918), 7; David James Burrell, "Love Your Enemies," _ibid._, LXXXVIII (August 29, 1918), 9-10.

evangelical community that made such rebukes necessary. But it is noteworthy that most fundamentalist leaders, far from feeding and justifying such a response, instead condemned it strongly. It was not Germans, but antibiblical hypotheses nurtured in Germany, that they abhorred. At least four years before the outbreak of war had begun to turn Americans against Germans, Dyson Hague had attacked these "German fancies" and had contended that "For hypothesis-weaving and speculation, the German theological professor is unsurpassed."[64] Having long considered these theories dangerous to religion and morality, fundamentalists after the war could point to Germany as positive proof of their ruinous effects. And as defeated Germany went on display, victorious America went on trial.

World War I increased the fundamentalists' desire to purify the nation in still another way. For the many premillennialists among them it seemed to bring into focus many scriptural prophecies concerning the last days, injecting a note of urgency into their postwar efforts.

The quickening pulse of world events at the turn of the century, including international alliances and rivalries, peace conferences, and proposed world federations, had stimulated the study of prophecy even before the war.[65]

---

[64]Dyson Hague, The Fundamentals, I, 90.

[65]See, e.g., Philip Mauro, Man's Day (London: Morgan & Scott Ltd., 1908), pp. 176-77. Note, too, that A. C.

But the outbreak of hostilities and the prospect of a worldwide holocaust had caused prophetic interest to mushroom to the extent that Arno C. Gaebelein had to caution his readers not to dogmatize on the significance of the war.[66]

But while premillennial spokesmen tried to be cautious in their interpretations, the conviction grew, nevertheless, that the conflict was at least the gateway to the last days. This conviction was strengthened immeasurably by the fall of Jerusalem and the Balfour Declaration in 1917, which re-established Palestine as a Jewish homeland. Learning of the British occupation of Jerusalem, aging millenarian C. I. Scofield wrote to William L. Pettingill, "Ah! at last a real 'sign'! . . . We may meet in the air before I sign this!"[67] A. E. Thompson, the former pastor of the American Church at Jerusalem, told the Philadelphia Prophetic Conference in 1918:

> . . . when Jerusalem was captured, we all said with one consent, "This is the climax of the ages." We have entered a prophetic era. We are looking upon the things which Moses, and the prophets, and Christ Him-

---

Gaebelein and James M. Gray organized a prophetic conference in Chicago early in 1914, A. C. Gaebelein, Introduction to Christ and Glory, p. 3.

[66][A. C. Gaebelein], "A Word of Caution," Our Hope, XXI (November, 1914), 262-65.

[67]William L. Pettingill, "The Fall of Jerusalem," Serving and Waiting, VII (February, 1918), 363.

self have foretold.[68]

At the New York Prophetic Conference later the same year, Gaebelein summed up the feelings of most millenarians when he said, "It seems then clear that divine providence has used this horrible war to take away Palestine from the Turk and make it possible for the Jewish people to return."[69] W. B. Riley agreed, asserting that the nations of the earth "have compelled history to run into 'the mould of prophecy,' that 'the last days' might be exactly as God said they would be."[70]

It is ironic that the fundamentalists, who have so often been accused of hating the Germans, were in 1918 accused by modernists Shailer Mathews and Shirley Jackson Case of being pacifists and subverting the war effort by teaching the second coming of Christ. Case in particular was merciless with the premillennialists, accusing them of "throwing up the sponge" and "raising the white flag of surrender." He charged them with IWW affinities and insinuated that they collaborated with the Germans.[71]

---

[68]A. E. Thompson, "The Capture of Jerusalem," in <u>Light on Prophecy</u>, p. 145.

[69]Arno C. Gaebelein, "The Capture of Jerusalem and the Great Future of that City," in <u>Christ and Glory</u>, p. 156.

[70]W. B. Riley, "The Last Days," in <u>ibid</u>., p. 163; cf. P. W. Philpott, "Coming Events Cast Their Shadows Before," in <u>Light on Prophecy</u>, pp. 206, 208.

[71]Shirley Jackson Case, "The Premillennial Menace,"

These obviously unfounded charges brought a swift reaction. W. H. Griffith Thomas, a native Englishman, termed pacifism "intolerable" and insisted that millenarians had been "the strongest and most determined advocates of this war."[72] Canadian P. W. Philpott called the charges "the most cowardly method of representation," and revealed that his four sons and three hundred men from his congregation were presently serving in France.[73] Such accusations were "laughable," claimed W. B. Riley, for premillennialists were, "by their very convictions of truth," opposed to Germany's theology and militaristic attitude. Riley pointed out that a hundred members of his Minneapolis church and two of his sons were serving in the army.[74] Veteran evangelist J. Wilbur Chapman, addressing the Phila-

---

The Biblical World, LII (July, 1918), 16-23. See Sandeen's fuller discussion of these charges. The Roots of Fundamentalism (Chicago: University of Chicago Press, 1970), pp. 235-36. Curiously, Carroll E. Harrington follows the lead of Mathews and Case, referring to a "wholesale display of pacifism at the New York and Philadelphia Prophetic Conferences . . . in open defiance of wartime patriotism." "The Fundamentalist Movement in America, 1870-1920" (Unpublished Ph.D. dissertation, University of California at Berkeley, 1959), p. 209.

[72]W. H. Griffith Thomas, "The Prince of Peace," in Christ and Glory, p. 226.

[73]Philpott, "Coming Events," in Light on Prophecy, pp. 203-4.

[74]W. B. Riley, "Premillennialism and Government Investigation," School and Church, II (January-March, 1919), 98-99; "The Gospel for War Times," in Light on Prophecy, p. 341. Cf. [A. C. Gaebelein], "Who is the Menace?" Our Hope, XXV (March, 1919), 521-24.

delphia conference, declared that

> . . . no people in this world . . . will be more faithful in upholding the government, in standing for a righteous peace, in giving of money or giving of life for the winning of this war than the people who are represented in this great gathering.[75]

Christ's return did not induce passivity, but millenarians believed God gave signs to spur them to greater evangelistic activity. Several, in fact, expressed the view that their energetic service could hasten the second coming. A prayer by D. M. Stearns at the Philadelphia Prophetic Conference illustrates this emphasis:

> We thank Thee for telling us there is just one thing to do if we are redeemed, and that is, to live to make Thee known as quickly as possible, and to make known this great salvation, so that Thy church, Thy body, shall be completed and the marriage of the Lamb come.[76]

Herbert Mackenzie told the same conference that "we have a commission which must be obeyed and completed in order that he may come again and receive us unto Himself."[77]

When they spoke of the Christian's duty, premillenialists normally emphasized evangelism of various types, and particularly foreign missions. Herbert Mackenzie reflected

---

[75] J. Wilbur Chapman, Remarks to the Philadelphia Prophetic Conference of 1918, in _Light on Prophecy_, p. 245.

[76] D. M. Stearns, "One of the Convention Prayers," _ibid._, pp. 360, 362.

[77] Herbert Mackenzie, "Does This Truth Paralyze or Energize?" in _ibid._, p. 275; cf. John M. MacInnis, "Where is Jesus Now, and What is He Doing?" _ibid._, p. 126; W. B. Riley, "Questions and Answers," _ibid._, p. 344; W. H. Griffith Thomas, "The Return of the Lord," _Serving and Waiting_, X (May, 1920), 21.

that, just as the Napoleonic wars had stimulated interest in missions, so perhaps God intended through the World War to do the same again.[78] It was understood, however, that the war must first be won if missionary work was to expand. While premillennialists sympathized with President Wilson's aim "to make the world safe for democracy," they were more concerned about making it safe for evangelism, for they believed that, in the absence of Christ, only the preaching of his gospel could "make democracy safe for the world."[79]

But should the Christian restrict himself to evangelism, or should he become involved in political and social questions as well? Here premillennialists disagreed among themselves. A minority, represented by A. C. Gaebelein, insisted that, in view of the inevitable deepening of apostasy, such concerns were a waste of time.[80] But most others, including Riley and Gray, apparently put patriotism ahead of theology at this point. Riley admitted that when someone argued with him that Christians had a higher mission than politics, "I confess . . . I hardly know who is the right man." But as for himself, "I vote with a venge-

---

[78]Mackenzie, "Does This Truth Paralyze or Energize?" pp. 274-75.

[79]W. B. Riley, "The Gospel for War Times," pp. 335-38.

[80]A. C. Gaebelein, "The Only Way," Our Hope, XXX (August, 1923), 76-78; "The Conflict and How to War," ibid., XXX (February, 1924), 459-62.

ance, and I fight for sobriety with all the ability that is in me."[81] Gray took as his guiding principle for political involvement the words of the hymn, "Hold the fort, for I am coming." He explained,

> I do not expect the church to take this world for Christ till Christ comes, but by His grace, the church can do something to hold the position He has given us, to "occupy" till He comes.[82]

This activist viewpoint of Gray and Riley came to dominate the fundamentalism of the next decade. If world evangelization was the most urgent need of the hour, it must have a base of operations. That base was an awakened American Protestantism in a purified American society. The sense of national mission was always present in the thinking even of those who claimed a heavenly citizenship.

In view of the premillennial interpretation of current events, it becomes meaningless to speak of "postwar disillusionment" as a cause of fundamentalism. Millenarians never had any illusions about the lasting value of the war or the Wilsonian program for peace. To them the war had already proven the inadequacy of humanism, and in such an environment, as Harrington has noted, they felt more confident than ever to promote evangelical doctrine as a

---

[81] W. B. Riley, "Questions and Answers," p. 349.

[82] Quoted by William M. Runyan, Dr. Gray at Moody Bible Institute (New York: Oxford University Press, 1935), p. 98.

more realistic alternative.[83] While expressing admiration for President Wilson, they voiced grave doubts about the success of his peace efforts.

The conflict had scarcely ended when millenarians began to warn idealistic America that man-made peace was at best temporary. W. H. Griffith Thomas reminded his New York audience in November, 1918 that cessation of hostilities was not necessarily peace, and that unless statesmen took sin into account they would be treating symptoms, not sores.[84] W. B. Riley told the same gathering that although he sympathized with present peace proposals, "I know my Book too well to expect that either peace or prosperity will be the universal portion until men have turned from their false gods . . . "[85] Reuben A. Torrey, observing the rising of a world-wide "red tide," predicted that a temporary peace due to League of Nations influence would give way to "the most awful universal war that this old world has ever seen."[86] The following year brought many more cautions, such as that of W. W. Fereday:

> Let all who love our Lord Jesus Christ cultivate a healthy outlook at the present crisis. Beware of men's

---

[83]Harrington, "Fundamentalist Movement in America," p. 283.

[84]Thomas, "The Prince of Peace," pp. 218, 222.

[85]Riley, "The Last Days," pp. 172-73.

[86]Reuben A. Torrey, "That Blessed Hope," in <u>Christ and Glory</u>, pp. 22, 33.

> vain hopes and expectations. Beware of the influence of the press. Stand aloof from the world's schemes for the putting right of all that is wrong. Let your eyes be heavenward . . .[87]

With such an attitude there was little chance of disillusionment when peace plans went awry and power politics replaced idealism. The premillennial fundamentalist would simply say, "I told you so."

World War I exercised a profound influence on the fundamentalism of the twenties, although not precisely in the manner some observers have believed. It may have left a residue of hatred or disillusionment in some minds, but to the bulk of the fundamentalists these generalizations do not apply. Instead, the war intensified their patriotism and deepened their sense of Christian responsibility to their country.

Encouraged by America's usefulness in a "righteous cause," they assumed that it could continue its divine mission if only it were freed from the antibiblical and secular philosophies threatening it. At the same time the war confirmed and intensified their hostility toward those philosophies which, in their view, had caused the conflict. How alarming it was to find America, on the threshold of

---

[87]W. W. Fereday, "After the Great War," Our Hope, XXVI (July, 1919), 38. See also [A. C. Gaebelein], "After the War--What?" and "The League of Nations," ibid., XXV (April, 1919), 586-88, 616; W. Leon Tucker, "Millennium? Not Yet," The Wonderful Word, XI (March, 1919), 247-48; "A New Age or the Same Old Age?" ibid., XI (June, 1919), 386-87.

moral and spiritual opportunity, flirting with the seductress of its fallen foe! Finally, international developments had convinced many fundamentalists that time was running out and the world must be evangelized quickly. If the United States was to play a significant role in this final thrust, it must be revived and purified. For some this purification was related only to the "spiritual" realm of the churches, but for a number of influential fundamentalists it was extended to other aspects of American culture, and they did not hesitate to use political means to accomplish it.

Fundamentalist militancy can therefore be understood only by considering both its theological and national context. If the Bible was divinely inspired and America was divinely commissioned, then logically America should embrace the Book. And while the dream of a Christianized America did not quite fit the premillennial view of the last days, most fundamentalists did not seem too troubled by the inconsistency. They would, with Gray, "hold the fort" and leave the outcome with God.

CHAPTER V

"THE FAITH" AND THE MINORITIES

The post-World War I years in America were plagued with fear-bred intolerance. Wartime experiences and propaganda had done their work, and a nation conditioned to look for traitors and spies found itself unable to drop its guard. Racial and ethnic tensions already present in the social fabric were both postponed and aggravated by the war. Ideological cleavages were exaggerated as radical groups refused to support the Great Crusade and expressed open support for the Bolshevik revolutionists of Russia. Wartime idealism quickly evaporated before the postwar realities of runaway prices, strikes, business depression, and unemployed veterans. Hopes for a democratic world and a lasting peace faded as the results of the Paris conference became known.

In short, many Americans felt confused and threatened by the strange new climate of the postwar era. The nation, their major point of identification, seemed on the verge of disaster, and in desperation they rose to its defense. The tense, self-conscious "100 percent Americanism" built up during the war was first violently released in the "Red

Scare" of 1919 and 1920. But it continued to spin itself out during the following decade in immigration restriction, anti-Semitism, distrust of Catholics and Negroes, and general dislike for anything "un-American." Wartime patriotic organizations, including the revived Ku Klux Klan, lived on and new ones were created to battle alleged threats to the American way of life. Even men with a reputation for scholarship, such as Madison Grant and Lothrop Stoddard, lent their support to what many considered to be Anglo-Saxondom's last stand.[1] In such an atmosphere of insecurity hysteria often replaced reason, rumor supplanted fact, and law gave way to lynching.[2]

The crucial question for this study is how fundamentalism was related to this climate of intolerance. Some

---

[1]Madison Grant, The Passing of the Great Race (New York: Charles Scribner's Sons, 1916); Lothrop Stoddard, The Rising Tide of Color (New York: Charles Scribner's Sons, 1920).

[2]Various writers have commented on the causes and manifestations of this intolerance. See, e.g., Stanley Coben, "A Study of Nativism: The American Red Scare of 1919-20," in New Perspectives on the American Past, ed. by Stanley N. Katz and Stanley I. Kutler (Boston: Little, Brown and Company, 1969), II, 203-22; John Higham, Strangers in the Land (New Brunswick, N.J.: Rutgers University Press, 1955), pp. 265-99, passim; Paul L. Murphy, "Sources and Nature of Intolerance in the 1920's," in The 1920's: Problems and Paradoxes, ed. by Milton Plesur (Boston: Allyn and Bacon, Inc., 1969), pp. 165-83; John Hope Franklin, "Postwar Upheaval: Racism and Riots," in The Impact of World War I, ed. by Arthur S. Link (New York: Harper & Row Publishers, 1969), pp. 91-99; Robert K. Murray, Red Scare: A Study of National Hysteria, 1919-1920 (New York: McGraw-Hill Book Company, 1955), pp. 3-17 and passim.

writers on the twenties see fundamentalism encouraging and even participating in violent measures to uphold Americanism. John D. Hicks declares, for example:

> Religious fundamentalists provided the backbone for the Ku Klux Klan; if the pleadings of the righteous and the law of the land failed to make people do the right thing, then private force might properly be employed.[3]

Others more cautiously assert that fundamentalism was a parallel form of intolerance, originating in a similar frame of mind and similar cultural conditions, but expressing its frustrations in less violent ways. Norman F. Furniss cites such fundamentalist characteristics as "vaguely-defined fear," "longing for certainty" in the midst of "unrelieved hardship," and "violence in thought and language."[4] The fears and tensions which the Klan and the American Legion expressed through threats and lynchings were sublimated by fundamentalists into verbal attacks on evolutionists and theology professors. Whichever of these

---

[3]John D. Hicks, Republican Ascendancy, 1921-1933 (New York: Harper & Row, 1960), pp. 182-83. Richard Hofstadter also maintains that they "gave heavy support" to the Klan. The Paranoid Style in American Politics (New York: Alfred A. Knopf, 1965), p. 73, note; cf. Walter Lippmann, A Preface to Morals (New York: Macmillan Company, 1929), p. 31.

[4]Norman F. Furniss, The Fundamentalist Controversy, 1918-1931 (New Haven: Yale University Press, 1954), pp. 35-37; cf. Ray Ginger, Six Days or Forever? Tennessee v. John Thomas Scopes (Boston: Beacon Press, 1958), pp. 10-12; George E. Mowry, The Urban Nation, 1920-1960 (New York: Hill and Wang, 1965), pp. 30-31; Clifford Kirkpatrick, Religion in Human Affairs (New York: John Wiley & Sons, Inc., 1929), p. 402.

two viewpoints one encounters, he is left with the impression that fundamentalists were possessed with the same blind Americanism which produced the anti-Red, anti-foreign, anti-Negro, anti-Catholic, and anti-Semitic outbursts of the decade.

An accurate portrayal of fundamentalist attitudes toward minority groups demands that we bear several facts in mind. First, prejudice is not easily defined, and the one who sees himself as an object of prejudice will obviously include more in the term than will the one he accuses of prejudice. Even if one accepts Simpson's and Yinger's definition of prejudice as an emotional, rigid attitude toward a group, including both prejudgment and misjudgment,[5] he must still determine whether a specific statement, action, or attitude fits this category. While this may be easily done with regard to the grosser manifestations of prejudice, there will always be disagreement as to whether certain ambiguous statements or acts should be regarded as prejudicial. Rather than attempting to resolve such questions with finality, therefore, this study will simply describe fundamentalist attitudes toward minority groups, state their reasons for holding them, and compare these attitudes with those of other Americans during the

---

[5]George Eaton Simpson and J. Milton Yinger, _Racial and Cultural Minorities_ (3d ed.; New York: Harper & Row, Publishers, 1965), pp. 10-12.

same period.

Secondly, a religious person's distrust of or hostility toward an outside group need not imply a general dislike for all outsiders. Bernhard Olson, for example, has discovered in a study of four Protestant Sunday School curricula, ranging from fundamentalist to liberal, that the lessons portrayed outside racial, ethnic, and national groups more favorably than they portrayed other religious groups. Olson has concluded that even strong theological commitment does not necessarily predispose a person to a general ethnocentrism.[6] To some extent this conclusion is illustrated by the fundamentalist leaders of the twenties. While their political and religious heritage inclined them to suspect both Communists and Catholics, they differed widely in their appraisal of foreigners, Negroes, and Jews. Furthermore, most of them were highly critical of the most ethnocentric organization of their time, the Ku Klux Klan.

A third fact to remember is that fundamentalists could not be "100 percent American" without compromising their theological commitment. As we have previously observed, their strong patriotism was usually tempered by the theological conviction that the nation deserved praise only as long as it retained biblical beliefs and morals.

---

[6] Bernhard E. Olson, Faith and Prejudice: Intergroup Problems in Protestant Curricula (New Haven: Yale University Press, 1963), pp. 27-29; cf. Simpson and Yinger, Racial and Cultural Minorities, pp. 397-400.

While some fundamentalists perceived threats to America in its changing population, this was really not their major concern, and much of their literature remained silent on such questions. They were far more alarmed by the inroads of heterodox religious teaching in churches and schools, for spiritual strength was believed to be essential to whatever challenges the nation might face.[7]

The World War and its aftermath caused fundamentalists, along with other Americans, to rethink the role of the immigrant in American life. The implication of recent arrivals in a number of violent and subversive incidents, combined with their adherence to unfamiliar religious traditions, seemed to indicate that the "melting pot" was overflowing and that large numbers of partially assimilated immigrants were threatening the nation's political and religious heritage. They therefore believed more care should be exercised in the admittance and education of future immigrants.

We have previously pointed out that some fundamentalists, like Cortland Myers, believed foreigners were partially responsible for the decline of religious influence in education.[8] David James Burrell more generally linked secularism with foreign influence, and wrote with consider-

---

[7]I have reserved a discussion of fundamentalists' views of communism for a later chapter.

[8]See page 127.

able irritation:

> The time has evidently come for the millions of patriotic people in our country to serve kindly but emphatic notice on all who seek shelter under the aegis of our free institutions that the fundamental principles of our American civilization have not been abrogated in their behalf; in other words, the guests at our fireside are expected to observe the common rules of hospitality.[9]

Other fundamentalists were disturbed by the anarchistic tendencies of foreigners shortly after the war. Arno C. Gaebelein felt that hitherto these "enemies of everything that is right and decent" had been treated far too leniently, and he hoped the "utmost force" would be used to rid the country of them.[10] David S. Kennedy gave his support to the policy of deporting alien radicals because he believed these "bright and determined" men posed a genuine threat to the government.[11] In the wake of the Wall Street bombing, Curtis Lee Laws complained bitterly, "We have flung wide our gates in generous hospitality and this infamy is a part of our reward." Laws insisted that "The miscreants must be hunted down and swift justice must

---

[9]David J. Burrell, "Our Christian Land," The Bible Champion, XXXII (February, 1926), 66. Mark A. Matthews expressed the same sentiments in almost identical terms in 1922. "The Logic of Deeds Is More Convincing Than the Rhetoric of Professions," The Wonderful Word, XIV (July, 1922), 460.

[10][Arno C. Gaebelein], "The Attempts to Overthrow Our Government," Our Hope, XXVI (January, 1920), 414.

[11][David S. Kennedy], "Ellis Island Reds Increasing," The Presbyterian, XC (July 22, 1920), 4.

be measured out to them."[12] Laws' mood in the early post-war years is further illustrated by his insistence that pastors of churches be either natural-born or naturalized American citizens.[13]

Only sporadically throughout the rest of the decade did fundamentalists criticize foreigners, and when they did it was usually in reference to their Roman Catholic religious affiliation. A. Reilly Copeland of Waco, Texas asserted in 1924 that two-thirds of the immigrants who came annually were "under Rome's complete control and . . . wholly unfit to become American citizens." He charged that Rome "herded" them into large cities where they could not be evangelized or Americanized.[14] Four years later, during Alfred E. Smith's presidential campaign, William B. Riley drew a sharp distinction between the Protestant Scandinavian population of the Northwest and the Catholic, South European inhabitants of New York. This latter group, claimed Riley, were "steeped in ignorance," had little respect for law, seldom educated their children in public

---

[12][Curtis Lee Laws], "Cruel and Senseless Assassination," _The Watchman-Examiner_, VIII (September 23, 1920), 1159.

[13][Curtis Lee Laws], "Our Pastors Should Be American Citizens," _ibid._, IX (April 28, 1921), 520.

[14]A. Reilly Copeland, "Copeland Exposes Plans of Romanism in America," _The Searchlight_, VII (August 8, 1924), 3; cf. J. Frank Norris, "The Menace of Romanism in Politics," _ibid._, VII (August 1, 1924), 3.

schools, and in general were a curse to the areas in which they settled.[15]

In view of such opinions, it is not surprising that many fundamentalists favored some degree of immigration restriction. Men as varied in temperament as J. Frank Norris and A. Reilly Copeland, on one hand, and James M. Gray and Melvin Grove Kyle, on the other, expressed support for restrictive measures.[16]

This advocacy of restriction was motivated more by cultural than by genetic considerations. Unlike the prominent racial theorists of their day, fundamentalists stressed the underlying unity of the diverse segments of mankind, for their theology emphasized the oneness of humanity in creation, in sin, and at least potentially in redemption. William B. Riley, therefore, was only being theologically consistent when he cautioned Americans not to despise the Hungarian, the Italian, or the Jew, since all

---

[15]W. B. Riley, "Shall Tammany Rule America?" The Fundamentalist, VI (October 12, 1928), 2; cf. "The Turn of the Tide or the Decline of Modernism," The Christian Fundamentalist, II (December, 1928), 8.

[16]Norris, "Menace of Roman Catholicism," p. 3; Copeland, "Plans of Romanism," p. 3; [James M. Gray], "Selective Immigration," Moody Monthly, XXVI (November, 1925), 99-100; [Melvin G. Kyle], Editorial, Bibliotheca Sacra, LXXXVI (April, 1929), 132-33. J. Gresham Machen on the other hand, opposed a proposal to enroll aliens, but he apparently was motivated by a fear of growing bureaucracy rather than a concern for the individual immigrant. Letter in New York Herald Tribune, December 7, 1925, p. 14.

were brothers in origin.[17]

Furthermore, fundamentalists professed to believe a certain amount of racial and national diversity was good for America. J. T. Larsen considered it one of the secrets of American greatness, and Curtis Lee Laws looked forward to the day when all nationalities found in his country would "intermingle their blood" and become "ideal Americans."[18] But for this to happen, newcomers were expected to sacrifice much of their past heritage and conform to the mold of the native majority. David James Burrell told a prospective immigrant in Naples he would have to leave Italy behind, with its "royal establishment, its musical tongue, its happy-go-lucky way of living, its boisterous Sundays and hilarious holy-days; its manner of dress and bibulous habits." To become a true American, he would have to submit to indoctrination in American principles, imbibe the American spirit, become naturalized, and stand ready to defend the American government and way of life.[19] Only

---

[17]W. B. Riley, The Bible of the Expositor and the Evangelist (40 vols.; Cleveland: Union Gospel Press, 1926-1938), New Testament, XVII, 97-100.

[18]J. T. Larsen, "What Makes the United States Great and What Detracts From Her Greatness," Moody Monthly, XXIX (July, 1929), 525; [Curtis Lee Laws], "American Blood in 1975," The Watchman-Examiner, VI (March 14, 1918), 329.

[19]David James Burrell, "An American," The Presbyterian, LXXXVII (August 15, 1918), 10; cf. Rudolph Malek, "America's Vulnerable Spot," Moody Monthly, XXII (November, 1921), 655-56; [Curtis Lee Laws], "A Stumbling-Block to Americanization," The Watchman-Examiner, VIII (February 26,

then would he cease being a mere "guest at the American fireside."

Some fundamentalists recognized, however, that an assimilation process that required learning a new language and adapting to a new culture was not quickly accomplished, and they stressed the need for patience in dealing with new arrivals. Editors James M. Gray and David S. Kennedy deplored the legal short cuts which summarily deported suspected radicals during the Red Scare, and they pled for fair trials for all.[20] In the same atmosphere of suspicion Henry J. Weber criticized those who demanded that foreigners learn English immediately. Such haste, he pointed out, was tearing parents and children apart instead of strengthening family units. What was needed, said Weber, was not force, but love and sympathy.[21] Nearly ten years later, when the Smith presidential campaign again brought foreigners under suspicion, Samuel G. Craig cautioned against a censorious attitude. Instead of condemning wet, Roman Catholic immigrants, he argued, Christians should

---

1920), 272; "Americanizing America," The Bible Champion, XXV (January, 1919), 19-20; Larsen, "What Makes the United States Great," p. 526; Riley, Bible of the Expositor, Old Testament, III, 24.

[20] [James M. Gray], "Honor the Courts," Moody Monthly, XXI (January, 1921), 206; [Kennedy], "Ellis Island Reds Increasing," p. 4.

[21] Henry J. Weber, "Be Ye Merciful With the Immigrants," The Presbyterian, LXXXIX (June 26, 1919), 9.

display an attitude which would inspire them to good citizenship and win them to evangelical Christianity.[22]

While cultural assimilation was regarded as essential to national unity and good citizenship, fundamentalists believed one further ingredient was needed. This was conversion of immigrants to evangelical Protestant Christianity. Receiving Jesus Christ as Savior would both unify immigrants with American believers and make them moral assets to the nation.

Fundamentalists frequently emphasized the spiritual unity produced by a common faith. The oneness of the Christian church far surpassed the effects of the American "melting pot." It was, according to Leon Tucker, "the supreme display of unity in all the universe of God," for here "the nations get together and are knit together and sit together in a new place--heavenly places--in Christ Jesus!"[23] Christianity was a great leveling force, claimed Mark Matthews. "There are no national distinctions . . . *we are one in Christ Jesus.*" (Italics in original.)[24] Conversion, then, was the door to true unity among nationalities, and all other attempts to make the immigrant feel

---

[22][Samuel G. Craig], "United States Immigration," *The Presbyterian*, XCVIII (September 27, 1928), 4-5.

[23]W. Leon Tucker, "Unity," *The Wonderful Word*, XI (June, 1919), 393-94.

[24]Mathews, "Logic of Deeds," p. 460.

"at home" in America were regarded as incomplete without it.

But fundamentalists saw conversion not only as a means of achieving unity in diversity, but also as a source of national strength, since they believed converted people became better citizens. They envisioned America as a "smelting pot" in which spiritually purified individuals, both native and naturalized, could add their moral fiber to other national resources.[25]

Evangelization of immigrants therefore became an important aspect of fundamentalist home missions. The aspirations of this work were well illustrated in the activities of the New York Bible Society in distributing free Bibles to the newcomers. A typical appeal for support of its work bore the caption, "When Tony Landed in New York," and related how the Scripture had changed an immigrant's life for the better. It concluded with a statement which would strike a responsive note in the patriotic Christian:

> Thousands of boys just like Tony . . . are pouring into America every month. Are you complaining about

---

[25]Charles L. White, "Facing the Future," The Watchman-Examiner, VI (March 14, 1918), 336-37; "Is Your Town Evangelizing Its Foreigners?" The Sunday School Times, LXIII (October 15, 1921), 562; [David S. Kennedy], "Americanization," The Presbyterian, LXXXIX (December 4, 1919), 3; "Christianize or Americanize?" ibid., XC (July 1, 1920), 7; [Gray], "Selective Immigration," pp. 99-100; [Gaebelein], "Attempts to Overthrow Our Government," p. 414.

> these immigrants coming here with their crimes? There is only one reason why they develop into criminals, law-breakers, Bolshevists, etc. WE DON'T SHOW THEM ANYTHING BETTER![26]

The new arrivals could enrich American life, but their contribution depended largely upon their conversion to the evangelical faith. To evangelize the foreigner was to strengthen America.

The same philosophy was expressed in a two-page advertisement for Moody Bible Institute in a 1920 issue of The Watchman-Examiner, which featured a photograph of students representing twenty-five foreign countries and the American Negro. It read: "Agitators of class hatred and revolutionary radicalism are busy from coast to coast. We appeal for your support in our work of training 'agitators' for righteousness." It further declared that the Christian gospel "makes men of whatever class or nationality upright, industrious and peaceable, whether educated or uneducated."[27]

Fundamentalists' attitudes toward immigrants thus included two contrasting, yet complementary, emphases. On one hand, the character of many of the foreign-born disturbed them, and they tended to agree with most Americans that, in their present condition and numbers, they threat-

---

[26] Moody Monthly, XXIV (May, 1924), 446.

[27] "The Answer to Labor Unrest," The Watchman-Examiner, VIII (July 15, 1920), 904-5.

ened the nation's stability. The prospect of cultural pluralism in America's future apparently contradicted their own version of national unity. On the other hand, they believed the assimilation of immigrants already present was both possible and desirable, and they paralleled sharp criticism of radical and Catholic elements with pleas for patience, fairness, and exemplary conduct toward them. But while they occasionally advocated the usual cultural means of assimilation, fundamentalists believed the real key to producing "ideal Americans" was evangelization and Christian teaching. In this characteristic emphasis they found an outlet for both their patriotism and their militant evangelical faith.

Closely tied to the question of immigration was that of Roman Catholic influence in America, for suspicion of Catholics, which had existed since colonial times, had become more pronounced as large numbers of Catholic immigrants entered American life. Not only had Catholic communicants become a sizable minority in the religious community by 1920, but the tendency of the new arrivals to remain segregated in large cities also aroused fears of their growing political influence. Already many had gained notoriety for their bossism in local politics and their opposition to the prohibition laws. When New York's Catholic governor, Alfred E. Smith, became the Democratic presidential nominee in 1928, therefore, much of Protestant America was already alarmed.[28]

Although one cannot ignore the historic religious tensions between Protestants and Catholics, their theological differences were overshadowed in the twenties by Protestant fears of Rome's political influence in America. This was true for several reasons. First, the majority of Americans were uninformed and unconcerned about doctrinal matters in religion. Secondly, fundamentalists and other Protestant conservatives who were still concerned with theology were facing what they considered to be a far greater theological peril in modernism. Thirdly, many Americans could not forget the Roman Catholic hierarchy's past reputation for political meddling.

Roman Catholic political influence was therefore being scrutinized, not only by conservative Protestants, but also by modernists and non-religious citizens. Editorials in the liberal Protestant Christian Century, while careful to disclaim any sympathy for the Ku Klux Klan, yet displayed an open distrust toward a papacy that had never renounced temporal power and an organization that owned vast amounts of property in the United States.[29] Simi-

---

[28]For a general background to the Catholic issue in the Smith campaign see Hicks, Republican Ascendancy, pp. 3, 206-7.

[29]"Why Be Surprised at Papal Claim?" The Christian Century, XL (December 20, 1923), 1645; "The Roman Menace," ibid., XLI (October 9, 1924), 1296-97; cf. Winfred Ernest Garrison, "Present Day Papal Ambitions," ibid., XLI

larly, sociologist John M. Mecklin, who personally believed most Catholic Americans to be loyal citizens, nevertheless detected an opportunism in the Roman Catholic system that used religious toleration to promote its worldwide religious and political aims and to eradicate its competitors.[30]

The same concerns occupied the minds of fundamentalists. The Fundamentals had said relatively little about the Catholic Church, but what it said was not complimentary. J. M. Foster of Boston, in an article entitled, "Rome, the Antagonist of the Nation," had criticized its theology, sacerdotal system, and political ambitions. He charged that in some municipalities the hierarchy controlled ninety-five percent of the political offices, that the American press was being censored by Jesuits, and that the parochial school system was a peril to the nation.[31]

The postwar years only added to such apprehensions. A Catholic claim to influence in the Wilson administration in 1919 prompted A. C. Gaebelein to name the Church as one

---

(May 1, 1924), 567-69.

[30]John Moffatt Mecklin, The Ku Klux Klan: A Study of the American Mind (New York: Russell & Russell, Inc., 1963), pp. 199-202.

[31]The Fundamentals: A Testimony to the Truth (12 vols.; Chicago: Testimony Publishing Company, [1910-1915]), XI, 113-26.

of America's most serious menaces.[32] Proposed diplomatic relations with the Vatican in 1921 brought a forceful reply from Curtis Lee Laws, who insisted it was his "solemn duty" to oppose Rome's "political and un-American" ambitions.[33] Laws and fellow New York fundamentalists David James Burrell, John Roach Straton, and Frank M. Goodchild were charter members of the Evangelical Protestant Society, founded in 1922 "to defend American democracy against the encroachments of Papal Rome."[34] Texan J. Frank Norris, spurred on by lax prohibition enforcement, the Eucharistic Conference in Chicago, and growing Catholic influence in large cities, opened a relentless barrage on the Church in 1926.[35]

The nomination of Al Smith in 1928 seemed to bring the worst Protestant fears within the range of probability. Already a successful politician, Smith was capable of solidifying the Catholic and immigrant vote through his positions on prohibition and immigration, and if he should

---

[32] [A. C. Gaebelein], "Romish Catholic Boasting, Is It true?" Our Hope, XXV (April, 1919), 616-19.

[33] [Curtis Lee Laws], "Roman Catholic Aggressiveness," The Watchman-Examiner, IX (May 5, 1921), 549; "Our Anti-Catholic Attitude," ibid., IX (May 12, 1921), 581.

[34] New York Times, April 6, 1922, p. 10.

[35] See, e.g., J. Frank Norris, "The Conspiracy of Rum and Romanism to Rule This Government," The Searchlight, IX (February 5, 1926), 1, 6; "Rome Invades Protestant America--The Eucharistic Conference in Chicago," ibid., IX (June 25, 1926), 1, 4, 5.

be elected, what Protestant American could predict the ultimate impact upon the nation? This was a rare occasion on which fundamentalists, modernists, and all Protestant shades of opinion between them stood together. J. Frank Norris, who normally would berate Southern Methodist University for its liberalism, found common cause with one of its theology professors in seeking Smith's defeat,[36] and editorials on the campaign in The Christian Century and Moody Monthly were strikingly similar.[37]

Some of the desperate efforts to defeat Smith were pitched on a purely emotional level and employed unscrupulous tactics to inflame prejudices. This campaign saw J. Frank Norris at his demagogic worst. He more than carried out his threat that, if Smith were nominated, "I will pull off my coat and campaign the South for the Republican nominee."[38] He not only spoke to large audiences daily at the height of the campaign, but also worked behind the scenes to influence Southern opinion. He offered to secure for a Texas member of the Republican National Committee the addresses of fifty thousand Texas Klansmen in order to

---

[36]Letter, J. Frank Norris to W. D. Bradfield, January 18, 1928, Archives, Southern Baptist Convention, John Franklyn Norris Papers.

[37]Examples will be adduced later. But note the observations of William E. Leuchtenburg, The Perils of Prosperity, 1914-32 (Chicago: University of Chicago Press, 1958), pp. 234-35.

[38]Norris, "Rum and Romanism," p. 6.

spread anti-Smith propaganda.[39] He also exploited Southern racial fears by circulating a photograph of Ferdinand Morton, a Negro official in New York City, in his office with a white secretary. It appeared in The Fundamentalist under the caption: "$7,500 A Year Tammany Negro Boss and His White Secretary." Upon first seeing the picture Norris called it a "knockout," and assured his supplier that he would "sow the state down" with copies. "This will mean 100,000 white votes for Hoover if we can get it before the people," wrote Norris.[40] He also urged that black members of the Republican National Committee be replaced by whites in order to carry the South.[41]

Few fundamentalist leaders followed Norris down this low road. Indeed, much of their literature was surprisingly silent on the campaign, and most of those who spoke out did so with restraint. With other Protestants, they

---

[39] Letters, J. Frank Norris to Lon F. Anderson, August 27, 1928; J. Frank Norris to Hon. R. B. Craeger [Creager], January 23, 1928, Archives, Southern Baptist Convention, John Franklyn Norris Papers.

[40] The Fundamentalist, VI (October 5, 1928), 8; Letter, J. Frank Norris to James Vance, September 18, 1928, Archives, Southern Baptist Convention, John Franklyn Norris Papers.

[41] Letter, J. Frank Norris to Hon. R. B. Craeger [Creager], April 2, 1928. See also letter of H[arvey] Beauchamp to J. Frank Norris, September 22, 1928, in which Beauchamp asked for proof that Smith was a "common drunkard." If this were available, he believed, it would clinch Hoover's victory in Texas. Both letters in Archives, Southern Baptist Convention, John Franklyn Norris Papers.

attempted to convince the public that not all opposition to Governor Smith's religion constituted intolerance or bigotry. They believed that in the light of Roman Catholic history they had the right to ask him how allegiance to a government that believed in religious freedom and separation of church and state was compatible with allegiance to a religion that did not. One writer declared:

> It is no fault of Protestants that the Roman Church chose to make history as we find it. To designate a man who has found nothing in that history to commend itself to his conscience an intolerant person is to display the art of intolerance to perfection.[42]

The question of Smith's alleged dual allegiance received widespread attention as the result of an exchange of articles in The Atlantic Monthly. In April, 1927 Charles C. Marshall, a retired New York lawyer, directed some questions to the Governor, and Smith submitted an admirable reply the following month.[43] But the issue refused to die, for, as a Christian Century editorial pointed out, Smith's answer expressed only his personal ideas and inclinations and settled nothing regarding canon law or papal pronouncements on church and state. The liberal organ asserted that Protestant Americans had a legiti-

---

[42] "Wayside Gleanings," The Bible Champion, XXXIV (October, 1928), 537.

[43] Charles C. Marshall, "An Open Letter to the Honorable Alfred E. Smith," The Atlantic Monthly, CXXXIX (April, 1927), 540-49; Alfred E. Smith, "Catholic and Patriot: Governor Smith Replies," ibid., CXXXIX (May, 1927), 721-28.

mate reason for not wanting a Catholic president, and that they had a right to their opinion "without justly incurring the accusation of bigotry or intolerance."[44]

Fundamentalists also labored to make their stand clear. "To be sure," said W. B. Riley, "it would not Romanize America to have Al Smith as president, and he could not make us entirely over in four years; but it would be a step in the wrong direction."[45] James M. Gray, who scrupulously avoided telling his readers for whom to vote, nevertheless stated the logic of the situation as he saw it. As a religion in a free country, said Gray, the Roman Catholic Church deserved the same rights as other religions. But as a political system, it opposed the American principle of separation of church and state. A Catholic president could not be free to uphold the American principle as long as he was bound by religion to obey the pope. This reasoning, insisted Gray, involved neither personal animosity nor religious intolerance, but simply a concern for the future of American institutions.[46]

---

[44] "What the Smith Reply Settled and What It Didn't," The Christian Century, XLIV (May 5, 1927), 549; "Browbeating the Protestants," ibid., XLV (October 11, 1928), 1217-19.

[45] [W. B. Riley], "Reasons Why Al Smith Should Not Be Elected President of the United States," The Christian Fundamentalist, II (October, 1928), 8.

[46] James M. Gray, "What Is Intolerance--And What Is Religion?" Moody Monthly, XXIX (December, 1928), 167-68; cf. "Governor Smith's Religion," ibid., XXVII (March,

From a political standpoint, then, fundamentalists distrusted the Roman Catholic Church and refused to consider any concessions to the hierarchy. They also differed with its doctrines and religious practices, but they never viewed it in the same sinister light as modernism, and at times even bestowed surprising compliments. J. Gresham Machen recognized a "profound gulf" between Protestantism and the Church of Rome, but added that this distance seemed almost trifling when compared with the "abyss" between evangelicals and liberals. "The Church of Rome may represent a perversion of the Christian religion," said Machen, "but naturalistic liberalism is not Christianity at all."[47] James M. Gray pointed out that much theological truth was retained by the Catholic Church. Catholics accepted the Bible as God's word, believed Jesus to be the Savior of mankind, and recognized the universal need for salvation. "We Protestants," said Gray, "ought to study their faith . . . to find out what is true or false about it, and then

---

1927), 324; "The Atlantic Monthly Makes a 'Scoop,'" ibid., XXVII (June, 1927), 471; "Governor 'Al' Smith As a Presidential Candidate," ibid., XXVII (August, 1927), 579-80; "National Politics," ibid., XXIX (November, 1928), 101. See also [Samuel G. Craig], "Relative to a Roman Catholic President," The Presbyterian, XCVIII (September 27, 1928), 13.

[47]J. Gresham Machen, Christianity and Liberalism (Grand Rapids, Michigan: Wm. B. Eerdmans Publishing Company, 1946 [originally published in 1923]), p. 52. A similar statement was made by David S. Kennedy, "The Fundamentalists and Romanism," The Bible Champion, XXX (July, 1924), 353-54.

with the Bible in our hands show them the right way."[48]

Fundamentalists on occasion complimented and even quoted Roman Catholics on points on which they could agree. James M. Gray praised the "Christian character" of a Greensboro, North Carolina, priest whose departure to another town was regretted by the city's Protestant populace, and he quoted with approval from a patriotic speech Cardinal Mundelein delivered in Chicago.[49] W. B. Riley reprinted an article condemning companionate marriage which had appeared in the Catholic publication, Our Sunday Visitor,[50] and J. Frank Norris (only four years after the Smith campaign!) quoted from an encyclical of Pope Pius XI warning against subversive atheists. It was a great sin, declared Norris, to continue to denounce former opponents even when they took a position "for God, home and native land."[51]

In the light of these facts, we can make several observations about fundamentalist attitudes toward Roman

---

[48][James M. Gray], "Be Fair to Roman Catholics," Moody Monthly, XXX (February, 1930), 290.

[49][James M. Gray], "Power of Character," Moody Monthly, XXV (October, 1924), 53-54; "Cardinal Mundelein's Americanism," ibid., XXIV (July, 1924), 543.

[50]Thomas M. O'Leary, "Companionate Marriage," The Christian Fundamentalist, III (April, 1930), 616-17; 631.

[51]J. Frank Norris, "The Red Menace of Communism in the United States," The Fundamentalist, X (June 10, 1932), 3.

Catholics in the twenties. First, they shared with other Protestants apprehensions about Rome's presumed political aspirations in America, and their opposition to Al Smith in 1928 was ostensibly motivated primarily by these misgivings. Second, whatever their private feelings toward Catholics may have been, fundamentalist leaders, with a few exceptions, discussed these issues with restraint and rarely employed _ad hominem_ argument. Some, in fact, did not even discuss them at all. In the third place, while fundamentalists never forgot their theological differences with Catholics, they also were aware of their common ground, for their current war against modernism placed their similarities in sharper focus. They were therefore more conciliatory toward Catholics theologically than would otherwise have been the case. While fundamentalists' concern for traditional American institutions led them to oppose Al Smith's candidacy, their concern for orthodoxy led them to rate Catholicism higher theologically than modernism--a discrimination in thinking not usually associated with hundred percent Americanism.

Another group often surrounded by suspicion during this decade were the Jews. By the beginning of the twentieth century many an American had stereotyped the Jew as a grasping, mysterious figure with international connections, wielding power through his wealth. The huge fortunes some Jews made during World War I reinforced the picture, and although Jewish participation in the Russian Revolution and the attraction of many American Jews to radical causes would seem to contradict this stereotype, these developments only heightened the alarm of many Americans. A sinister conspiracy seemed to be in operation.[52]

Fortifying these suspicions was the appearance in 1920 of a book entitled The Protocols of the Learned Elders of Zion, which purportedly had originated in Russia in 1905. This document revealed the alleged plans of Zionist Jews to control the world through economic manipulation. In the same year Henry Ford's The Dearborn Independent issued a series of articles, later published as The International Jew, to "expose" the plot.[53] Although the Ford-sponsored articles were often denounced and the Protocols were widely held to be a forgery, they provided excellent fuel to fan latent anti-Semitism into flame. Throughout the decade Jews were favorite targets for the hostility of the Ku Klux Klan and other superpatriots.

---

[52]Oscar Handlin discusses the background of this stereotype in "American Views of the Jew at the Opening of the Twentieth Century," in At Home in America, Vol. V of The Jewish Experience in America, ed. by Abraham J. Karp (5 vols.; Waltham, Mass.: American Jewish Historical Society, 1969), pp. 1-22. See also Karp's introductory chapter in the same volume, esp. pp. viii-ix.

[53]See esp. chaps. 8-10 in The International Jew: The World's Foremost Problem (Dearborn, Mich.: Dearborn Publishing Co., 1920). The articles continued through January 14, 1922 and eventually comprised four published volumes.

An even stronger wave of anti-Semitism arose in 1933 and the following years, due to the Depression, an increase in revolutionary sentiment, opposition to New Deal policies, and the rise of Nazism in Germany. One student of anti-Semitism has calculated that while only five anti-Semitic organizations were founded in the United States between 1915 and 1932, nine sprang up in 1933 alone and 105 came into being between 1934 and 1939.[54]

The degree to which anti-Semitism existed among fundamentalists will be determined to some extent by how one defines his terms. If he, with Simpson and Yinger, views anti-Semitism as "any activity that tends to force into or hold Jews in an inferior position and to limit their economic, political, and social rights,"[55] few fundamentalist leaders would qualify for the label. If he broadens it to include any stereotyped mental image of Jews, whether complimentary or uncomplimentary,[56] the number would increase considerably. And if he broadens it still further to include religious proselytizing of Jews, hardly a prominent fundamentalist in the twenties would escape the charge of

---

[54]Donald S. Strong, Organized Anti-Semitism in America, quoted by Simpson and Yinger, Racial and Cultural Minorities, p. 216.

[55]Simpson and Yinger, Racial and Cultural Minorities, p. 197.

[56]Gertrude J. Selznick and Stephen Steinberg, The Tenacity of Prejudice: Anti-Semitism in Contemporary America (New York: Harper & Row, Publishers, 1969), pp. 3-21.

anti-Semitism or attitudes contributing to it.[57]

However others may have viewed their dealings with Jews, many fundamentalists genuinely regarded themselves as their friends. This was especially true of the millenarians, who believed not only that ancient Israel was "God's chosen people," but that God was gradually bringing to fruition a program for modern Israel that would eventually leave them in control of Palestine. The Zionist movement, followed by the fall of Jerusalem in the World War, had convinced them that Israel was soon to reclaim its ancient inheritance, and they watched every new development with expectancy, for they believed these trends presaged the return of Christ and the millennial kingdom.[58]

But fundamentalist interest in Jews was not limited to a curiosity about their future. Many felt indebted to this ancient people for their spiritual contributions to the world, and warned Americans that to malign or attack

---

[57]A close relationship between Protestant theology and anti-Semitism is seen by Arthur Gilbert, A Jew in Christian America (New York: Sheed and Ward, 1966), pp. 199-207; and Rodney Stark, et al., Wayward Shepherds: Prejudice and the Protestant Clergy (New York: Harper & Row, Publishers, 1971), pp. 57-58. Bernhard Olson, however, (Faith and Prejudice, pp. 104, 271-74), draws a sharp distinction between the two, though criticizing careless ways in which theology is sometimes taught.

[58]See, e.g., Philip Mauro, "After This" (Boston: Hamilton Bros., 1918), p. 149; J. Frank Norris, "World War Needed to Fulfill Word of Bible, Says Norris," The Searchlight, II (July 3, 1919), [3-4]. The King's Business and Our Hope devoted special sections to Jewish and Palestinian news every month.

them was to invite the judgment of God. William L. Pettingill declared that "I cannot, for the life of me, see how a Christian can do otherwise than love the Jew, when he remembers that everything . . . worth while came to him through the Jews."[59] "The nations will never pay the debt they owe to the Jew," wrote Arno C. Gaebelein, "and it is feared that but few Christians realize their indebtedness to the peculiar people."[60] "Such men as Henry Ford . . . should remember the ancient words of the eternal God and save themselves the maledictions of God," advised Leon Tucker, "for it is still unchanged and unaltered that God 'will curse them that curse thee.'"[61]

Fundamentalists believed God was sovereignly preserving the Jewish people for a significant role in the climax to human history. Meanwhile, individual Jews needed the same gospel as everyone else in order to enjoy God's salvation. Fundamentalists therefore undertook special efforts

---

[59] W. L. Pettingill, "The Coming Glory," in Light on Prophecy: The Proceedings and Addresses at the Philadelphia Prophetic Conference, May 28-30, 1918 (New York: Christian Herald, 1918), p. 253.

[60] [A. C. Gaebelein], "The Jews of Roumania," Our Hope, XX (June, 1914), 759.

[61] W. Leon Tucker, "Anti-Semitism," The Wonderful Word, XIII (July, 1921), 439; cf. "Nothing Jewish in my house," ibid., XVIII (January, 1926), 147-48; Thomas M. Chalmers, "Why Increasing Hatred of the Jews?" The Sunday School Times, LXV (October 20, 1923), 621-22; J. Frank Norris, "Love vs. Hate," The Searchlight, X (January 7, 1927), 3.

to convert them. Early in his ministry A. C. Gaebelein directed a New York City mission for Jewish immigrants, and he retained a strong interest in this type of work throughout his life. Both the Bible Institute of Los Angeles and Moody Bible Institute gave Jewish evangelism a prominent place among their extension ministries. Moody established a Department of Jewish Missions with a converted immigrant Jew to direct it, and aired Yiddish broadcasts over its radio station. Leon Tucker established funds for the support of missionaries to the Jews, in both New York City and Palestine. Charles G. Trumbull vigorously promoted Jewish evangelism through The Sunday School Times.[62]

When they invited Jews to become "Christians," fundamentalists meant something more specific than giving up Judaism and identifying with a Protestant church. They were asking them to accept Jesus as their Messiah and trust him personally for the forgiveness of sins. Some, in fact, deliberately minimized the institutional implications of

---

[62] Arno Clemens Gaebelein, Half a Century: The Autobiography of a Servant (New York: Publication Office "Our Hope," 1930), pp. 75-76; The King's Business, XV (January, 1924), 29-30; S. Birnbaum, "Americanization of the Unassimilated," Moody Monthly, XXIII (July, 1923), 524; Jacob Gartenhaus, "Methods of Mission Work Among the Jews," ibid., XXIV (July, 1924), 556-57; ibid., XXVII (January, 1927), 270; The Wonderful Word, XIII (January, 1921), 182; and XV (April, 1923), 323; [Charles G. Trumbull], "Time to Make Plans," The Sunday School Times, LX (March 30, 1918), 177; "How a Christian Became Interested in the Jews," ibid., LX (May 18, 1918), 283-84; "Will God Favor the Jews?" ibid., LX (December 14, 1918), 710.

Jewish conversions. A. C. Gaebelein taught that "The Jew has no need whatever of the organizations and institutions of historical (i.e. Gentile and denominational) Christianity. All he needs is personal saving faith in his own Jewish Messiah."[63]

To Jews whose ancestors had suffered at the hands of professing Christians, however, proselytizing was unwelcome, and Jewish religious leaders joined with liberal Protestant churchmen in condemning efforts to convert them. They claimed that such activity caused prejudice by portraying Jews as "Jesus-killers."

Fundamentalists stoutly denied any intention of breeding hatred or ill will, and insisted that love and a sense of duty compelled them to evangelize Jews. "Every true minister of the gospel," wrote Jacob Gartenhaus, a Baptist missionary to Jews, "will gladly lend his support to encourage and cultivate a better understanding . . . among all races." But this effort could not rule out evangelism. Gartenhaus maintained that

> The only motive that prompts Baptists to give the gospel to their Jewish neighbors is the debt of gratitude which they feel they owe to them for the very gospel they are trying to preach, believing . . . that it will make them happier and holier men and women.[64]

---

[63]Gaebelein, Half a Century, pp. 75-76.

[64]Jacob Gartenhaus, "Jews and the Federal Council of Churches of Christ in America," Moody Monthly, XXVIII (July, 1928), 504; cf. Aaron Judah Kligerman, "Shall We Scrap Jewish Missions to Please the 'Good-Willers'?" ibid.,

J. Gresham Machen stated the case for proselytizing even more strongly. Addressing a meeting of the Fellowship of Reconciliation in 1924, he expressed hope that Jews and Christians could cooperate in promoting tolerance. But as to the legitimacy of evangelism, Machen had no doubts.

> The plain fact is that we Christians regard all of you who are not Christians as lost under the guilt of sin. . . . what do you expect us to do? Do you expect us to promise that we will avoid proselytizing? Do you not see that such a promise would involve, from our point of view, the most awful bloodguiltiness of which a man could ever possibly be guilty? . . . we should, if we ceased to proselytize among you, be not kind and considerate but guilty of the most heartless neglect that could possibly be conceived.[65]

From the fundamentalist viewpoint, then, evangelizing Jews was an act of kindness and a performance of duty, and even when others interpreted their efforts differently, they considered them too important to be abandoned for the sake of goodwill.

Religious differences with Jews did not prevent several prominent fundamentalists from objecting to the current verbal attacks against them. The charge of a worldwide "Jewish peril," wrote Thomas Chalmers, director of the New York Jewish Evangelization Society, could be "dismissed

---

XXIX (June, 1929), 482-83; [James M. Gray], "Converting the Jew," <u>ibid</u>., XXIV (February, 1924), 282.

[65] J. Gresham Machen, "Relations Between Jews and Christians," in <u>What Is Christianity?</u> (Grand Rapids, Mich.: Wm. B. Eerdmans Publishing Company, 1951), p. 112.

utterly from the realm of serious discussion."[66] If such a "peril" existed, James M. Gray declared, it was the same as the Gentile peril, which was sin, and he branded anti-Semitism as alien and hostile to both American and biblical principles.[67] John Roach Straton, in rejecting Henry Ford's conclusions about Jews, attributed Jewish growth and influence to divine providence, rather than a conspiracy. J. Frank Norris agreed, asserting that it was "unfair, unjust, un-Christian and un-American to criticize the Jew because he is a Jew."[68]

The fact remains, however, that in their zeal to restore America to Christian orthodoxy and morals, fundamentalists did sometimes criticize Jews. As a rule, it was not the devout Jew but the irreligious one who was singled out for blame, for they believed he was contributing to the very secularism they were trying to combat. Thomas

---

[66]Thomas M. Chalmers, "Is Henry Ford Correct?" The Sunday School Times, LXVI (September 20, 1924), 555.

[67]James M. Gray, "The 'Jewish Peril' and How to Meet It," Moody Monthly, XXI (July, 1921), 469-71. Gray repeated essentially the same statement fourteen years later in "The Jewish Protocols," Moody Monthly, XXXV (January, 1935), 230.

[68]John Roach Straton, New York Times, December 29, 1924, p. 17; J. Frank Norris, "The Jewish Question--The Greatest Question of the Age," The Searchlight, IV (April 7, 1922), 2. Later publications and correspondence show that Norris never altered his view. See, e.g., his letter to Rexford G. Tugwell, September 18, 1933, and a letter to Norris from William D. Kaufman of the American Zionist Emergency Council, June 25, 1948, Archives, Southern Baptist Convention, John Franklyn Norris Papers.

Chalmers, for example, charged that Jews were among those who were commercializing Sunday, disregarding prohibition laws, and corrupting youth through morally questionable journalism and theatrical productions. Although he rejected the Ford "revelations," Chalmers suggested that Jews read them as a stimulus to moral reform.[69] Mark Matthews seemed more troubled by their gravitation toward radical philosophies. Professing a deep affection for Jews, he nevertheless concluded that their present revolutionary activities made them a curse to the world instead of a blessing.[70] While such criticisms were usually tempered by reservations or coupled with predictions of Israel's ultimate conversion, they did present contemporary Jews in an unfavorable light.

There were also those who could not dismiss the Protocols from their thinking. They read in the continuing spread of communism and the economic collapse of the early thirties the diabolical design of sinister forces, and it was tempting to accept the Protocols as at least a partial explanation. One writer claimed that the same "International Jew" that had been assailing Christianity for twenty

---

[69]Chalmers, "Is Henry Ford Correct?" p. 555; cf. David J. Burrell, "The Blue Laws," The Bible Champion, XXIX (August-September, 1923), 388; [A. C. Gaebelein], "Aspects of Jewish Power in the United States," Our Hope, XXIX (August, 1922), 103.

[70]Mark A. Matthews, Gospel Sword Thrusts (New York: Fleming H. Revell Company, 1924), pp. 142, 147.

centuries was now attempting to assimilate it into Judaism. Another declared that Jewish Bolshevists were presently following the plan of conquest outlined in the Protocols point by point. Still another associated apostate Jews with "a mysterious world-wide but invisible potency called Finance," whose "unseen meshes, strong as steel, hold firmly the destinies and policies of nations."[71]

The authenticity of the Protocols was accepted, surprisingly, by prophecy lecturer Arno C. Gaebelein. Gaebelein's statements about Jews leave the reader perplexed at times as to his real feelings. Being a strong premillennialist, he believed Israel would occupy a prominent place in the world's future. Furthermore, he sometimes made eloquent pleas for "reason over blind prejudice" and condemned the evils of stereotyping. Yet, on another occasion, he declared that "There is nothing so vile on earth as an apostate Jew."[72]

It was apparently Gaebelein's growing nervousness

---

[71] W. MacNicholl, "Cogitations of a Fogy," The Bible Champion, XXX (July, 1924), 371-77; Elizabeth Knauss, "Is Bolshevism a Menace?" The Christian Fundamentalist, III (September, 1929), 338-40, 352; Philip Mauro, "The Empire of Finance: The Black Horse Rider," The Bible Champion, XXXVI (January, 1930), 5. During the twenties Mauro came to believe that Israel had no further purpose in God's prophetic plan. See The Hope of Israel, What Is It? (Boston: Hamilton Bros., 1929).

[72] A. C. Gaebelein, "The Middle Wall of Partition," Our Hope, XXXV (August, 1928), 49-55; cf. "Aspects of Jewish Power in the United States," ibid., XXIX (August, 1922), 103.

about communism that led him to take the Protocols seriously. He doubted that the document's authorship would ever be known, and he studiously avoided placing the responsibility for it on the entire Jewish people. But he was convinced it was not a forgery. Behind it, he declared, were "hidden, unseen actors, powerful and cunning, who follow the plan still, bent on the overthrow of our civilization," and large numbers of these radicals were Jews.[73]

Gaebelein's thinking seemed to take a more pro-Jewish direction after reports of Nazi anti-Semitism reached the United States in 1933. For several months he suspended judgment, but by the spring of 1934 his sympathies lay clearly with the German Jews. In the sixth printing of The Conflict of the Ages in 1936, he specifically absolved the Jewish people from responsibility for the Protocols, and in 1939 he joined other fundamentalists in signing a manifesto condemning all forms of anti-Semitism.[74]

---

[73] Arno Clemens Gaebelein, The Conflict of the Ages (New York: Publication Office "Our Hope," 1933), pp. 95-100.

[74] [A. C. Gaebelein], "An Unbiased Report on the Conditions in Germany," Our Hope, XL (January, 1934); "The Religious Chaos in Germany," and "The Approaching Night for Israel," ibid., XL (March, 1934), 549-50; Gaebelein, Conflict of the Ages (6th printing, 1936), p. 99. The manifesto is mentioned by Ralph Lord Roy, Apostles of Discord (Boston: Beacon Press, 1953), p. 47. James M. Gray also withheld a judgment on the German situation in 1933 ("Jews in Germany," Moody Monthly, XXXIII May, 1933 , 392), but his 1935 article, "The Jewish Protocols," leaves no doubt

William B. Riley initially held views of Jews that matched those of Gaebelein, but ultimately became more thoroughly critical. Like Gaebelein, he extolled past Jewish contributions and predicted a significant Jewish role in the fulfillment of prophecy.[75] He also agreed that the Protocols could not absolutely be traced to Jewish origins, although he accepted the document as genuine. But unlike Gaebelein, who condemned all acts of violence against Jews, Riley was content to philosophize that such attacks were a part of divine judgment for crucifying Jesus and rejecting Christianity.[76] Also unlike Gaebelein, Riley eventually rejected Jewish evangelism as "the most hopeless of all Christian enterprises," since he believed the Jews would remain apostate until the return of Christ.[77]

Although he expressed these views fully only after 1933, Riley pointed out at least two earlier considerations which led him to his later skepticism. First, his unpleasant experiences with "converted" Jewish evangelists who

---

as to his pro-Jewish verdict. Other fundamentalists condemned Hitler's actions from the beginning. See, e.g., Donald Grey Barnhouse, "Which Way Germany?" Revelation, II (March, 1932), 103-5, 134; Louis S. Bauman, "Dictatorship Over the Souls of Men," The King's Business, XXIV (June, 1933), 182; J. Frank Norris, "The Persecution of the Jews in Germany," The Fundamentalist, XI (April 7, 1933), 3, 5.

[75] W. B. Riley, Bible of the Expositor, New Testament, XII, 33; Old Testament, XIX, 185-86.

[76] Ibid., New Testament, IV, 201; VIII, 216.

[77] Ibid., Old Testament, XV, 152-54.

turned out to be thieves or fakes had dampened his earlier enthusiasm for Jewish missions. Secondly, his fear of Marxist influence in America, coupled with his observation that Jews always seemed to be involved in radicalism, led him to blame them disproportionately for the ills of the nation. He never personally advocated proscription of Jews, but his refusal to condemn Nazi Jewish policies give the impression that he tacitly approved of them.[78]

What Riley implied tacitly, Gerald B. Winrod of Wichita, Kansas championed openly. His support of Hitler during the late thirties made Winrod's name practically synonymous with anti-Semitism, and his publication, The Defender, came under constant government surveillance during World War II for its Nazi sympathies.[79] Winrod's anti-Jewish attitudes came to fruition only in the Depression years. Like many other fundamentalists, he was a premillennialist, and as late as 1929 he was warning against persecuting the "chosen people."[80] But at the same time an

---

[78]Riley fully expressed his views and rationale in a letter to C. V. O'Neill, December 9, 1937. Cf. letters to Riley from Louis B. Schwartz, a Jewish lawyer in Minneapolis, September 7 and September 29, 1934. Correspondence is found in Minnesota State Historical Society, Jewish Community Relations Council of Minnesota Papers. Riley's views are also discussed in Roy, Apostles of Discord, pp. 46-47.

[79]For an extended discussion of Winrod's activities, see Roy, Apostles of Discord, pp. 26-37 and passim.

[80]Gerald Winrod, Science, Christ and the Bible (New York: Fleming H. Revell Company, 1929), pp. 78-81, 94.

ambiguity pervaded some of his statements, such as the following:

> I love the Jews. I do not like all of their deeds. Because of the strong delusion in which the Jew lives at the present time, it is dangerous for him to have too much power in his hands. Being of a superior type of mind, his cleverness makes him the greater sinner. But some day the overshadowing hand of God will be vindicated in this unique people.[81]

By 1930 Winrod assumed a harsher tone, and in 1933 he was leveling the familiar charge of a worldwide conspiracy. A visit to Hitler's Germany in 1934 completed the transformation, and from that time on he was a Nazi apologist. Under the guise of religious journalism he consistently peddled anti-Semitism to a large fundamentalist reading public.[82]

German persecution proved to be a dividing line between fundamentalists in their thinking about Jews. While it induced Winrod to exploit the possibilities of the new anti-Semitic wave and led Riley to expound smugly the doctrine of Jewish guilt, it sobered many others into taking a firm pro-Jewish stand. Gaebelein was only one of "dozens of fundamentalist leaders," according to Roy, who declared their opposition to anti-Semitism in 1939. A number of familiar fundamentalist names also appeared the same

---

[81]Gerald B. Winrod, Mussolini and the Second Coming of Christ (Wichita, Kans.: Defender Publishers, 1928), p. 40.

[82]Roy, Apostles of Discord, pp. 28-29, 35-36.

year in favor of organized relief for the Jews of central Europe.[83] Fence-sitters were forced to take sides, and the majority of them joined Jewish sympathizers in denouncing anti-Semitism.

It becomes clear from the foregoing evidence that fundamentalists had no standard viewpoint toward Jews. Their attitudes ranged from sympathetic concern for the "chosen people" to dire warnings of their machinations. While practically all of them favored evangelization of Jews, this activity was, from their viewpoint, a gesture of kindness rather than an evidence of hostility. Many anticipated the day when a restored and converted Israel would welcome her returning Messiah in her ancient homeland, and they seemed genuinely grieved at the hostility meted out to Jews, whether in Palestine, Germany, or the United States. These men apparently were free of malicious intent in their Jewish relationships. Perhaps their chief fault was a failure to comprehend why their proselytizing efforts were often interpreted unfavorably.

Some, on the other hand, saw contemporary Jews as a threat to the nation or the world. But these men solidi-

---

[83] *Ibid.*, pp. 45-46, 378-79. The appeal for relief was endorsed by fundamentalists William Biederwolf, Lewis Sperry Chafer, Clarence E. Macartney, Mark A. Matthews, Harry Rimmer, Charles G. Trumbull, Louis A. Bauman, H. A. Ironside, Stewart MacLennan, and Wilbur M. Smith. See Joseph Taylor Britan, "An Appeal for Persecuted Israel," *Moody Monthly*, XXXIX (February, 1939), 345.

fied their hostility not so much in the immediate postwar years as during the early thirties, when the rigors of the Depression and the increase in revolutionary sentiment again cast suspicion on the Jews. It was then that they took a closer look at the Protocols and the Ford articles, and, fortified by them, plunged into the new wave of anti-Semitism. Yet, even as this wave gained momentum, men of the same theological persuasion rose up to condemn it. Ultimately, personal preference rather than religious reference group determined whether a fundamentalist felt sympathy or hostility toward Jews.

In ferreting out threats to America, the "hundred percenters" did not confine their suspicions to those of "foreign" citizenship, religion, and financial connections. Many distrusted the American-born Negro as well. Legally emancipated but laboring under political disabilities, social taboos, and economic hardships, the nation's black population was by 1920 struggling for identity and self-sufficiency. World War I had encouraged them in at least two ways. On one hand, black veterans returned home with the exhilaration of victory and a new sense of importance. On the other, civilian Negroes had followed war industry to Northern cities, and their newly found prosperity lured others to follow in the postwar years.

But the "new Negro" was not received kindly by many in the dominant white society. Southerners resented the newly-confident black veteran and feared economic dislocations from the rapid exodus of sharecroppers and tenant farmers. Northerners were alarmed by the rising black tide in urban centers, and white unemployed veterans found themselves competing with Negro laborers for jobs. As a result, lynchings and race riots reached a new high in 1919, and despite increasing attempts at interracial understanding, a residue of mutual distrust remained throughout the decade.[84] Meanwhile, apologists for white supremacy penned the rationale for the "color line." With contemporary scientific interpretation on their side, such scholars as Madison Grant and Lothrop Stoddard alarmed many Americans about the potential dangers in black expansion.[85]

The racial attitudes of fundamentalists at that time are difficult to define because they commented on the subject so rarely and because their opinions varied so widely.

---

[84] Thomas R. Frazier (ed.), Afro-American History: Primary Sources (New York: Harcourt, Brace & World, Inc., 1970), pp. 249-51; Leslie H. Fishel, Jr. and Benjamin Quarles, The Black American: A Documentary History (Revised ed.; Glenview, Ill.: Scott, Foresman and Company, 1970), pp. 403-10.

[85] Grant, Passing of the Great Race, pp. 14-16; Stoddard, Rising Tide of Color, pp. vi, 90, 100-103. Stoddard wrote more directly on black-white relations in America in The Forum, LVIII (October, 1927), 510-19 (portions reprinted in Fishel and Quarles, Black American, pp. 422-25). The relationships between racism and evolutionary science are explored by John S. Haller, Jr., Outcasts from Evolution: Scientific Attitudes of Racial Inferiority, 1859-1900 (Urbana, Ill.: University of Illinois Press, 1971). The preface to Madison Grant's book was written by the eminent scientist, Henry Fairfield Osborn.

Almost the whole range of thinking on race was represented in fundamentalism, and there was nothing distinctive in their views except an effort on the part of some to relate the subject to biblical teaching. Exponents of virulent racial bigotry were rare, but almost as rare were the advocates of complete racial equality. Most fundamentalists apparently followed a middle course--condemning lynching and other injustice and professing a desire for spiritual equality in the church, but expressing reservations or remaining silent on details of social equality.

Since fundamentalists rejected evolution, they were not affected much by contemporary theories of race, although some accepted Anglo-Saxon supremacy on purely patriotic grounds. But at least a few spokesmen allowed their estimation of blacks to be conditioned by a popular interpretation of Genesis 9:25. They believed that for an indiscretion, Noah's son, Ham, and all his descendants were relegated to a perpetually inferior position. Dyson Hague observed that historically Hamites had been "degraded, profane, and sensual."[86] Gerald B. Winrod conceded the early cultural achievements of the black race, but maintained that their civilizations had disappeared suddenly and that they had become servants as prophesied.[87]

---

[86] Fundamentals, VIII, 88.

[87] Winrod, Science, Christ and the Bible, pp. 74-75.

Donald Grey Barnhouse also believed the curse on Ham helped to explain black subjection, but he insisted that the curse had been abrogated by the death of Christ. "Today, in God's sight," said Barnhouse, "there is no such thing as an inferior race."[88]

But most fundamentalist leaders apparently preferred to leave questions of racial origins aside and to confine their comments to present problems, and here their perspectives varied. J. Frank Norris typified the racial attitudes of the white South--sometimes paternalistic, sometimes threatening, but always conscious of the color barrier. Norris apparently felt some responsibility for the spiritual welfare of Negroes, for he occasionally preached in Fort Worth's black churches and at least once addressed a black congregation in Chicago. He also invited a black chorus to sing in his church and counted some Negro ministers among his admirers.[89] But Norris also was zealous for white supremacy, and warned that if Negroes wanted peace and prosperity they should stop advocating social, political, or "any other kind" of equality. He once related how

---

[88]Donald Grey Barnhouse, "The Three Sons of Noah: The Black Man," Revelation, II (July, 1932), 311.

[89]Telegrams, J. C. Austin to J. Frank Norris, May 23, 1927, and J. Frank Norris to J. C. Austin, May 27, 1927; Letters, W. N. Beard to J. Frank Norris, April 23, 1929; J. W. Bailey to J. Frank Norris, January 22 and May 15, 1929; C. Thompson-George to J. Frank Norris, September 7, 1929. Archives, Southern Baptist Convention, John Franklyn Norris Papers.

he had frightened two black workers in the church auditorium and convinced them the place was haunted. With rather curious logic he reasoned that this was a "righteous act" to shake them up, make them forget their troubles, and provide a chance to tell them about the end of the world.[90]

Georgia-reared John Roach Straton shared Norris' paternalism, but took a positive stand against violence inflicted on blacks, most of whom he considered "harmless." "It is a shame," said Straton, "to have taken these simple-minded children of the human race from Africa and enslaved them . . . and now to terrorize and intimidate them."[91] Kentucky-bred William B. Riley took a considerably longer step toward racial equality, but ultimately stopped short of it. As a boy Riley had ruffled his elders by suggesting that blacks be organized into a Sunday School class instead of being left in the church gallery to "pick up the crumbs from the white man's Bible table," and as an adult he considered himself unprejudiced, since he believed the death

---

[90]Letters, J. W. Bailey to J. Frank Norris, October 9, 1929, and J. Frank Norris to Jane Hartwell, December 28, 1928, Archives, Southern Baptist Convention, John Franklyn Norris Papers.

[91]New York Times, December 4, 1922, p. 4; December 11, 1922, p. 4. Other fundamentalists who condemned lynching and other forms of intimidation were Howard A. Banks, "Two Significant Meetings in Philadelphia Five Blocks Apart," Serving and Waiting, XXI (July, 1931), 77; W. Leon Tucker, "The White Flag," The Wonderful Word, XII (November, 1919), 53; and David S. Kennedy, "The Lynching and Race Problems," The Presbyterian, XCII (August 17, 1922), 4-5.

of Christ made all men brothers, either potentially or actually. But Riley did not think this principle alone could decide questions of social and political standing, and he personally felt racial intermarriage was unbiblical.[92]

James M. Gray, who took a moderate position on many social issues, displayed the same sympathetic yet equivocal viewpoint. He declared that the Negro had been an asset to American life, both in economic contributions and in his "innate endowments of emotion, optimism, patience and religious fervor." He utterly condemned lynching and unscrupulous economic practices that plunged Negroes into debt, and encouraged the conquest of racial prejudice. But he himself questioned whether blacks' economic and political opportunities should be broadened at present, due to "questions of manners, cleanliness and intelligence."[93]

A few fundamentalists took a more positive stand on racial equality. David S. Kennedy lauded the "remarkable" progress of blacks since emancipation and urged a swift end

---

[92]Riley, Bible of the Expositor, New Testament, XIII, 258-60; Old Testament, XII, 200-3. Southern-born Mark A. Matthews also declared, "There is no place for racial prejudice in the church," but how he would have applied this principle is not clear. Building the Church (New York: American Tract Society, 1940), p. 67.

[93][James M. Gray], "The American Negro," Moody Monthly, XXI (October, 1920), 54; "Negro Rights," ibid., XXI (July, 1921), 467; "Power of Character," ibid., XXV (October, 1924), 53-54; "The Plight of the Negro," ibid., XXXIV (December, 1933), 146.

to Jim Crow laws and other forms of discrimination. He was willing to regard racial intermarriage as "lawful," although he discouraged it for social reasons.[94] Melvin Grove Kyle approached the race question from a broader, but no less positive, standpoint. He condemned "Anglo-Saxon supremacy" as "a racial delusion that is causing no little of the confusion in the world today; its real name is pride."[95] Kyle declared that nothing was more inimical to the spirit of Christ than racial prejudice, and he urged his readers to deal with it personally instead of viewing it as someone else's problem.

> We are all in favor of this <u>elsewhere</u>--but let fifty Chinese or Japanese or Indians or Negroes appear at the front door of <u>our</u> Church to come in and worship!!--there would be an exodus at every exit available.[96]

Fundamentalists tended to view racial antagonism as a spiritual problem demanding spiritual solutions. Some, like Leon Tucker, believed much would be accomplished through the evangelization of the Negro. In praising a black evangelist, he wrote, "May God bless any man who seeks to evangelize the colored folk of the South. There

---

[94] [David S. Kennedy], "The Negro's Progress in Business," <u>The Presbyterian</u>, XC (November 4, 1920), 5; "The Federal Council on Race Relations," <u>ibid</u>., XCI (November 17, 1921), 4-5.

[95] [Melvin Grove Kyle], Editorial, <u>Bibliotheca Sacra</u>, LXXXIII (July, 1926), 251.

[96] [Melvin Grove Kyle], Editorial, <u>ibid</u>., LXXXVIII (July, 1931), 260; cf. <u>ibid</u>., LXXXVI (January, 1929), 5-6.

is great need. There are many who are praying for a million blacks who are drifting away from God."[97] Among Tucker's many evangelistic enterprises was a home missionary work among blacks in New York City, with a worker teaching Bible classes for both children and mothers and attempting to alleviate their poverty as well.[98]

Others, however, sensed that a solution demanded equal spiritual adjustments on the part of whites. Matthew F. Smith implied this when he wrote:

> This problem we brought upon ourselves by importing these people from Africa. We must face the problem courageously and endeavor to solve it by giving them the gospel of peace and brotherhood.[99]

A. William Lewis counseled Christians to apply Jesus' "good Samaritan" teaching to race relations. "It is fundamental in Christianity," wrote Lewis. "It wipes out the color line. It obliterates caste. It makes human sympathy universal. Within the bounds of the Kingdom there cannot be any adverse discrimination."[100]

---

[97] W. Leon Tucker, "A Colored 'Billy Sunday,'" The Wonderful Word, XI (May, 1919), 345.

[98] Ibid., XIII (December, 1920), 135; XIII (March, 1921), 280.

[99] Matthew F. Smith, "Imperiled Foundations," The Bible Champion, XXIX (March, 1923), 167.

[100] A. William Lewis, "The Unprejudiced Friend," ibid., XXXIV (April, 1928), 223; cf. A. Z. Conrad, Comrades of the Carpenter (New York: Fleming H. Revell Company, 1926), p. 159; [David S. Kennedy], "Lynching and Race Problems," pp. 4-5.

Some fundamentalists believed they owed Negroes the opportunity for an education. William H. Johnson, citing the great contributions of blacks to the war effort, urged in 1918 that returning black veterans be given a chance to get a Christian education on a college level.[101] To what extent fundamentalists followed his advice we do not know, but at least some of the Northern Bible institutes frequently enrolled blacks.[102] One of these, Roderick Toombs, later expressed his appreciation for the education and the atmosphere of the school he attended:

> I am so glad that I ever had the pleasure of associating with such a company of live Christians as are at Philadelphia School of the Bible. Both students and faculty are just like one big family of brothers and sisters; no color line; they treated their brother in black the same as their brother in white.[103]

Whether Toombs' experience was typical or exceptional is impossible to say. Indeed, the fragmentary nature of our evidence discourages any broad generalizations about fundamentalist racial attitudes. These attitudes ranged from the most backward to the most advanced of their day,

---

[101] William Hallock Johnson, "The Negro and Christian Education," The Presbyterian, LXXXVIII (December 26, 1918), 19.

[102] See, e.g., Moody Bible Institute's advertisement in The Watchman-Examiner, VIII (July 15, 1920), 904-5; and Philadelphia School of the Bible's pictures of graduates in Serving and Waiting, XII (August, 1922), and XIII (August, 1923).

[103] "News of Former Students," Serving and Waiting, XII (November, 1922), 311.

with most fundamentalists apparently settling for a compromise between their biblical ideals of unity and brotherhood and the prevailing American social mores. Many expressed appreciation of and sympathy for blacks, but few were able to shed the remnants of paternalism and insist on equal treatment of Negroes on a broad scale.

Hundred-percent Americanism reached its apex in the revived Ku Klux Klan. Originating in Georgia in 1915, the Klan eventually operated nationwide and enjoyed its greatest strength in the Southwest, Midwest, and Far West. At its height it exercised enough influence to produce anti-parochial school legislation in Oregon and to control the statehouse in Indiana. The Klan thrived on wartime and postwar fears of alien influence and worked to restore "native, white, Protestant supremacy" to America. Although its leaders disclaimed violence, its hooded figures, fiery crosses, and general secrecy produced an atmosphere in which violence both thrived and went unpunished.[104]

Some contemporary observers and many later students of the twenties have associated fundamentalism with the Klan, for several reasons. First, the Klan was Protestant in membership and philosophy. Second, some conservative

---

[104]For summaries of the Klan's aims and methods see Leuchtenburg, Perils of Prosperity, pp. 209-13; George E. Mowry (ed.), The Twenties: Fords, Flappers & Fanatics, Spectrum Books (Englewood Cliffs, N.J.: Prentice-Hall, Inc., 1963), pp. 136-53.

Protestant ministers joined or supported the organization.[105] Thirdly, Klansmen and many fundamentalists supported some of the same causes, including anti-evolution laws, prohibition, and the anti-Smith campaign of 1928. Fourthly, both professed similar codes of personal morality. Fifthly, it is often assumed that, since both were conservative protest movements, their adherents represented a similar mentality, class status, and geographical area. In the sixth place, it has been further assumed that both were gripped by blind patriotism and therefore feared the same types of enemies.

But those who allege a close connection between them almost invariably argue from similarity, probability, or insufficiently supported generalizations, rather than from solid historical evidence. John M. Mecklin, for example, wrote in 1924, "It is probable that the majority of the Baptist ministers in the small towns and countryside are . . . sympathetic with the Klan," and proceeded further, without citation of proof, to attribute to Klansman and fundamentalist alike fear, drabness of life, mental servility to a "simple faith," middle-class status, and rural or

---

[105] Robert Moats Miller finds that at least 69 ministers associated in some way with the Klan, and that, of its 39 national lecturers, 26 were clergymen. "A Note on the Relationship between the Protestant Churches and the Revived Ku Klux Klan," <u>Journal of Southern History</u>, XXII (August, 1956), 356, note.

small-town origins.[106] Richard Hofstadter alleges that fundamentalists gave "heavy support" to the Klan, while John Hicks calls them the "backbone" of the organization.[107]

A detailed study of the sources yields a somewhat different picture, however. Robert Moats Miller has found that the Klan received the endorsement of no Protestant religious body and the condemnation of many; that it received treatment ranging from silence to denunciation from a variety of religious periodicals; and that both liberal and fundamentalist clergymen took a stand against it. He concludes that "the Fundamentalist crusade and the Ku Klux Klan were parallel but independent currents in American history."[108] Lipset and Raab, in their study of right-wing extremism, reach a similar conclusion. While the Klan invoked the moral standards of fundamentalism to justify its activities, these authors conclude, the congruence of the two movements was a "historical accident." If fundamentalism had not existed, right-wing advocates would have created their own code of morality to support them.[109]

---

[106]Mecklin, Ku Klux Klan, pp. 100-106, passim.

[107]Richard Hofstadter, The Paranoid Style in American Politics (New York: Alfred A. Knopf, 1965), p. 73, note; Hicks, Republican Ascendancy, pp. 182-83.

[108]Miller, "Protestant Churches and the Ku Klux Klan," pp. 355-68.

[109]Seymour Martin Lipset and Earl Raab, Politics of

The findings of the present study confirm these conclusions. While a few prominent fundamentalists endorsed the Klan, the large majority of them either ignored it or opposed it openly.

One of the most open supporters of the Klan was J. Frank Norris. Although he denied Klan membership, Norris found common cause with it in the crusade against "rum and Romanism," and he insisted that Protestants had as much right to belong to the Klan as Catholics did to be Knights of Columbus. He asserted that local Klan leaders were "some of the most honorable citizens of Fort Worth," and characterized their opponents as "a bunch of low-browed, disreputable leeches on society."[110]

Norris' cordial association with the Klan is evident from a letter of the local organization, reprinted in The Searchlight, which congratulated him for efforts to make the city "a better place to live." Norris also claimed that during an anti-Catholic campaign in San Antonio in 1924 his safety was insured by six thousand Klansmen, who vowed that if he were harmed they would hang every priest

---

Unreason: Right-wing Extremism in America, 1790-1970 (New York: Harper & Row, Publishers, 1970), pp. 113-18.

[110] J. Frank Norris, "Judge Wilson, K. C.'s, Ku Klux Klan and Bootleggers," The Searchlight, IV (May 12, 1922), 1; "Roman Catholicism versus Protestantism," ibid., V (July 14, 1922), 1-2; "The Menace of Roman Catholicism in Politics," ibid., VII (August 1, 1924), 3; "A Reply to the N.Y. World on Stirring Up Strife," ibid., X (February 25, 1927), 3.

in the city. His access to the names of fifty thousand Klansmen in 1928 further illustrates the closeness of the tie.[111]

Other fundamentalist literature, however, reveals little sympathy for the Klan. James M. Gray allowed both sides of the question to be aired in Moody Monthly in 1923, but he personally remained critical. In one Monthly article, A. R. Funderburk of Palestine, Texas, took the organization to task for violating the biblical principles of love for one's neighbor, love for one's enemy, and respect for civil authority. He pointed out that it would exclude even Jesus from membership, since he was a Jew.[112] Funderburk was answered by John Bradbury of Lancaster, Pennsylvania, who, using the Klan's own pronouncements, held it to be a friend and ally of the church.[113] Later, Bob Shuler of Los Angeles wrote that, in spite of its mistakes, which eventually would be corrected, there was no "more hopeful secret society" in America than the Klan.[114]

---

[111]Reprinted letter, Fort Worth Knights of the Ku Klux Klan to J. Frank Norris, The Searchlight, V (September 15, 1922), 4; Norris, "Menace of Roman Catholicism," p. 3; Letter, J. Frank Norris to Hon. R. B. Craeger [Creager], January 23, 1928, Archives, Southern Baptist Convention, John Franklyn Norris Papers.

[112]A. R. Funderburk, "The Ku Klux Klan--Is It of God?" Moody Monthly, XXIII (March, 1923), 291-92.

[113]John Bradbury, "Defending the Ku Klux Klan--A Reply to Mr. Funderburk," ibid., XXIII (May, 1923), 420-21.

[114]Bob Shuler, "Investigate the Ku Klux Klan," ibid.,

But Gray editorially remained skeptical. Examining the stated objectives of the Klan, he found moral principles he could agree with. "But why," he asked, "cannot such a mission be carried out without secrecy, without increasing race and religious animosity, and without going about the country in disguise?"[115] Gray maintained that the church need not resort to a secret, oathbound organization guilty of "follies and misdemeanors" to make its principles effective in public life. The very type of people the Klan attracted was a warning that such an alliance was an "unequal yoke."[116]

Gray's objections were voiced repeatedly by other leading fundamentalists. William B. Riley, who facetiously remarked that the Klan was more acceptable theologically than the liberal wing of the Northern Baptist Convention, nevertheless indicted it for its appeal to prejudice, secrecy, vulnerability to hypocrisy, and violent tendencies. While careful to affirm his own Americanism, Riley objected to the Klan's blind, narrow opposition to foreigners. David S. Kennedy went farther and turned the tables on these superpatriots, labeling them "un-American"

XXIV (December, 1923), 182.

[115][James M. Gray], "The Ku Klux Klan," _ibid._, XXIII (February, 1923), 240.

[116]James M. Gray, "The Ku Klux Klan," _ibid._, XXIV (December, 1923), 163.

because of their secrecy and violence.[117]

John Roach Straton of New York City was forced to declare himself on the Klan in 1922 when his Calvary Baptist Church was accused of being a "Klan nest." This allegation was based on the activities of Dr. Oscar Haygood, a retired minister and "general evangelist" for the church. But Straton quickly secured Haygood's dismissal and vehemently denounced "lame duck pastors" who went about "saving the country." He declared that "the man in the mask" had no place in America, and repudiated all attempts to stir up racial and religious prejudice.[118]

In addition to their objections to the Klan's methods, many fundamentalists condemned it for its secrecy. While some prominent fundamentalists were lodge members,[119] others considered all secret societies unbiblical. It was primarily on this basis that William L. Pettingill opposed the Klan. "Although there are doubtless many well

---

[117] Riley, Bible of the Expositor, New Testament, XIII, 253-78. This chapter is a reprinted sermon, "Crime and the Ku Klux Klan," delivered in 1924 when the Klan was at its height. [David S. Kennedy], "The Ku Klux Klan," The Presbyterian, XCI (September 15, 1921), 4.

[118] New York Times, November 20, 1922, p. 2; November 25, 1922, p. 1; December 4, 1922, p. 4; December 9, 1922, p. 4; December 11, 1922, p. 4; December 18, 1922, p. 17; December 29, 1922, p. 1. Straton later joined the nationalistic Supreme Kingdom, but severed his ties when criticism arose. New York Times, January 7, 1927, p. 4; January 20, 1927, p. 1.

[119] See Appendix A. At least five of the leaders included were Masons.

intentioned people within its ranks," wrote Pettingill, "I have no doubt of its Satanic origin. It is just another *unequal-yoke* scheme which is opposed to the Word of God." (Italics in original.)[120]

Fundamentalists also opposed the Klan-inspired Oregon school law, which required children to attend public schools. J. Gresham Machen deplored the loss of freedom and the standardization it imposed. James M. Gray warned that such legislation could cut two ways, giving Catholics the incentive to outlaw public schools if they should ever become a majority. W. B. Riley, though he had championed anti-evolution legislation in several states, rejoiced when the Oregon law was declared unconstitutional in 1925.[121]

Thus, with a few exceptions, fundamentalist leaders criticized, condemned, or ignored the Ku Klux Klan. For them its secrecy, intolerance, and questionable methods far outweighed any agreement in morals or ideology which might

---

[120] William L. Pettingill, "Ku Klux Klan and Anti-Ku Klux Klan," *Serving and Waiting*, XIV (November, 1924), 319; cf. "Rome and the Ku Klux Klan," *ibid.*, XIII (October, 1923), 275; "Ku Klux Klan," *ibid.*, XVI (May, 1926), 9. Riley and Straton also advanced the same argument and Gray hinted at it. See Riley, *Bible of the Expositor*, New Testament, XIII, 263-65; Straton, *New York Times*, December 4, 1922, p. 4; Gray, "Ku Klux Klan," *Moody Monthly*, XXIV (December, 1923), 163.

[121] Machen, *Christianity and Liberalism*, p. 12; [James M. Gray], "Oregon School Case," *Moody Monthly*, XXV (June, 1925), 447-48; "The Oregon and Tennessee Laws," *Christian Fundamentals in School and Church*, VII (October-December, 1925), 33-34.

have brought the two movements together.

To what extent, then, can we identify fundamentalism with the "hundred percent American" mentality which regarded certain minority groups as national threats? Statements by some of its leaders unquestionably reveal attitudes similar to those of the hundred percenters—uneasiness about immigrant influence, suspicion of Catholic motives, wariness of growing Jewish power, and paternalism toward Negroes. Without doubt fundamentalists shared in the distrust of the postwar decade.

Yet this pattern of thinking was neither consistent nor prominent throughout the movement as a whole. Each fundamentalist spokesman formed his own opinions, and no two men among them held identical viewpoints regarding all the groups in question. Neither did individual leaders see all the minorities in the same light, for one who voiced criticism of one group sometimes expressed sympathy or praise for another. Furthermore, not a single minority group was uniformly viewed in an unfavorable light by all fundamentalists. It should also be remembered that fundamentalist leaders often failed to comment at all on certain minorities, even when they were most controversial.[122]

---

[122]Among fundamentalist editors, for example, Melvin G. Kyle, William Pettingill, Charles G. Trumbull, and Leon Tucker ignored Catholic issues, even during the Smith presidential campaign. Kyle and David S. Kennedy did not discuss Jews, Pettingill said nothing about immigrants, and Arno C. Gaebelein, Pettingill, and Trumbull made no

Rarely did any of them advocate the curtailment of a group's political rights, and most of those who discussed the Ku Klux Klan opposed its activites.

These findings suggest that fundamentalism as a movement adopted no uniform viewpoint toward controversial minorities and, because of the diversity of opinion within it, could not have been a major promoter of hundred percent Americanism during the twenties. Some individual fundamentalists either promoted or fell victim to the trend, but others, through their tolerance, doubtless became a moderating influence in the spheres in which they moved. The silence of still others suggests that, for all their patriotism, fundamentalists believed America's biggest problems were spiritual, not social or political, and that their time was best spent in fighting heresy, not social minority groups.

J. Gresham Machen wrote to his mother in 1920, "The gospel of Christ is a blessed relief from that sinful state of affairs commonly known as hundred per-cent Americanism."[123] In this statement lies a clue to the difference between the hundred percenter and the fundamentalist. The hundred percenter had but one object of loyalty and point

---

reference to black-white relationships.

[123]Ned B. Stonehouse, J. Gresham Machen: A Biographical Memoir (Grand Rapids, Mich.: Wm. B. Eerdmans Publishing Company, 1954), p. 304.

of reference--his nation with its cherished way of life. When he perceived a threat to the nation, he had to fight to retain his security.[124] The fundamentalist, on the other hand, divided his loyalty between his nation and his religious faith, so that even when he believed the nation was endangered he could still find security in his faith and react with some moderation. For most fundamentalists, therefore, the minorities threatening the social and political status quo in the twenties did not pose a critical problem. The point at which they did become militant was when they perceived, as in modernism and evolution, threats to both their nation and their faith.

---

[124] Coben develops this point at some length in "American Red Scare," pp. 204-9.

CHAPTER VI

"THE FAITH" AND SOCIAL CONCERN

> The world needs new control of nature and society and is told that the Bible is verbally inerrant.
> It needs a means of composing class strife, and is told to believe in the substitutionary atonement.
> It needs a spirit of love and justice and is told that love without orthodoxy will not save from hell.
> It needs international peace and sees the champions of peace incapable of fellowship even at the table of the Lord . . .
> It needs faith in the divine presence in human affairs and is told it must accept the virgin birth of Jesus Christ.
> It needs hope for a better world order and is told to await the speedy return of Jesus Christ . . .[1]

This is how Shailer Mathews portrayed fundamentalism in 1924. To him and many other observers it was a theological system totally removed from the needs of the modern world, indifferent and sometimes hostile to progressive social reforms.[2] Some even insinuated, though never proved, that vested economic interests promoted fundamentalism in order to reduce the interference of the liberal

---

[1]Shailer Mathews, The Faith of Modernism (New York: Macmillan Company, 1924), p. 10.

[2]See, e.g., Carroll Edwin Harrington, "The Fundamentalist Movement in America, 1870-1920" (Unpublished Ph.D. dissertation, University of California at Berkeley, 1959), pp. iii-iv; Henry F. May, The End of American Innocence (New York: Alfred A. Knopf, 1959), pp. 127-29.

"social gospel" in business affairs.[3]

Mathews correctly identified fundamentalism's chief interest as theological and evangelistic, rather than social. But the extent to which this emphasis implied indifference or hostility to social reform is open to question. To understand the fundamentalists' relationship to the reform ideology of the early twentieth century requires that we both examine the reform movements of that era and compare fundamentalist approaches to social problems with them.

The social gospel, which is usually regarded as fundamentalism's antithesis in reform philosophy, was born amid the urban and industrial problems of the post-Civil War years and reached maturity in the first two decades of the twentieth century. Buoyed up by an optimistic interpretation of Darwinism and a strong belief in environmental influence on character, its advocates attempted to banish economic injustices by applying Jesus' ethical teachings to the industrial order. While few of them were radicals, they did at times advocate political intervention in the economic process, thus challenging laissez-faire individu-

---

[3]Kirsopp Lake, The Religion of Yesterday and Tomorrow (London: Christophers, 1925), p. 161; "Shaker Fundamentalism Shaking," The Christian Century, XXXIX (November 9, 1922), 1383-84; Norman F. Furniss, The Fundamentalist Controversy, 1918-1931 (New Haven: Yale University Press, 1954), p. 28; Winthrop S. Hudson, American Protestantism (Chicago: University of Chicago Press, 1961), p. 149.

alism and time-honored "economic laws." Nineteenth-century evangelical revivalism was a part of the social gospel's theological heritage, but its theology eventually acquired a distinctly liberal flavor. It focused on the immanence of God, the goodness of man, the superiority of Christian ethics, and the possibility of achieving the kingdom of God on earth through human efforts.[4]

Social gospel preachers were not alone in their campaign for social righteousness and order. By 1900 a variety of other civic-minded Americans had become involved in reform--agrarians, politicians, muckraking journalists, professors, businessmen, labor unionists, and white-collar professionals. This diverse group, commonly called "progressives," was united neither by common social and political connections nor by a unified program, but simply by a common desire to preserve America's historic values of individualism and equality in the highly organized industrial setting of the twentieth century.[5] As they sought to

---

[4]One of the most complete studies on the social gospel is C. Howard Hopkins, The Rise of the Social Gospel in American Protestantism, 1865-1915 (New Haven: Yale University Press, 1940). Its revivalist origins are explored by Timothy L. Smith, Revivalism and Social Reform (New York: Abingdon Press, 1957). See also Robert T. Handy (ed.), The Social Gospel in America, 1870-1920 (New York: Oxford University Press, 1966); Benjamin G. Rader, "Richard T. Ely: Lay Spokesman for the Social Gospel," The Journal of American History, LIII (June, 1966), 61-74.

[5]The complexity of progressivism is reflected in the many interpretations of it by historians. As examples of this variety, see Richard Hofstadter, The Age of Reform

make their nation a more democratic, orderly, efficient, and healthful place, they approached their task with a moral idealism inherited from evangelical Protestantism. In fact, progressives not only drew inspiration from their Protestant heritage to combat economic and political evils, but also attacked practices offensive to Protestant personal morality, such as the liquor trade and prostitution.[6]

Historians differ in describing the fate of "progressivism" during and after World War I, but all generally agree that the reform impulse declined during the business-oriented and fear-ridden twenties.[7] Not until prosperity

---

(New York: Alfred A. Knopf, 1956); George E. Mowry, The Era of Theodore Roosevelt, 1900-1912 (New York: Harper & Row Publishers, 1958); Robert H. Wiebe, Businessmen and Reform: A Study of the Progressive Movement (Chicago: Quadrangle Books, 1962); Gabriel Kolko, The Triumph of Conservatism: A Reinterpretation of American History, 1900-1916 (New York: Macmillan Company, 1963). See also George E. Mowry, The Progressive Era 1900-1918: Recent Literature and New Ideas (2d ed.; Washington, D.C.: American Historical Association, 1964), p. 3. Because of the vagueness of "progressive" aims, the bewildering variety of people involved, and the diverse and even contradictory solutions they proposed, I tend to agree with Peter G. Filene that while there may have been a diffuse progressive era there was never a progressive movement. "An Obituary for 'The Progressive Movement,'" in Twentieth-Century America: Recent Interpretations, ed. by Barton J. Bernstein and Allen J. Matusow (2d ed.; New York: Harcourt Brace Jovanovich, Inc., 1972), pp. 35-51.

[6]James H. Timberlake, Prohibition and the Progressive Movement, 1900-1920 (Cambridge, Mass.: Harvard University Press, 1963), p. 2 and passim; Mowry, Era of Theodore Roosevelt, pp. 104-5; Hofstadter, Age of Reform, pp. 203-5.

[7]See, e.g., Hofstadter, Age of Reform, pp. 273, 280ff.; Arthur S. Link, "What Happened to the Progressive Movement in the 1920's?" American Historical Review, LXIV

had passed and the Depression had taken a heavy toll did reform regain a prominent place in American thinking, and when it did, it lacked much of the crusading idealism that had marked the earlier efforts. In place of moral appeals or lectures to businessmen and politicians, the New Deal stressed corporate organization to produce results, and the economic aid extended to the beleaguered citizen contained little hint of moral uplift. This is not to suggest that the New Dealers lacked moral principles or motivation in their reforms, but their immediate goal was a practical one --economic reconstruction as quickly as possible.[8]

Fundamentalism, which exerted its greatest influence between the progressive and New Deal eras, did not pose as a reform movement. If social reform means direct participation in corporate institutional processes to change a social environment in the interests of human welfare, few fundamentalists were consistent reformers. They were preachers who saw their primary duty as one of converting individuals to Christ, rather than revising the social structure. They rejected the premise of Bushnell and the social gospel that the environment made the individual.

(July, 1959), 833-51; Paul W. Glad, "Progressives and the Business Culture of the 1920s," The Journal of American History, LIII (June, 1966), 77-89.

[8]Hofstadter, Age of Reform, pp. 318, 323-25; Paul K. Conkin, The New Deal (New York: Thomas Y. Crowell Company, 1967), pp. 28, 80-81.

For them the opposite was nearer the truth, and until individuals were made new by conversion, they believed society would remain seriously flawed.

This did not mean that fundamentalists were indifferent to contemporary social inequities. Their writings evidenced a concern that social gospelers could hardly improve upon, not only about defections from personal morality but also about corporate political and economic abuses. Neither did they necessarily believe institutional reforms were wrong. A few strong premillennialists, to be sure, considered them a waste of the Christian's time, since they believed only Jesus' return could accomplish complete social regeneration. But the majority, including other prominent premillennialists, believed collective efforts were necessary to curtail, if not to eliminate, the social products of sin.

But ultimately, they believed, the solutions to social problems had to be moral and spiritual. This was true whether they were dealing with excessive liquor consumption or the rigors of the Depression. If Americans, like Israel of old, would leave their idols and restore God to his deserved position among them, he would honor their faith with prestige, peace, and prosperity. Even a substantial minority of true Christians might, through the pervasive influence of their faith, eliminate the nation's worst political and economic evils.

Since they proposed a basically religious solution for America's ills, fundamentalists are not neatly categorized as political liberals or conservatives. The same person who, for religious reasons, saw weaknesses in collective reform efforts, might also, for religious reasons, oppose economic exploitation of the poor. Nevertheless, their conservative theology, combined with their loyalty to American traditions, made many of them skeptical toward drastic innovations. They shared the moral ideals of the progressives, supported many of their reforms, and drew inspiration from progressivism for their own anti-evolution crusades. But they were somewhat more skeptical about socialism, and uniformly denounced communism. Similarly, they admired Herbert Hoover, who was in many respects the final embodiment of progressivism, but were cautious and sometimes critical toward Franklin Roosevelt and his innovative, secularly-oriented New Deal.

Social concern in the progressive tradition thus ran deep among fundamentalists, but their theological views on the human condition and hope prevented them from becoming full-fledged liberal reformers. It is necessary to explore these views further in order to comprehend their attitudes toward specific social questions which confronted them.

The fundamentalist saw man as perfectly created but severely marred. He accepted literally the biblical account of Adam's sin, and believed the tendency to do evil was passed on to all his descendants. While not denying the influence of environment, he blamed social evils primarily on this inherited downward pull. William B. Riley called it the "tap-root" of all social disorder.[9] This was a pessimistic view of human nature, as J. Gresham Machen was quick to admit. But pessimism was unhealthy, maintained Machen, only when it did not square with the facts, and those who hoped to renew society would do well to acknowledge its faulty human foundation.[10]

From this premise of inherited sin followed several logical conclusions. First, whatever other needs men might have, their basic need was a spiritual one. This spiritual defect alienated them not only from God but also from one another and from their own true potential, sowing the seed for social problems. It was this spiritual need, claimed fundamentalists, that many reformers tended to overlook. James M. Gray, while lauding the work of the Family Welfare Association, lamented its lack of spiritual emphasis. Gray wrote:

> Money, health, education, training, advice in business affairs, how valuable and necessary they are, and yet how far short of meeting humanity's fundamental need.

---

[9] William B. Riley, <u>The Perennial Revival: A Plea for Evangelism</u> (Revised ed.; Philadelphia: American Baptist Publication Society, 1916), p. 204.

[10] "Does Fundamentalism Obstruct Social Progress?" <u>Survey</u>, LII (July 1, 1924), 391-92. This article includes affirmative arguments by Charles P. Fagnani and negative arguments by J. Gresham Machen.

> On the other hand, when that need is met, how frequently the other handicaps disappear![11]

J. Gresham Machen concurred wholeheartedly. If relief and physical improvement should become the only concerns of the race, he declared, "then mankind will have sunk to the level of the beasts."[12]

Many pointed out that the recent World War had resulted from just such spiritual neglect, and they warned that a lasting peace must be based on spiritual as well as material reconstruction. W. H. Griffith Thomas exhorted his readers in 1920:

> Let us do all we can to assist human progress and to be forward-looking and do all we can to make this world better; but . . . let us not forget that sin is in the human heart and sin has not been altered . . . since July, 1914.[13]

Fundamentalists reasoned, secondly, that since the tendency to sin that lay at the root of social evils was an individual problem, it had to be attacked on that level before constructive social change could begin. On the one hand, the individual sinner was a menace to the entire social fabric, for every larger societal unit, even the family, was affected by its individual component parts. On

---

[11] [James M. Gray], "Social Welfare Work," <u>Moody Monthly</u>, XXX (August, 1930), 575.

[12] "Does Fundamentalism Obstruct Social Progress?" p. 427.

[13] W. H. Griffith Thomas, "The Return of the Lord," <u>Serving and Waiting</u>, X (May, 1920), 21.

the other hand, the converted individual became a social asset because his faith propelled him into society to "battle for the right." Fundamentalists argued that it made little sense to speak of improving the mass unless the units of the mass were changed.[14]

But how could individuals be changed? Fundamentalists maintained, thirdly, that since sin was an internal problem, individuals could not be changed for the better simply by manipulating their environment. An inner regeneration alone could bring lasting improvement. If asked what kind of environment made better people, said Amzi C. Dixon, he would have difficulty deciding, for both in the tenement house and the mansion piety and profanity lived side by side.[15] G. J. Rousseau insisted that "a good environment has never made a man good who wanted to be bad," and, conversely, "a bad environment could never make a man bad who wanted to be good."[16] "Soap and sunshine are

---

[14] J. C. Massee, The Ten Greatest Chapters in the Bible (Nashville, Tenn.: Sunday School Board of the Southern Baptist Convention, 1924), pp. 73, 76; "Does Fundamentalism Obstruct Social Progress?" p. 392; Hugh R. Monro, "The World's Last Hope," Our Hope, XXXI (July, 1924), 54; A. Z. Conrad, Jesus Christ at the Crossroads (New York: Fleming H. Revell Company, 1924), p. 123; [Charles G. Trumbull], "How Shall We Defend the Gospel?" The Sunday School Times, LXIII (August 20, 1921), 445-46.

[15] A. C. Dixon, Evangelism Old and New (New York: American Tract Society, 1905), pp. 42-43.

[16] G. J. Rousseau, "The Social Gospel," The Bible Champion, XXIX (August-September, 1923), 417.

good," observed A. Z. Conrad, "but they never yet changed a heart. The change of direction from down to up is not wrought by a better parish house."[17]

It was at this point, fundamentalists claimed, that the social gospel was making a fatal mistake. It was treating symptoms without touching the disease, a procedure both self-defeating and harmful to humanity. Since it drew attention away from the basic problem of sin, it also concealed the only permanent solution, regeneration. Fundamentalists fully believed that evangelical Christianity would bring humanitarianism, education, honest politics, and ethical economics in its wake. But when social gospel advocates raised these by-products to the level of major and immediate goals, they were leading churches away from their true task and leaving them neither product nor by-product, neither regeneration nor reformation. In short, the social gospel was not Christianity, for in John Roach Straton's words, Jesus did not say, "Ye must be reformed again," but "Ye must be born again."[18]

---

[17] A. Z. Conrad, "A City Church and the Unchurched," The Missionary Review of the World, LII (March, 1929), 174.

[18] John Roach Straton, The Gardens of Life (New York: George H. Doran Company, 1921), p. 144; cf. David S. Kennedy, "Politicalizing the Church," The Bible Champion, XXIX (June-July, 1923), 317-18; Earl Dubbel, "A Humanitarian Fallacy," Our Hope, XX (January, 1914), 416; The Fundamentals: A Testimony to the Truth (12 vols.; Chicago: Testimony Publishing Company, [1910-1915]), X, 37-38; "Does the 'Social Gospel' Save?" The Sunday School Times, LXVI (August 23, 1924), 502; Donald Grey Barnhouse, "True Liber-

Spiritually reborn individuals would inevitably exercise a beneficial influence on their surroundings, the fundamentalists reasoned. Baptist fundamentalist ministers at the 1921 Northern Baptist Convention published a statement of faith which endorsed the personal gospel of regeneration, but added, "We believe that all human betterment and social improvement are the inevitable by-products of such a gospel."[19] To fail to show social concern was to deny one's Christian profession. "We cannot pray and prey at the same time," warned Leon Tucker. "We cannot wait upon God and lie in wait for our neighbor . . ."[20] J. Gresham Machen declared that without service for others it was impossible to be true disciples of Jesus, and William Biederwolf asserted even more strongly, "Social service means serving society, and if a man is not saved for that he is not saved at all."[21] Social concern was a natural

---

alism," Revelation, II (August, 1932), 327; Charles F. Reitzel, "The Church and Her Calling--Is She Still Ringing True," Serving and Waiting, XIX (July, 1929), 79-81; John Horsch, The Failure of Modernism: A Reply to Harry Emerson Fosdick (Chicago: Bible Institute Colportage Association, 1925), pp. 30-31.

[19] "A Confession of Faith," The Watchman-Examiner, IX (June 30, 1921), 805.

[20] W. Leon Tucker, "Shall We Pray or Prey?" The Wonderful Word, XI (August, 1919), 482.

[21] J. Gresham Machen, "The Claims of Love," in God Transcendent and Other Selected Sermons, ed. by Ned B. Stonehouse (Grand Rapids, Mich.: Wm. B. Eerdmans Publishing Company, 1949), p. 66; William E. Biederwolf, Evangelism: Its Justification, Its Operation and Its Value (New

consequence and proof of conversion.

Hence fundamentalists were led by this line of reasoning to a final conclusion: If the basic human need was spiritual and individual, and if a new birth was essential to personal and social improvement, they must devote the bulk of their time and resources to evangelism. As an ambassador for Christ the Christian minister would not be indifferent to politics, economics, or other aspects of the social order, declared James M. Gray, "but first, last and all the time he will be seeking to reconcile men unto God."[22]

One must also bear in mind that the primary motive behind this "ministry of reconciliation" was not the improvement of society but the eternal welfare of the individual. If social improvement followed the gospel, fundamentalists rejoiced, but they regarded this as a secondary benefit. Treating Christianity as a "tool" to accomplish useful things was to them a prostitution of its real purpose. It could be used to combat Bolshevism, unify the

---

York: Fleming H. Revell Company, 1921), p. 72; cf. [Curtis Lee Laws], "Evangelism and Social Service," The Watchman-Examiner, VIII (January 29, 1920), 133-34; [William B. Riley], "Social Fruits From Fundamentalism," The Christian Fundamentalist, I (February, 1928), 24; Paul M. Tharp, "The Man on the Median Line," Moody Monthly, XXXIII (October, 1932), 53-54.

[22][James M. Gray], "'Al' Smith among the Prophets," Moody Monthly, XXXIV (September, 1933), 3; cf. "'Progress and Poverty,'" ibid., XXXII (February, 1932), 279-80.

nation, produce healthy communities, or promote international peace, observed J. Gresham Machen, but if adopted for any of these reasons it ceased to be Christianity, for the Christian gospel was a message of personal redemption.[23]

This, in general outline, is the way fundamentalists viewed their relationship to social problems and their solution. But beneath the agreement in general philosophy one discovers differences of application, particularly in regard to how much time and attention a Christian should devote to social questions and what specific reforms should receive his endorsement. Lay fundamentalist William Jennings Bryan apparently sensed no contradiction between conservative Christianity and wide-ranging reform efforts, according to recent studies.[24] For the minister, however, the dilemma could become more acute, for to neglect the needs of the soul while stressing those of the body was to betray his calling. It is therefore surprising to discover how many fundamentalist preachers devoted generous attention to the need for social amelioration. Not all could wholeheartedly endorse Melvin Grove Kyle's statement,

---

[23]Machen, <u>Christianity and Liberalism</u>, p. 152.

[24]See, e.g., Willard H. Smith, "William Jennings Bryan and the Social Gospel," <u>The Journal of American History</u>, LIII (June, 1966), 41-60; Lawrence W. Levine, <u>Defender of the Faith. William Jennings Bryan: The Last Decade, 1915-1925</u> (New York: Oxford University Press, 1965), pp. 197-210, 358-59, 362-64.

"Church members should all be reformers and the Church should teach them to be so,"[25] but the majority believed the minister should at least call their attention to social sin and exhort them to eliminate it.

Among advocates of social righteousness none was more consistently outspoken than John Roach Straton, the colorful and controversial pastor of New York City's Calvary Baptist Church. With consummate oratorical skill, Straton inveighed against dancing, women's fashions, theater attendance, sex, gambling, sabbath-breaking, materialism, jazz, and prizefighting. But he made no distinctions in guilt between these and the "public sins" of commercialized vice, slums, economic injustice, political corruption, child labor, crime, inadequate education, and the liquor trade. He reserved some of his harshest words for the idle and unethical rich.[26]

With his flair for the sensational, Straton attracted widespread attention in 1920 when, in disguise, he visited and obtained evidence against illegally-operating liquor establishments in New York. The information he gathered led to a police raid, a grand jury investigation of vice conditions, and widespread suspicions of corruption in

---

[25][Melvin Grove Kyle], Editorial, Bibliotheca Sacra, LXXX (January, 1923), 3. (Italics in original.)

[26]John Roach Straton, The Menace of Immorality in Church and State (New York: George H. Doran Company, 1920), passim; Gardens of Life, pp. 55, 141-43, 225-26.

enforcement agencies. Straton himself used the occasion to berate the churches for their moral laxity and to urge preachers to take more positive leadership in mobilizing public opinion.[27]

Across town from Straton, his aging but highly respected colleague, David James Burrell, attacked social evils from the pulpit of the Marble Collegiate Church. Burrell especially deplored the "survival of the fittest" philosophy that operated in both business trusts and labor unions. As an alternative he proposed "Christian Socialism," which would "level up" the less fortunate.

> It goes out into the highways and hedges and lends a hand. It aims to put paupers in the way of earning a livelihood, to strengthen the weak, befriend the friendless and save Society by so bettering the environment that its unfittest may survive.[28]

Burrell also took an active interest in moral legislation and civic affairs. Journalist William G. Shepherd described him as "a massive figure in the civic life of the city."[29]

In New Jersey, prominent Methodist Harold Paul Sloan

---

[27] New York Times, April 5, 1920, p. 17; April 6, 1920, pp. 1, 3; April 12, 1920, p. 5; April 26, 1920, p. 2.

[28] David J. Burrell, "Down and Out," The Bible Champion, XXX (November, 1924), 556.

[29] William G. Shepherd, Great Preachers As Seen By a Journalist (New York: Fleming H. Revell Company, 1924), p. 25. Burrell's strong interest in moral legislation is evident from his article, "The Blue Laws," The Bible Champion, XXIX (August-September, 1923), 386-89.

combined a strong apologetic for orthodoxy with an equally strong social concern. Sloan revealed his philosophy as he recounted his conversation with a theological liberal:

> In the course of our conversation he discovered that we shared fully his social passion; that we were devoted to the same great social objectives as he was. And then it seemed to dawn upon him as a new discovery: he saw that from our point of view the Christian faith, with its virgin born and death conquering Christ, its supernaturals, its authoritative Scriptures, is the chief explanation of all social progress.[30]

And what were those "great social objectives" Sloan had in mind? They included the abolition of unemployment and extreme poverty, the reduction of vocational diseases and industrial accidents, the conquest of racial prejudice, the elimination of international war, the permanent disappearance of the liquor traffic, the reduction of crime and corruption, and the recovery of Sunday as a day of worship and rest.[31]

A. Z. Conrad, pastor of Boston's Park Street Congregational Church, expressed similar aims. He believed the church had a fivefold duty: (1) to "gospelize the world," which meant both to evangelize and to apply "gospel ideals" to human problems; (2) to "harmonize society," eliminating all divisive tendencies; (3) to "ethicalize industry" so

---

[30]Harold Paul Sloan, "What are we Imperilling?" Christian Faith and Life, XXXVII (February, 1931), 66.

[31]Harold Paul Sloan, "The Crisis of Civilization," ibid., 57-61; "The Religion the World Needs," ibid., XXXVII (July, 1931), 339-42.

that workers' conditions might be improved; (4) to "capitalize influence," or organize to achieve any given reform; and (5) to "internationalize politics," stressing human brotherhood above nationalism.[32]

The practical application of the gospel demanded that the minister and the church be instruments of social improvement, according to Conrad. "No minister can excuse himself from an active participation in . . . social and political questions . . . on the ground that his business is purely spiritual," he insisted. "Spiritual leadership can never fulfill its duty until it forms contacts with all sorts and conditions of men and deals with all sorts of evils which have to be corrected."[33] As long as crime, political corruption, economic injustice, and the liquor industry existed, the minister's social task was unfinished.

It is tempting to reason that the fundamentalists who evidenced strong social concern either were postmillennialists or had no strong interest in millennial or prophetic questions. But one finds interest in social questions just as intense among premillennialists. This was particularly

---

[32] A. Z. Conrad, "The Colossal Task of the Modern Church," The Bible Champion, XXXIII (August, 1927), 400-401; cf. Comrades of the Carpenter (New York: Fleming H. Revell Company, 1926), p. 136.

[33] A. Z. Conrad, "Leadership in America's Moral Crisis," The Bible Champion, XXXVI (December, 1930), 626.

true of Anglican W. H. Griffith Thomas, founder of Wycliffe College in Toronto and popular Bible lecturer. Thomas bristled whenever anyone suggested that premillennialists were pessimists or opposed progress. In answer to one such charge he said, "Well, I have only to ask you to notice the temperance movement, and the movement for social reform, and the great ethical and moral and social effects . . . of missions."[34]

Thomas believed the pastor should concern himself with the problems of poor living conditions, ill effects of charity, unequal distribution of wealth, the extravagance of the wealthy, and the evil effects of drink. He urged his readers to join, and influence others to join, organizations which discussed such problems, to influence public opinion on temperance, and to cooperate actively with the movement for peace. He praised clergymen who sided with the oppressed and promoted economic righteousness. In short, Thomas believed that since almost every social problem had its moral aspect, every minister should share the responsibility for its solution.[35]

Another socially-conscious millenarian was Mark A. Matthews, whose early pastorates in Georgia and Tennessee

---

[34] W. H. Griffith Thomas, "The Prince of Peace," in Christ and Glory, p. 227.

[35] W. H. Griffith Thomas, The Work of the Ministry (London: Hodder and Stoughton, n.d. [between 1910 and 1919]), pp. 346-51.

and thirty-eight-year ministry at the First Presbyterian Church of Seattle formed one continuous story of social involvement. Matthews' interests were many and varied. In Jackson, Tennessee he organized a night school of 600, built a hospital and a library, and fought against legalization of slot machines and prize fights. His church in Seattle organized the first anti-tuberculosis work, kindergarten, and day nursery in the city. His congregation organized a Red Cross unit in 1917 and Matthews presided over the Seattle Red Cross Chapter for twenty years. He considered any institution that aided the disadvantaged and disabled a deterrent to crime and other social problems.[36]

Matthews also became deeply involved in local politics, and as early as his ministry in Georgia he locked horns with corrupt public officials. It was in Seattle, however, that his most spectacular battles occurred. From 1910 to 1917 he fought mayors, police chiefs, bootleggers, gamblers, and other beneficiaries of commercialized vice. The recall of a mayor and the criminal conviction of a police chief were partially due to his influence. "I would see my city burning in ashes," Matthews wrote later, "before I would permit again the establishment of segre-

---

[36]Ezra P. Giboney and Agnes M. Potter, The Life of Mark A. Matthews (Grand Rapids, Mich.: Wm. B. Eerdmans Publishing Company, 1948), pp. 20-21, 28; Mark A. Matthews, Gospel Sword Thrusts (New York: Fleming H. Revell Company, 1924), p. 83.

gated districts and the recognition by civil authorities of licensed vice."[37]

Matthews' self-acquired legal knowledge and long membership in the Tennessee Bar Association also proved valuable in more positive undertakings. He organized the first juvenile court in Seattle and his church paid the salary of the first juvenile officer. As one of those chosen to revise the city charter in 1926, he unsuccessfully tried to introduce a city manager type of government. Matthews believed the preacher had both the right and duty to speak out on all social issues, always being sure, however, to have sufficient legal evidence for any charges he made.[38]

J. Frank Norris, pastor of Fort Worth's First Baptist Church, shared Matthews' view of the ministry. Although he rarely paused to philosophize during his stormy career, his incessant political activity on all levels gave evidence of his broad view of pastoral duty.[39] Norris was a thoroughgoing premillennialist, even conducting an annual "Premillennial Bible School" at his church; yet many of his prophetic sermons were interlaced with denunciations of cur-

---

[37]Matthews, Gospel Sword Thrusts, pp. 80-81; Giboney and Potter, Mark A. Matthews, pp. 20, 29-35.

[38]Giboney and Potter, Mark A. Matthews, pp. 28-29, 37; Mark A. Matthews, Building the Church (New York: American Tract Society, 1940), p. 108.

[39]James M. Gray commented on (and gently criticized) Norris' broad concept of the ministry. "Dr. Norris' Acquittal," Moody Monthly, XXVII (March, 1927), 324.

rent social evils. A 1927 list of local grievances will illustrate Norris' points of attack: bootlegging, gambling, pool halls, vice in "hell's half acre," inequality of taxation, a ten-cent car fare that worked hardship on the poor, and Sunday plays and movies. He carried his fight against gambling to the state legislature, and opposed illegal liquor on all governmental levels.[40]

Such a mixture of moralistic and economic issues did not seem incongruous to Norris and his fellow fundamentalists, for they regarded both types of behavior as equally contrary to biblical principles. Throughout his entire ministry Norris consistently sided with the working classes against economic exploitation.[41] Unfortunately, it is sometimes difficult to determine whether he was sincerely battling for a cause or engaging in political controversy for publicity or sheer enjoyment.[42]

Still another premillennialist with strong interests

---

[40] [J. Frank Norris], "Has the Time Come for a House-cleaning?" The Searchlight, X (March 11, 1927), 1; Letter, J. Frank Norris to J. C. Duvall, January 19, 1929, Archives, Southern Baptist Convention, John Franklyn Norris Papers.

[41] Further detail will be given on this point later. See esp. "Why the Grand Jury Didn't Call Norris Again," The Searchlight, II (April 2, 1919), [1], [4]; J. Frank Norris, "The Church and the Poor," The Fundamentalist, XI (January 20, 1933), 3-4.

[42] Norris once confided to his vacationing secretary that politics was "a great game." Letter, J. Frank Norris to Kate Tarleton, July 8, 1930, Archives, Southern Baptist Convention, John Franklyn Norris Papers.

in social issues was William B. Riley, pastor of Minneapolis' First Baptist Church and head of the World's Christian Fundamentals Association. To Riley Jesus was the greatest social reformer of all time, and he believed evangelical Christianity produced permanent social advances wherever it took root. He urged Christians to avoid making distinctions between bodies and souls in their service, and simply to concentrate on meeting needs of "men and women."[43] His own social emphasis stressed democracy and morality. His humble Kentucky childhood gave him a strong sympathy for the common man, and he believed the church should take the lead in demolishing social distinctions. He also spoke out strongly against the saloon, crime, vice, and gambling.[44]

Riley's social emphasis flagged somewhat, however, as he became increasingly absorbed in the theological contro-

---

[43]William B. Riley, Perennial Revival, p. 203; "What Manner of Persons Ought We to Be?" in Light on Prophecy: The Proceedings and Addresses at the Philadelphia Prophetic Conference, May 28-30, 1918 (New York: Christian Herald, 1918), pp. 305-6; "The Crisis of the Hour," Serving and Waiting, X (August, 1920), 213-14; The Bible of the Expositor and the Evangelist (40 vols.; Cleveland: Union Gospel Press, 1926-1938), New Testament, II, 249-62.

[44]Ferenc M. Szasz, "William B. Riley and the Fight Against Teaching of Evolution in Minnesota," Minnesota History, XLI (Spring, 1969), 202-3; Marie Acomb Riley, The Dynamic of a Dream: The Life Story of Dr. William B. Riley (Grand Rapids, Mich.: Wm. B. Eerdmans Publishing Company, 1938), pp. 60-99, passim. In a book on evangelism, Riley devoted an entire chapter to the necessity of eliminating pew rents. Perennial Revival, pp. 143-56. See also Robert Sheldon McBirnie, "Basic Issues in the Fundamentalism of W. B. Riley" (unpublished Ph.D. dissertation, State University of Iowa, 1952), pp. 104-5.

versies and anti-evolution crusades of the twenties.[45] His growing fear of radicalism in his later years also made him more cautious. He could march in step with progressivism, but he perceived in both socialism and the New Deal threats to traditional American values.[46]

James M. Gray, president of Moody Bible Institute, although less swayed by fears than Riley, was probably more consistently conservative--temperamentally, theologically, and politically. His conservatism, however, allowed room for active social concern. Gray wrote:

> Because the Institute is conservative . . . and . . . premillennial . . . it is sometimes carelessly classed with mystics or idealists who are said to be indifferent to the claims and responsibilities of earthly citizenship, and the calls of social service. But nothing is further from the truth, if only these claims . . . are given their proper place in the divine scheme of the salvation of mankind.[47]

He condemned Christian "laissez-faireism," or indifference to political questions. For the Christian citizen the voting booth was just as important as the place of prayer. "No man has a moral right," declared Gray, "to ask protection from a government to which he is indifferent, and for

---

[45]Riley, however, regarded his fight against evolution as just another "progressive" reform in the interests of democracy and morality. See "Progress of Anti-Evolution," <u>The Christian Fundamentalist</u>, II (January, 1929), 12-14.

[46]Szasz, "Riley and Evolution," p. 203; McBirnie, "W. B. Riley," p. 104.

[47][James M. Gray], "Chicago Crime Commission," <u>Moody Monthly</u>, XXII (April, 1922), 956.

which he will not use his influence to make it as good as possible."[48]

Law enforcement and clean government were therefore twin concerns for Gray. He contributed to the first by serving as a trustee on the Chicago Crime Commission in the early twenties. Yet he recognized that law enforcement was no better than the officials who administered it, and he called for "radical legislation" to prohibit the lightening of sentences and the intimidation of juries. He also urged citizens who complained about high taxes for law enforcement to stop complaining, vote out the officials who condoned crime, and enjoy both reduced crime and reduced taxes. He further recommended municipal reform as an excellent outlet for the creative energy of young citizens.[49] For Gray an interest in the future life did not preclude an attempt to improve the present one.

These socially concerned fundamentalists differed in emphasis and method, but all displayed basic similarities in thinking. For one thing, each believed that any social problem which could be related to biblical moral principles was a legitimate field for Christian activity and influ-

---

[48]James M. Gray, The Teaching and Preaching that Counts (New York: Fleming H. Revell Company, 1934), p. 120; cf. pp. 121-22, 126-28.

[49][James M. Gray], "'Sanctified Squander'" and "The Baumes' Laws," Moody Monthly, XXVIII (August, 1928), 544; "Cost of Crime," ibid., XXIX (January, 1929), 224; "Municipal Government," ibid., XXXI (May, 1931), 438.

ence. Secondly, none made sharp distinctions between personal and public morals, for they viewed corporate standards as extensions of individual tendencies. They therefore inveighed against political corruption and economic injustice as frequently as against private sins. In the third place, they believed absolutely that evangelical Christianity could meet the social needs of their day, through both individual conversions and a general pervasive influence in community and nation. Fourthly, they believed the American political process was equal to the social challenges it faced, and they never advocated the overturn, even peaceably, of the existing system. But this political faith was possible only because they believed Christian influence in America was still strong enough to condition politics.

In this way, biblicism and nationalism walked hand in hand, determining for fundamentalists both the problems and the proper methods of solution. They drew inspiration from the reforms of the progressive years and continued to crusade for their biblically-oriented version of a better America.

But in spite of their strong advocacy of Christian influence in national life, these men tended to restrict severely the political role of the institutional church. They frequently criticized ecclesiastical bodies for circulating petitions, lobbying, mediating in labor disputes, making official pronouncements on social problems, and using the pulpit for political propaganda. Only as private citizens, they insisted, should Christians attempt to influence politics. The corporate church's duties lay elsewhere. James M. Gray, one of the most zealous watchdogs for this distinction, explained his reasoning:

> When the church seeks to influence political action in the way now under consideration, she stands in her own light and awakens a prejudice against herself which makes it harder to reach men with the gospel of salvation.[50]

Others also pointed out that the wall between church and state was being jeopardized. To bring Christian influence into politics was commendable, but to bring institutional religion into politics was damaging to both church and republic.[51]

A few fundamentalist leaders drew the distinction between the church and the world even more sharply, and questioned the legitimacy of any social service for the Christian. They argued that, in God's present economy for

---

[50] "Dr. Clarence True Wilson Replies to the Monthly," Moody Monthly, XXVII (April, 1927), 373. See also [James M. Gray], "Church and State," ibid., XXX (January, 1930), 232.

[51] J. C. Massee, The Ten Greatest Christian Doctrines (New York: George H. Doran Company, 1925), p. 143; William L. Pettingill, "The Church and Reform Movements," Serving and Waiting, XVIII (May, 1928), 17; Donald Grey Barnhouse, "The Church and Politics," Revelation, I (June, 1931), 200; [Melvin Grove Kyle], Editorial, Bibliotheca Sacra, LXXXIV (October, 1927), 372; [David S. Kennedy], "Social Service," The Presbyterian, LXXXIX (January 30, 1919), 3.

the earth, the church was instructed to evangelize, not to reform. Only the return of Christ and the onset of the millennium could effect social redemption. A writer of Sunday School lessons for The Wonderful Word faced the topic, "Making the Nation Christian," with these comments: "We do not feel warranted in making the attempt, for we cannot find any quotation in God's Word that puts it in the purpose of God for to-day." Again, summarizing the lesson, "The Social Task of the Church," he concluded, "The 'Social Task' is a great one, and it will take the King Himself to round it up in all its fullness."[52]

The hopelessness of human reforms was sometimes expounded in tones bordering on fatalism. Isaac M. Haldeman, pastor of New York City's First Baptist Church, declared:

> The Church is not here to make the world better. On the contrary, the Church is here to testify the world cannot be made better: that so far from being made better it will go from bad to worse. (Italics in original.)[53]

Prophecy lecturer Arno C. Gaebelein similarly reasoned that to try to counteract a divinely-predicted moral slump was useless. He even indirectly criticized some of his funda-

---

[52]A. H., "Bible School Department," The Wonderful Word, XIII (May, 1921), 379-80, 384.

[53]I. M. Haldeman, The Mission of the Church in the World (New York: Book Stall, 1917), p. 4; cf. Professor Rauschenbusch's "Christianity and the Social Crisis" (New York: Charles C. Cook, n.d.), pp. 25-31.

mentalist colleagues when he wrote:

> Our postmillennial friends may continue their well meaning efforts in trying to legislate crime and vice out of the world, or, attempt through pacifism to abolish war, or stop the teaching of infidelity by law enactments; they will find out anew what all history teaches, that all reformation by legislation leads to greater deformation.[54]

Advocates of this view sometimes maintained that Christian reform efforts were not only useless but positively sinful. Christians engaging in reform were neglecting evangelism; neglect of evangelism postponed the coming of Christ; and the postponement of Christ's return postponed the world's golden age and prolonged its woes. Socially concerned Christians were like Lot in Sodom--patching up a condemned civilization and becoming contaminated by it at the same time.[55]

Fundamentalism, then, contained two strains of thought regarding the place of social reform in Christian thinking. All agreed that external changes could not change man or meet his inner needs. But a majority believed Christians still were responsible for alleviating and restraining the effects of evil. A smaller group coun-

---

[54]A. C. Gaebelein, "The Better Way," Our Hope, XXXII (March, 1926), 525-26; cf. "Will Christ Come Again?" ibid., XXIV (January, 1918), 406-16; Arno Clemens Gaebelein, The Conflict of the Ages (6th printing; New York: Publication Office "Our Hope," 1936), pp. 45-47.

[55]Paul Riley Allen, "The Mission of the Church," The Wonderful Word, XIV (February, 1922), 204-8; Ernest G. Crabill, "The Folly of Man's Efforts to Reform This Age," ibid., XII (November, 1919), 63-67.

seled single-minded concentration on evangelism, believing this was the shortest route to Christ's return and the socially transformed world of the millennium. The presence of both viewpoints in fundamentalism demonstrates the inadequacy of seeking its unity in a common social or cultural outlook. Instead, it was their agreement on central theological tenets that led them to cooperate on issues most important to all of them--evangelizing the sinner, building the church, and defending the faith.

This intramural conflict over the proper social role of Christians became evident in the support or non-support fundamentalists voiced for specific causes. Most of them were attracted to movements and measures through which they could exert a moral and spiritual influence on American life, and they discerned such opportunities in prohibition and the crusades against the teaching of evolution in public schools.[56] A minority, however, either opposed or remained silent on these issues.

Prohibition was one of those rare causes in which fundamentalists and modernists could join hands, for the drive to outlaw alcoholic beverages had been gaining momen-

---

[56]It may be argued that such measures were not "reforms" in the present usage of this term. But the fact remains that large numbers of "progressive" Americans saw prohibition as one of the outstanding national reforms of their time (Timberlake, Prohibition and the Progressive Movement, p. 2). Fundamentalists also viewed their fight against evolution as a continuation of the progressive tradition.

tum among a broad segment of American Protestantism since the Civil War, and had already produced thirty-three dry states by 1920. The drive for a dry nation was supported by social gospelers Walter Rauschenbusch, Josiah Strong, and Charles Stelzle, as well as by the liberal-oriented Federal Council of Churches.[57] Throughout the fourteen-year duration of the "noble experiment," The Christian Century editors gave the Eighteenth Amendment their unwavering support. A 1922 editorial praised it as "the consummation of a generation of heroic effort to rid the land of its worst menace," and a 1932 call for a new progressive political party proposed a platform that included disarmament, diplomatic recognition of Russia, racial equality, socialization of industry, nationalization of banking--and prohibition![58]

Prohibition also enjoyed the support of most leading fundamentalists. Some, in fact, had campaigned for it for many years before it became law. Mark Matthews, W. B. Riley, and James M. Gray all had carried the torch as young men.[59] In the twenties many others, including Kyle,

---

[57]Timberlake, Prohibition and the Progressive Movement, pp. 21-29.

[58]"Fighting the Prohibition Law," The Christian Century, XXXIX (November 9, 1922), 1381; "A Platform for a Disinherited Party," ibid., XLIX (June 8, 1932), 728-30.

[59]Giboney and Potter, Mark A. Matthews, p. 18; [W. B. Riley], "Progress of Anti-Evolution," The Christian Fundamentalist, II (January, 1929), 13; William M. Runyan, Dr.

Straton, Kennedy, Conrad, Norris, Massee, Keyser, Pettingill, and Laws, joined them in advocating strict enforcement of the prohibition law, and the World's Christian Fundamentals Association annually went on record in its favor as well.[60]

If it be asked why people with a strongly personal view of conversion and an apocalyptic view of social redemption would support a measure seeking to legislate corporate morality, the answer is found in several directions. First, their patriotism told them that prohibition was proof of moral progress in a Christian nation. Looking ahead in 1918, Curtis Lee Laws exulted, "Glory, hallelujah! It seems too good to be true, but it will be true if Chris-

---

Gray at Moody Bible Institute (New York: Oxford University Press, 1935), pp. 38-39.

[60]As examples of this widespread fundamentalist support see [Melvin Grove Kyle], Editorial, Bibliotheca Sacra, LXXXVI (July, 1929), 256-57; John Roach Straton, "Why I am a Prohibitionist," The Bible Champion, XXXV (April, 1929), 197-201; [David S. Kennedy], "The American People and Prohibition," The Presbyterian, XC (September 30, 1920), 7; A. Z. Conrad, "Leadership in America's Moral Crisis," The Bible Champion, XXXVI (December, 1930), 626-28; [J. Frank Norris], "The Tragedy of American History--Doom of the Eighteenth Amendment," The Fundamentalist, XI (January 6, 1933), 8; J. C. Massee, Evangelistic Sermons (New York: Fleming H. Revell Company, 1926), p. 88; Leander S. Keyser, "Regulation does not Regulate," Christian Faith and Life, XXXVIII (September, 1932), 433; William L. Pettingill, "Worldwide Prohibition--World's Temperance Sunday," Serving and Waiting, XIII (October, 1923), 291-94; [Curtis Lee Laws], "Democracy and the Prohibition Amendment," The Watchman-Examiner, VIII (February 19, 1920), 241-42; "Resolutions and Reports," Christian Fundamentals in School and Church, VI (July-September, 1924), 15.

tian America does its duty."[61] By early 1920 America had seemingly done its duty, and some, like John Roach Straton, began to envision the even more glorious prospect of world-wide prohibition. The nation which so recently had exemplified democracy to the world was now bearing the torch of Christian morality.[62] William B. Riley may have been engaging in wishful thinking when he predicted in 1932 that "booze will never come back in America," but he was more likely expressing a sincere conviction that a basically Christian America would not allow it to happen.[63]

But if Americans really wanted a dry country, why were violations of the Amendment increasingly frequent? Fundamentalists advanced several answers. One was that many Americans, including prohibitionists, were rapidly forgetting the reasons underlying the measure. James M. Gray warned that sheer enforcement without "educative propaganda" was leaving "a shell without a kernel."[64] They also blamed the lukewarmness of enforcement officials, the

---

[61] [Curtis Lee Laws], "Nation-wide Prohibition in 1920," The Watchman-Examiner, VI (August 22, 1918), 1074-75.

[62] Straton, "Why I am a Prohibitionist," pp. 197, 201.

[63] W. B. Riley, "Can Prohibition Be Enforced?" The Christian Fundamentalist, V (April, 1932), 354.

[64] [James M. Gray], "Ontario's Liquor Control Act," Moody Monthly, XXXI (June, 1931), 486; cf. A. Z. Conrad, "Putting Intelligence into Religion," The Bible Champion, XXXV (January, 1929), 5.

poor examples of prominent citizens, and the liquor industry's influence over the press for falsely implying wholesale violation.[65] Some, like J. Frank Norris, also saw part of the difficulty in the hordes of unassimilated aliens. When he heard a speaker cheered in Carnegie Hall for saying, "What we want is our beer and our wine and our liquor, and to hell with the Constitution," Norris reacted sharply:

> Out beyond this metropolis, this wicked city, with five times as many foreigners as native-born Americans, I thought of the rolling prairies . . . I said, "Come on with your Liberty Leagues, come on and trample the Constitution under your feet, but by the grace of God and in the name of our heroic voters we will meet you at the Mississippi and roll you back into the Atlantic where you came from."[66]

Fundamentalists thus reasoned that a basically moral America wanted prohibition, but was being deceived by its own success or intimidated by a vocal minority.

Fundamentalists supported prohibition, secondly, because they regarded alcohol as a deadly social menace. Like a community misfit, it had to be incarcerated for the safety of the citizenry. Donald Grey Barnhouse claimed he opposed the liquor traffic simply because his children had

---

[65] Riley, "Can Prohibition Be Enforced?" p. 353; [Melvin Grove Kyle], Editorial, Bibliotheca Sacra, LXXXVII (April, 1930), 128; [James M. Gray], "Iniquity in Wet Newspapers," Moody Monthly, XXX (October, 1929), 58.

[66] J. Frank Norris, "A Reply to the N.Y. World on Stirring Up Strife," The Searchlight, X (February 25, 1927), 6.

to cross streets where motorists were driving. A stand for prohibition, according to A. Z. Conrad, was a stand for "the hearts and homes of the American people; for justice, sanity and sobriety; for purity, peace and progress."[67]

Thirdly, fundamentalists endorsed prohibition because they believed Christians should further an atmosphere conducive to upright living. To be sure, prohibition could not make people good. But it could make it harder for them to do evil, and to many fundamentalists this was a worthy goal. It was inconsistent to preach salvation from sin, argued James M. Gray, while at the same time voting to put temptation in the sinner's way. Although being spared a temptation would not save the sinner, it might ultimately provide for him a better chance to receive the saving message.[68]

In spite of their strong and consistent support for prohibition, fundamentalists refused to consider it a panacea. They warned against raising it to the level of the gospel or viewing it as the gateway to the millennium. It

---

[67] [Melvin Grove Kyle], Editorial, Bibliotheca Sacra, LXXXIII (October, 1926), 373-74; [David S. Kennedy], "Prohibition Must Be Enforced," The Presbyterian, XCV (December 3, 1925), 5; Donald Grey Barnhouse, "Repeal," Revelation, III (December, 1933), 446; A. Z. Conrad, "America's Moral Crisis," p. 628.

[68] Runyan, Dr. Gray, pp. 38-39; [James M. Gray], "Taking a Beating," Moody Monthly, XXX (February, 1930), 276; [Melvin Grove Kyle], Editorial, Bibliotheca Sacra, XC (July, 1933), 268.

was a tragedy, wrote Alva J. McClain, that church bodies which concentrated on unseating wet legislators had left their own apostate preachers unmolested and therefore had no gospel left to preach. Donald Grey Barnhouse added, somewhat satirically, that when prohibition was repealed the Bible preachers would continue to preach the same message, but those who had preached the gospel of prohibition would have to find a new cause.[69]

Prohibition's limitations did not discourage most fundamentalists from supporting it, but an apparently small minority refused to endorse the measure at all. The total silence of Leon Tucker, Charles G. Trumbull, Lewis Sperry Chafer, and J. Gresham Machen on an issue of such magnitude causes one to suspect either disapproval or lack of interest. With a few others one is not left to speculation, for they disapproved openly, largely because they felt prohibition was a human scheme that ignored God's plan for the present age. I. M. Haldeman counseled the minister to teach sobriety but not to link himself with "a movement which is part of the self-gratulating civilization of the

[69]Alva J. McClain, "The New President Quotes Scripture," Serving and Waiting, XXIII (June, 1933), 36, 44; Donald Grey Barnhouse, "The Eighteenth Amendment," Revelation, III (August, 1933), 288; cf. A. C. Dixon, "The World Movements of To-Day in the Light of the Bible," Serving and Waiting, X (December, 1920), 492; James M. Gray, "Enforcing Prohibition," Moody Monthly, XXIV (December, 1923), 162-63.

hour."[70] A. C. Gaebelein saw it in the same light:

> Though the ban has been put on intoxicating drinks, drunkenness continues. Yea these reform laws have led to increased lawlessness . . . But here we are face to face with the foolish inventions [sic] that legislation on moral lines is going to check these evils. As if the evil heart of man could be legislated out of the world.[71]

But perhaps a Finnish contributor to Moody Monthly expressed this viewpoint most succinctly when he predicted the imminent demise of prohibition in 1933: "The disappointment may be less keenly felt if we realize that the modern prohibition laws were never God's way. . . . We cannot take short cuts to Paradise."[72]

Fundamentalists who endorsed prohibition did so in cooperation with persons of other theological viewpoints. This was true to a much lesser extent in the war on evolution. Although this wide-ranging crusade received support from many besides active fundamentalists,[73] fundamentalist

---

[70] Haldeman, The Mission of the Church, pp. 39-41.

[71] [A. C. Gaebelein], "Moral Conditions and Reform," Our Hope, XXVII (February, 1921), 449-50; cf. "The Hopelessness of Reform to Save Man," ibid., XXX (April, 1924), 613.

[72] O. Eklund, "Prohibition Experiments Abroad," Moody Monthly, XXXIII (March, 1933), 309.

[73] See, e.g., Miriam Allen De Ford, "The War Against Evolution," The Nation, CXX (May 20, 1925), 565-66; "Organized Religious Groups Form Political Bloc in Country, Is Charge of Publicist," The Christian Fundamentalist, I (November, 1927), 3-7. A Literary Digest poll of Minnesota ministers in 1923 revealed that 115 opposed evolutionary teaching in public schools and 77 supported it. Of those who opposed it, 62 (almost 54%) were Lutherans. Lutheran

leadership organized and publicized it, writing, debating, introducing denominational resolutions, and most prominently, influencing state legislatures to consider anti-evolution bills. Between 1921 and 1929, thirty-seven such bills found their way into twenty legislatures, and even though only five won approval, they greatly alarmed evolutionary scientists and liberal thinkers in general.[74]

It is noteworthy that fundamentalists viewed anti-evolution laws precisely as they viewed other reforms. Optimistically predicting the ultimate Christianization of learning, business, and sport, Melvin Grove Kyle added, "Perhaps when that day comes, the action of the legislature of Tennessee in forbidding materialistic evolution to be taught in the public schools . . . will not seem so bigoted as it now seems to some people!"[75] W. B. Riley saw his own anti-evolutionism as an exact parallel to his long prohibitionist stand, and hoped to see evolutionary teaching suf-

---

groups rarely identified themselves with fundamentalism. "Shall Moses or Darwin Rule Minnesota Schools?" The Literary Digest, LXXVI (January 13, 1923), 31-32, 50-56. The Lynds discovered that, of 556 high school students questioned in "Middletown," 19% favored evolution, 48% favored the biblical creation account, 26% were uncertain, and 7% did not answer. Lynd and Lynd, Middletown, pp. 204-5.

[74]Willard B. Gatewood, Jr. (ed.), Controversy in the Twenties: Fundamentalism, Modernism, and Evolution (Nashville, Tenn.: Vanderbilt University Press, 1969), pp. 31-36, passim.

[75][Melvin Grove Kyle], Editorial, Bibliotheca Sacra, LXXXII (July, 1925), 257.

fer the same fate as alcohol.[76] Although historians have never regarded anti-evolution legislation as a "progressive" reform, it was clearly an offspring of the same rationale that produced religio-political legislation earlier in the century. Gatewood observes that

> . . . during the two decades prior to 1920, liberal churchmen, imbued with the Social Gospel, had expanded the scope of religious affairs to include a more positive stand on political questions. If the liberal could use the state to fulfill the aims of the Social Gospel, the defenders of orthodoxy reasoned that they could employ the same secular authority to foster their credo.[77]

In doing this, fundamentalists had to contend with charges that they were tampering with others' consciences, undermining the wall between church and state, and stifling scientific investigation. Walter Lippmann called their legislative efforts "a shrill insistence that men ought to feel that which no man can feel who does not already feel it in the marrow of his bones."[78] Some of their own number refused to cooperate because of church-state questions, and sociologist Clifford Kirkpatrick voiced the familiar charge that they were trying to "strangle" science.[79]

---

[76] [Riley], "Progress of Anti-Evolution," p. 13.

[77] Gatewood (ed.), Controversy in the Twenties, p. 28.

[78] Walter Lippmann, A Preface to Morals (New York: Macmillan Company, 1929), p. 64.

[79] On the church-state question see Donald Grey Barnhouse, "Tennessee and Evolution," Revelation, I (October, 1931); cf. Gatewood (ed.), Controversy in the Twenties, p. 28. On the charge of stifling science see Clifford

The leaders of anti-evolution countered each of these charges vigorously. First, they disclaimed any intention of forcing anyone to accept creation. "To teach creation runs up against the convictions of many non-Christian people, and is not treating them fairly," wrote Leander Keyser. "Let it be understood that Christian folk do not want to force their religion into the public, tax-supported schools; neither . . . do they want to be dragooned into accepting evolution."[80] Fundamentalists saw themselves not as inquisitors but as defenders. They believed, with Straton, that "monkey men make monkey morals," and it therefore was imperative that they protect the young from this damaging teaching.[81]

Secondly, they argued that their use of state power was legitimate because they represented a majority of American taxpayers, and the majority could not be coerced into supporting what they did not believe. Gerald B. Winrod spoke for many fundamentalists when he wrote,

> Here in democratic America an intellectual oligarchy has no right to control twenty-five millions of school children annually, at an expenditure of two billions of dollars, and teach them theories contrary to the wishes

---

Kirkpatrick, Religion in Human Affairs (New York: John Wiley & Sons, Inc., 1929), p. 405.

[80]Leander S. Keyser, "Let us Stick to Facts," The Bible Champion, XXXIII (June-July, 1927), 310.

[81]John Roach Straton in New York Times, April 16, 1928; cf. Philip Mauro, Evolution at the Bar (New York: George H. Doran Company, 1922), p. 72.

> of that great body of taxpayers who support the schools. The hand that writes the pay-check should control the school.[82]

Legislation, they believed, was presently the only way to secure redress of this injustice. It was not a matter of establishing a state religion, they contended, but of protecting the rights of religious people whose convictions had been outraged. The Minnesota Anti-Evolution League stressed this point:

> As American citizens we believe in the complete separation of church and state, and are opposed to religious teaching in public schools--higher or lower.
>
> As those who wish to teach Christianity must support their private schools, we therefore believe it just that those who wish to teach anti-Christian theories should be forbidden to use tax-supported schools for propagating their opinions.[83]

While thoughtful critics warned that such an approach would foster a mediocre education, they had to admit that fundamentalists were operating under a valid political principle. Walter Lippmann, for example, pointed out the agreement between the Tennessee anti-evolution law and Jefferson's law on religious toleration, in that both freed an individual from supporting opinions which he disbelieved, and he concluded that the American theory of lib-

---

[82]Gerald B. Winrod, Christ Within (3d ed.; Wichita, Kans.: Defender Publishers, 1929), p. 118.

[83]"Notes and Comments," The Bible Champion, XXIX (April, 1923), 197; cf. "'Will Christian Taxpayers Stand for This?'" Moody Monthly, XXIII (August, 1923), 557; Gatewood (ed.), Controversy in the Twenties, pp. 28-29.

erty could not refute such legislation.[84]

But was a statehouse the proper place to settle scientific questions? Were not fundamentalist efforts, however legal, simply obscurantist attempts to stifle modern scientific research? No, answered the fundamentalists, for evolution was not a proven scientific fact. If it were, conceded the Moody Monthly, "our mouths would be closed." But to teach hypothesis as fact and weaken the faith of youth in so doing was inadmissible both scientifically and religiously.[85] They asserted that they had no desire to stop free investigation or even the presentation of evolution as a theory. But they did object to dogmatic, one-sided presentations in tax-supported schools, and it was to protect students from this, not to settle scientific questions, that legislation was being introduced.[86]

The rationale for anti-evolution laws was not always clearly understood, however, and the blame for misunderstanding must rest with both sides in the controversy. The fundamentalists, for their part, often were too prone to

---

[84]Walter Lippmann, American Inquisitors (New York: Macmillan Company, 1928), pp. 10-12; cf. Kirkpatrick, Religion in Human Affairs, p. 405.

[85]"'Will Christian Taxpayers Stand for This?'" p. 557; George McCready Price, "Shall the Taxpayers Support Darwin?" The Bible Champion, XXX (April, 1924), 211-12.

[86]Edwin Deacon, "Taxed, but not Represented," The Bible Champion, XXXIV (May, 1928), 277-78; Riley, "Defense of Fundamentalism," p. 11.

simplify arguments for popular consumption, too ready to press an advantage and belittle opponents, and too hasty to draft legislation. Deeply disturbed by the circumstances and outcome of the Scopes trial in 1925, James M. Gray urged state legislators to inform themselves carefully what evolution was and to what extent it should be barred. He counseled his fundamentalist colleagues, "Let us appeal to reason, to thoughtful argument, to calm logic and limit ourselves to statements of fact," lest winners be losers in the end.[87] Unfortunately, Gray's advice often went unheeded as mobilizers of public opinion appealed to the emotions of fear, hate, or sympathy for the fallen William Jennings Bryan.

But supporters of evolution did not always react in a scholarly or gentlemanly manner either. No fundamentalist could have been more dogmatic or intolerant than a 1925 New Republic article, for example, which proposed barring from public school teaching anyone who refused to accept the present conceptions of man's origins.[88] It is not surpris-

---

[87] [James M. Gray], "William Jennings Bryan," Moody Monthly, XXVI (September, 1925), 3; "The Fight Against Evolution," ibid., XXVI (April, 1926), 364; cf. [Melvin Grove Kyle], Editorial, Bibliotheca Sacra, LXXXII (January, 1925), 5-6.

[88] "The Cure for Fundamentalism," The New Republic, XLIII (June 10, 1925), 58-60; cf. Gatewood (ed.), Controversy in the Twenties, p. 32; Paul Shorey, "Evolution--A Conservative's Apology," The Atlantic Monthly, CXLII (October, 1928), 481.

ing that fundamentalists and evolutionists alike felt their arguments were falling on deaf ears.

What the anti-evolution crusade gained temporarily in restrictive legislation was more than offset by the long-range loss of influence and respectability it cost fundamentalism. It is ironic that the reform many fundamentalists regarded as their greatest opportunity to serve society became their greatest liability. The national attention it attracted, especially through the Scopes trial, tended to identify a theological movement of varied endeavors with a single negative issue. The prominence of a folk hero like William Jennings Bryan left the impression that nationwide fundamentalism really belonged to the Southern hills and Midwestern plains. Its political appeal to the masses allowed critics to label fundamentalism demagogic, and Bryan's inability to defend his faith intelligently projected an anti-intellectual image. The war on evolution, more than any other single factor, fixed the stereotypes that have plagued fundamentalism ever since.

The results of this crusade, however, should not be allowed to obscure the familiar idealistic forces that gave it birth. First, the theological conviction of biblical inerrancy led the fundamentalist to oppose a theory he deemed inimical to that credo, for to compromise inerrancy at any point was to jeopardize the basis for his faith. Second, his belief in a basically Christian America combined with his faith in democratic processes to produce a militant political crusade. Third, the apparent effectiveness of other recent moral legislation, notably prohibition, encouraged him to seek a solution for the evolution problem in the same direction.

The emphasis on abstract moral principles that permeated fundamentalist thinking on prohibition and anti-evolution extended also to their views on economic issues. Most fundamentalists were naive about economic theory, and accepted without serious question the basic framework of American capitalism. But within that framework they believed biblical standards should rule. The laborer should be worthy of his reward, the employer should be a wise and generous steward of his wealth, and unselfish motives should guide them both in their relationships.

Liberal critics of fundamentalism sometimes insinuated that their opponents were collaborating with big business. A Christian Century editorial in 1922, for example, accused "wealthy fundamentalists and their militant ecclesiastical spokesmen" of insincere grasping at worldly wealth while professing to await Christ's return.[89] Fundamentalism did, indeed, enjoy the support of some businessmen, notably the Stewart brothers, who held a controlling

---

[89] "Shaker Fundamentalism Shaking," The Christian Century, XXXIX (November 9, 1922), 1384; cf. [Curtis Lee Laws], "Unitarians to the Rescue," The Watchman-Examiner, X (March 9, 1922), 295.

interest in the Union Oil Company. These "two Christian laymen" who underwrote the publication of The Fundamentals also contributed generously to other fundamentalist enterprises. Milton Stewart devoted much wealth to overseas evangelism, while Lyman founded and presided over the board of the Bible Institute of Los Angeles. One of Arno C. Gaebelein's friends and supporters was Amos K. Gordon, vice president of Standard Oil Company of Louisiana. Charles L. Huston, a prominent official in the Lukens Steel Company, became president of Philadelphia School of the Bible in 1921, and Henry P. Crowell, chairman of the board of Quaker Oats Company, presided over the board of Moody Bible Institute. John Roach Straton dedicated one of his books to a New York businessman, Edward C. Miller.[90]

But such associations alone prove nothing, and may indicate only that certain businessmen were deeply religious. Furthermore, fundamentalists had no monopoly on rich friends. If the Bible Institute of Los Angeles was financed by an oil magnate, so also was the University of Chicago and Harry Emerson Fosdick's Riverside Church, which taught an opposite point of view. To understand the funda-

---

[90] "The Stewarts as Christian Stewards," The Missionary Review of the World, XLVII (August, 1924), 595-602; Arno Clemens Gaebelein, Half a Century: The Autobiography of a Servant (New York: Publication Office "Our Hope," 1930), pp. 122-23; William L. Pettingill, "The New President of the School," Serving and Waiting, XI (December, 1921), 495; Runyan, Dr. Gray, pp. 132-36; Straton, Gardens of Life, p. [v].

mentalists' relationship to wealth it is necessary to examine their stated views as well as their associations.

Wealth to fundamentalists was amoral in itself; its tendency toward good or evil depended on how it was gained and used. The holding of wealth was a God-given stewardship, a privilege to be used but not abused. The businessman's primary goal should not be to make money but to glorify God, and this lofty aim would preserve him from dishonesty in the pursuit of wealth and selfishness in its use. On the other hand, to ignore this important responsibility was to invite spiritual ruin for himself, his family, and his society. They believed, therefore, that Christianity should neither oppose nor avoid business, but should constantly provide its proper motive.[91]

This logically implied that neither rich nor poor was intrinsically better or entitled to higher respect. The minister "should never be afraid of the rich, cow-tow to the mighty, or neglect the poor," advised Mark Matthews. "The prince and the peasant are both his companions, both

---

[91]A. C. Dixon, Present Day Life and Religion (Chicago: Bible Institute Colportage Association, 1905), pp. [55-57]; The Young Convert's Problems and Their Solution (New York: George H. Doran Company, 1906), pp. 64-68; [Curtis Lee Laws], "Christianity and Business in 1921," The Watchman-Examiner, VIII (December 30, 1920), 1605-6; "Most Wealth an Anti-Climax," The Sunday School Times, LXII (September 18, 1920), 501-2; Massee, Evangelistic Sermons, p. 90; [David S. Kennedy], "Christianity and Business," The Presbyterian, XCIII (November 8, 1923), 3; Harold John Ockenga, "Do Men Have Rights?" Christian Faith and Life, XXXVIII (May, 1932), 263.

his subjects, and both the objects of his pity and love."[92]

But since an expanding industrial nation tended to glorify the rich, fundamentalist preachers saw more need to aid and encourage the lower classes. A. C. Dixon urged Christians to use their influence to abolish class barriers in the churches they joined, and many influential fundamentalist city churches set an example of social inclusiveness. Moody Memorial Church, for instance, took the motto, "Ever welcome to this house of God are strangers and the poor," and concentrated on ministering to the masses of downtown Chicago. David James Burrell, John Roach Straton, and William B. Riley all attempted to erase social distinctions in their churches.[93]

Fundamentalists also contributed generously to relief and charity for the poor, but they abhorred the thought that charity should ever substitute for economic justice. John Roach Straton scoffed at New York's elite paying fifty dollars for admission to a charity ball. "If these leaders . . . will put more of their time and strength on correcting the industrial and social wrongs of the day, there

---

[92]Matthews, Building the Church, p. 107.

[93]Dixon, Young Convert's Problems, p. 11; P. W. Philpott, "A Church That Draws the Masses," The Missionary Review of the World, LII (July, 1929), 535-38; "Moody Church's New Home," Serving and Waiting, XV (January, 1926), 485-86; Shepherd, Great Preachers, p. 24; New York Times, May 25, 1919, p. 14; October 27, 1923, p. 4; Szasz, "Riley and Evolution," pp. 202-3.

would be less need of charity," contended Straton. "What the great masses of humanity want is not charity but justice . . ."[94] The obvious inequality of wealth in the United States proved to fundamentalists the need for drastic changes in the business world. When industrial complexes swallowed up the small businessman, when animals were better cared for than humans, when some lived in opulence while others starved, something in the economy must be out of joint.[95]

The crux of the problem, as fundamentalists saw it, was the moral irresponsibility of individual capitalists. They scourged the profiteers of the war and postwar years who enriched themselves at the physical and moral expense of others. A. C. Gaebelein wondered in 1916 whether manufacturers of war materials ever thought of the misery they were causing, and as food prices soared the following year, Leon Tucker complained that "The trusts triumph and the people perish."[96] When the postwar years brought no relief

---

[94]Straton, Menace of Immorality, pp. 27, 197; cf. Massee, Evangelistic Sermons, pp. 50, 56.

[95][Melvin Grove Kyle], Editorial, Bibliotheca Sacra, XC (January, 1933), 3-4; William Edward Biederwolf, The New Paganism (Grand Rapids, Mich.: Wm. B. Eerdmans Publishing Company, 1934), pp. 62-72; Carlton R. Van Hook, "Jesus Passes By," Christian Faith and Life, XXXVII (January, 1931), 40-41; George F. Kenyon, "Be Patient Therefore, Brethren," Moody Monthly, XXXI (April, 1931), 404; Carey S. Thomas, "God's Outline of Future History," Serving and Waiting, XXIII (November, 1933), 52-54.

[96][A. C. Gaebelein], "The Enrichment of the United

and frustrated workers were goaded into striking, fundamentalists again laid a large share of the blame on "heartless, profiteering capitalists."[97]

They believed the insatiable desire for profits not only produced material inequities but also degraded the quality of American life. The low moral tone of commercial movies and stage, the lack of human concern in industry, the excesses of advertising, and the close relationship between women's low wages and prostitution all drew critical remarks from fundamentalists.[98] They deplored the effects of prosperity on the American people, believing that it dulled their sense of spiritual need and weakened their moral stamina. A way of life that measured achievement in purely materialistic terms, they argued, tacitly discouraged spiritual and intellectual pursuits and stand-

---

States," Our Hope, XXII (November, 1916), 294; W. Leon Tucker, "The Famine Fight," The Wonderful Word, IX (April, 1917), 294.

[97][A. C. Gaebelein], "The Increasing Unrest," Our Hope, XXVI (August, 1919), 108; [James M. Gray], "Retailers Blamed," Moody Monthly, XXI (June, 1921), 428; W. E. Biederwolf, "Lessons from the Japanese Earthquake," The Bible Champion, XXX (February, 1924), 100.

[98]New York Times, December 9, 1922, p. 4; "Elder Hays a Little Hazy," The King's Business, XV (April, 1924), 196-97; Straton, Menace of Immorality, pp. 74, 94-96, 232-33; [James M. Gray], "The Automobile Toll," Moody Monthly, XXXI (May, 1931), 438; [Melvin Grove Kyle], Editorials, Bibliotheca Sacra, LXXXIV (October, 1927), 373-74; LXXXVI (April, 1929), 134-35.

ardized culture at a mediocre level.[99]

Furthermore, capitalistic excesses, if unchecked, would eventually drive working people to Communism. Russia's woes, according to W. B. Riley, began not with the "Reds" but with the "Rich," who had mercilessly exploited the workers, and he was convinced by 1932 that such men had also brought America to the verge of revolution.[100] "You stop labor unrest in the sweep of Bolshevism," J. Frank Norris maintained, "when you go after the higher-ups who are reaping ungodly gains and enormous profits."[101]

At times fundamentalists were downright cynical about big business. Philip Mauro called capitalism a "gigantic fraud," and W. B. Riley declared that the rich man in any community took the wrong side of an issue nine times out of ten. Riley wrote bluntly:

---

[99]See, e.g., Machen, What Is Faith? p. 212; "Does Fundamentalism Obstruct Social Progress?" p. 426; Christianity and Liberalism, pp. 14-16; [Melvin Grove Kyle], Editorial, Bibliotheca Sacra, LXXXIV (October, 1927), 372; cf. A. C. Gaebelein, "Lovers of Money," Our Hope, XXX (July, 1923), 57-58; [Charles G. Trumbull], "America's Peril," The Sunday School Times, LXVIII (December 11, 1926), 753.

[100]W. B. Riley, "Standardized Schools and Sovietism!" The Christian Fundamentalist, I (January, 1928), 5; "The Eighteenth Amendment," ibid., VI (July-August, 1932), 9; cf. Straton, Menace of Immorality, 195-96; Philip Mauro, James: The Epistle of Reality (Boston: Hamilton Brothers, 1923), pp. 108-11.

[101]"Why the Grand Jury Didn't Call Norris Again," The Searchlight, II (April 2, 1919), [1]; cf. J. Frank Norris, "The Coming World War," The Fundamentalist, VIII (October 10, 1930), 2.

> We do not happen to be enamored of the money crowd. We believe that many of our millionaires are men whose methods are under the condemnation both of God and of men. We have never had any sympathy with the greed of rich corporations, and we have hated the oppressive measures that some of them have employed.[102]

A. Z. Conrad remarked sarcastically that big business in general did not "waste time" considering ethics, and Mark Matthews warned prospective preachers never to follow a businessman's advice on how to run a church. They believed the capitalist too often was blinded to moral issues because of his preoccupation with efficiency and profits.[103] Men who expressed such views could hardly have been courting the favor of big business.

At the same time, fundamentalist sympathy for the laborer was both widespread and deep. It was only natural that it should be so, reasoned Melvin Grove Kyle, for most churches were made up of working class people. Kyle maintained that his wide circle of ministerial acquaintances almost without exception favored better distribution of wealth among the poor and exploited.[104] "Until we are able

---

[102]W. B. Riley, "The Sacco-Vanzetti Excitement," The Christian Fundamentalist, I (October, 1927), 12; "An Offense to Big Business," The Searchlight, X (April 1, 1927), 4; Mauro, James, pp. 113, 117.

[103]A. Z. Conrad, "Putting Religion into Intelligence," The Bible Champion, XXXV (February, 1929), 58; Matthews, Building the Church, p. 109; cf. Biederwolf, The New Paganism, pp. 69-70.

[104][Melvin Grove Kyle], Editorial, Bibliotheca Sacra, LXXXVI (October, 1929), 375-76.

to ethicalize industry we shall not have fulfilled our mission," A. Z. Conrad declared. "Competitions are fierce. Labor is not adequately rewarded. . . . The multitudes have never had their full share."[105]

Under such conditions fundamentalists recognized labor unions as both legitimate and necessary. While they sometimes criticized certain union tactics, they never questioned the propriety of their aims. "We have not a word to say against them in principle, but very much to say in their favor," remarked James M. Gray.[106] Melvin Grove Kyle gave much of the credit for the prosperity of the twenties to the unions, which had insisted that high wages be retained after the war.[107] Even when labor drew sharp criticism in 1919, J. Frank Norris praised the American Federation of Labor and spoke of the unions as "America's Gibralter against the spread of Bolshevism and anarchy."[108]

Indeed, labor never had a more consistent friend than

---

[105] A. Z. Conrad, Comrades of the Carpenter, p. 54; cf. pp. 56-57. See also Straton, Menace of Immorality, p. 207; William H. Bates, "The Book of Philemon," The Bible Champion, XXX (January, 1924), p. 25; Riley, Bible of the Expositor, Old Testament, XII, 137-41; Roy Talmage Brumbaugh, "Thy Kingdom Come," The King's Business, XXII (March, 1931), 103.

[106] [James M. Gray], "'At the Mercy of the Workers,'" Moody Monthly, XXIII (November, 1922), 92.

[107] [Melvin Grove Kyle], Editorial, Bibliotheca Sacra, LXXXIII (October, 1926), 374-76.

[108] "Dr. J. Frank Norris Champions Cause of Electrical Workers," The Searchlight, II (May 29, 1919), [4].

Norris. In 1919 he defended the Brotherhood of Electrical Workers in their dispute with the Texas Power and Light Company. In 1929 he opposed the appointment of Texas Governor Pat Neff to the United States Board of Mediation, claiming that "labor never had a worse enemy in the governor's chair." In 1932, when reminded by a local labor official that his church was employing nonunion labor in the construction of a new building, he promised to meet with him and make any adjustments within his power. Even at the time of the misunderstanding the local official acknowledged that Norris' relations with labor over the years had been "friendly, more than friendly, you have defended our position in times of trouble . . . "[109]

But other fundamentalists, while sympathizing with the worker, were not always ready to give a blanket endorsement of organized labor. David S. Kennedy praised "reasonable" labor leaders who would postpone a strike for the public good, but feared that the postwar rash of strikes was inspired by Communists. John Roach Straton detected within organized labor "the growth of a wrong spirit" which led unionists to disregard the rights of the

---

[109]Ibid.; J. Frank Norris, "Rich Must Meet Labor Issues," ibid., II (June 5, 1919), [1], [4]; Letters, J. Frank Norris to W. N. Doak, January 10, 1929; W. P. Butcher to J. Frank Norris, June 22, 1932; J. Frank Norris to Fort Worth Trades Assembly, June 24, 1932. All correspondence in Archives, Southern Baptist Convention, John Franklyn Norris Papers.

public. Melvin Grove Kyle also objected to unions' dictatorial methods, which he believed could lead to an oligarchy of the working class.[110] James M. Gray likened unions to trusts which must recognize their lawful limits under government regulation. Yet he expressed appreciation for their essential patriotism. "The American Federation of Labor may be fighting enemies of our free government of which many of us know very little," Gray observed, "and when we are irritated by local conditions chargeable to a so-called labor chief, it may be comforting to feel that the federation itself would be for us rather than against us."[111]

As fundamentalists felt free to criticize both business and labor on moral grounds, they usually saw the industrial struggles of the twenties as cases of mutual greed. Norris, it is true, took labor's side in every dispute, and Riley also felt that capitalists, being the stronger party, should yield more."[112] But most others

---

[110][David S. Kennedy], "True Men in Capital and Labor," The Presbyterian, LXXXIX (October 9, 1919), 6; "The Strikes and Their Treatment," ibid., LXXXIX (October 16, 1919), 6; Straton, Menace of Immorality, p. 207; [Melvin Grove Kyle], Editorials, Bibliotheca Sacra, LXXXI (July, 1924), 257; LXXXVI (October, 1929), 376; cf. [Curtis Lee Laws], "Will Massachusetts Endorse Her Governor?" The Watchman-Examiner, VI (October 30, 1919), 1507.

[111][Gray], "'At the Mercy of the Workers,'" p. 92; "The Soviet and the Labor Unions," Moody Monthly, XXIX (January, 1929), 224.

[112]Riley, Bible of the Expositor, Old Testament,

reasoned, with Herbert Magoun, that if "legalized piracy" was wrong for business, it was also wrong for labor. The two parties should see themselves as hands that needed each other, and apply the Golden Rule to their problems. While purely economic remedies had their place, none of them could succeed until service replaced selfishness.[113]

How could such a change in attitudes be effected? It sounded simple enough when James M. Gray said, "All that is necessary is for employers and employed to have a little more confidence in each other's integrity, and a little more integrity to justify that confidence."[114] But where did that begin? It might help, as Gray suggested, for churches to make a public example of a few profiteers and labor leaders by excommunicating them, or for the government to set up an industrial court to outlaw the "industrial duel," as Melvin Grove Kyle recommended.[115] But

---

XIII, 148-49.

[113]Herbert W. Magoun, "Some Phases of the Industrial Problems," The Bible Champion, XXVI (August, 1920), 309-10; [David S. Kennedy], "Employer and Employee," The Presbyterian, LXXXIX (September 25, 1919), 6-7; [Melvin Grove Kyle], Editorials, Bibliotheca Sacra, LXXX (October, 1923), 416-18; Bates, "Philemon," pp. 24-25; Harold Paul Sloan, "The War to End War," The Bible Champion, XXXIV (January, 1928), 9; Straton, Menace of Immorality, p. 212.

[114][James M. Gray], "Government Control," Moody Monthly, XXII (December, 1921), 696.

[115][James M. Gray], "The Georgia Baptist Convention," ibid., XXIII (March, 1923), 282; [Melvin Grove Kyle], Editorial, Bibliotheca Sacra, LXXIX (October, 1922), 395-96.

external controls could at best only regulate or suppress antagonism. Furthermore, some fundamentalists were wary of centralizing more political control in Washington.
J. Gresham Machen and James M. Gray both warned of the dangers to personal liberty inherent in federal intervention in economic issues.[116]

The solution they ultimately proposed, therefore, was a spiritual one: transform both businessman and employee through the gospel of Christ and instill in them the economic implications of their faith. Building on this foundation, they could work out specific problems in an atmosphere of love and respect.[117] Fundamentalists thus remained true to their theology of conversion as the means of solving a social problem.

It is curious, though, that many fundamentalists failed to see a contradiction in their thinking about the role of government. If it was right to legislate morals concerning drink, why not concerning working standards? Not all were inconsistent here: Kyle, for example, favored

---

[116] J. Gresham Machen, Letter to New York Times, November 18, 1924, p. 24; "Child Labor and Liberty," The New Republic, XLI (December 31, 1924), 145; [James M. Gray], "Government Control," Moody Monthly, XXIII (September, 1922), 4; "Government, Hands Off!" ibid., XXIII (November, 1922), 92.

[117] Riley, Bible of the Expositor, New Testament, XI 183-99; Straton, Gardens of Life, p. 114; New York Times, October 9, 1922, p. 5; Sloan, "War to End War," p. 9; Marion H. Reynolds, "Work in the Shops," The King's Business, XV (December, 1924), 780.

both prohibition and industrial control, while Machen apparently favored neither.[118] But why did men like Gray support vast governmental control over the individual in prohibition, yet oppose it in labor relations? Perhaps several reasons were involved. First, prohibition appeared to be the capstone of an indigenous American movement, growing out of American mores and self-imposed by representative democratic processes. But a tightly-regulated economy under a powerful government seemed foreign to a nation in which free economic enterprise had always prevailed. Already existing regulatory legislation was deemed sufficient to provide necessary ground rules. Secondly, fundamentalists may have been reacting against the social gospel's strong advocacy of political remedies for economic problems. Thirdly, the growth of governmental control over the economy brought to some minds pictures of existing socialistic states in which strong government meant complete social regimentation and anti-Christian Marxist materialism.

Fundamentalists could be extremely critical of capitalists, but the failures they detected lay not in the economic system but in its abuse by selfish individuals and groups. And because selfishness existed in workers and

---

[118]I have been unable to discover Machen's views on prohibition, but his abhorrence of government intrusion on personal liberty, combined with his utter silence on the subject, imply disapproval.

politicians as well as businessmen, they generally refrained from advocating a new economic system like socialism, for the evils accompanying it might well outweigh the relief from profiteering it would bring. The church should concentrate on changing men, not methods, for, as Melvin Grove Kyle stated it, "not even an ideal plan works in this world as it now is: as sin and selfishness have made it, it is not an ideal world."[119]

Such a philosophy lent itself to conservative politics, and those familiar with the "fundamentalist-radical right" combination of the fifties and sixties are prone to see the earlier fundamentalists in the same role, as militant defenders of the political status quo. But this is not strictly accurate, for most fundamentalists took pains to avoid alliances between the church and any political or economic system. "However much we may appreciate the present social order," David S. Kennedy warned, "we should never suppose that Christianity stands or falls with it."[120] Paul Carter, observing their inconclusive and even contradictory political views, says, " . . . in deepest essence this was not what the fundamentalist controversy

---

[119] [Melvin Grove Kyle], Editorial, Bibliotheca Sacra, XC (January, 1933), 8.

[120] [David S. Kennedy], "Christianity and the Social Order," The Presbyterian, XC (December 16, 1920), 6.

was about."[121] The fundamentalist ideal, however imperfectly achieved, was to let the church be the church, unhindered by worldly ideologies and free to speak to society on the authority of the Bible alone.

For this reason they had no consensus about socialism, but rather formed opinions largely based on personal predilections. As early as the writing of The Fundamentals one detects this difference of opinion. Philip Mauro deplored the whole modern democratic movement of which socialism was a part, and predicted it would end in a condition of worldwide lawlessness.[122] Charles R. Erdman, however, expressed a more conciliatory view. As an economic theory, said Erdman, socialism could be neither praised nor condemned by the church, for the two were in wholly different categories.

> While Socialists may adopt many of the Christian principles and feel impelled by Christian motives, they must remember that Christianity is something other than a social propaganda and far more than an economic theory. . . . The Church leaves its members free to adopt or reject Socialism as they deem wise.[123]

Erdman viewed the American public school system and post

---

[121]Paul A. Carter, "The Fundamentalist Defense of the Faith," in Change and Continuity in Twentieth-Century America: The 1920's, ed. by John Braeman, Robert Bremner, and David Brody (Columbus, Ohio: Ohio State University Press, 1968), pp. 190-94.

[122]The Fundamentals: A Testimony to the Truth (12 vols.; Chicago: Testimony Publishing Company, [1910-1915]), V, 7-8; cf. II, 97.

[123]Ibid., XII, 110-11.

office department as applications of the socialistic principle, and saw no reason why Christians should raise religious questions about the extension of government ownership to railroads, mines, public utilities, or factories. While he criticized "popular socialism" for emphasizing men's material needs above the spiritual and for identifying Christianity with corrupt capitalism, Erdman believed socialism's protest against social wrongs should challenge the church to practice more consistently the social implications of its gospel.[124]

As The Fundamentals were being compiled, other fundamentalist spokesmen showed the same openmindedness in discussing socialism. W. H. Griffith Thomas cautioned that socialism could not be a final solution, but he praised socialists highly for their efforts. "Christianity urges personal reform, Socialism cries out for corporate action," said Thomas. "One emphasizes regeneration, the other legislation. Now the latter is great and important, but the former is still greater. We must insist on both."[125] W. B. Riley, in one of his early works, also portrayed both socialism and Christianity as striving to recover the biblical scheme of social order.[126]

---

[124]Ibid., XII, 112-19.

[125]Thomas, Work of the Ministry, pp. 348-49.

[126]Riley, Perennial Revival, p. 209.

But the postwar years were to bring more critical voices, aggravated perhaps by the American Socialists' refusal to support the World War, the alarming revolutions in Russia and other European countries, and the tendency of many American Socialists to support the Third Communist International.[127] The resulting confusion and suspicion in American minds led to such rabid attacks as that of R. S. Beal, who, putting socialism together with Darwinism, modernism, and communism, accused it of wrecking society and predicted its culmination in the Antichrist.[128]

More subdued, though no less pointed, were the criticisms of J. Gresham Machen, who discerned in his society a slowly constricting "tyranny of a democratic collectivism" which would eventually stifle liberty of conscience. He believed socialism would mean nothing less than physical, intellectual, and spiritual slavery to the individual.[129] Furthermore, it was purely materialistic. "It is not altogether selfish," conceded Machen. "But--at least in its most consistent forms--it errs in supposing that the proper distribution of material wealth will be a panacea."

---

[127]Leuchtenburg, Perils of Prosperity, pp. 66-70.

[128]R. S. Beal, "The Eternal Searchlight Turned on Modern Socialism," Christian Fundamentals in School and Church, VIII (January-March, 1926), 38-50; cf. John Roach Straton, New York Times, October 9, 1922, p. 5.

[129]Machen, "Does Fundamentalism Obstruct Social Progress?" p. 392; "Prophets False and True," in God Transcendent, pp. 115-16.

A society without the higher spiritual ideals of Christianity, in Machen's estimation, would be mediocre in spite of its material achievements.[130] But although he strongly opposed socialism, Machen defended the liberties of Socialists. He especially denounced New York's Lusk laws for licensing teachers, which were aimed against them.[131]

Equally fearful of a drift toward socialism was James M. Gray, who considered it "antagonistic to the philosophy of the Christian religion and the gospel of grace." The increase in government paternalism had become necessary, said Gray, because Christian principles had not been applied to economic problems. But he doubted that socialism would be any improvement over capitalism. Its ambiguous record elsewhere, he believed, should cause Americans to pause before adopting it, and besides, the weaknesses of human nature would plague it no less than capitalism.[132]

But Gray, like Machen, believed in fair play, and he published in a 1933 issue of Moody Monthly an article

---

[130] J. Gresham Machen, What Is Faith? (New York: Macmillan Company, 1925), p. 212.

[131] J. Gresham Machen, What Is Christianity? (Grand Rapids, Mich.: Wm. B. Eerdmans Publishing Company, 1951), pp. 114-15; cf. "Social Progress," p. 392.

[132] [James M. Gray], "Government Control," p. 4; "Would Socialism Bring Relief?" Moody Monthly, XXXII (November, 1931), 103-4; "The Law of Supply and Demand," ibid., XXXIII (November, 1932), 98; "Our Economic Life in the Light of Christian Ideals," ibid., XXXIII (July, 1933), 481-82.

claiming a moral superiority of socialism over capitalism. Its author contended that while socialism was not necessarily Christian, capitalism was definitely anti-Christian, and concluded that "We must govern ourselves; then let us do it in a way consistent with our profession of following the Lord Jesus Christ."[133] In editorial comments on this article, Gray conceded that if New Testament conditions could be reproduced socialism might be practicable. But since those conditions did not presently prevail, it held no advantage over capitalism. Sin must be dealt with as a precondition for the success of either one.[134]

While few fundamentalists espoused socialism, most of those who discussed it were willing to recognize its good intentions, if nothing more. The same can hardly be said for their approach to Russian Communism. Here there were no discussions of strengths and weaknesses--only condemnation. They opposed it not so much for economic reasons as for its militant atheism, revolutionary method, and sinister means of infiltration, all of which contradicted their Christian principles and American ideals.

Unlike many liberal churchmen of the twenties and thirties, fundamentalists found nothing to admire in the

---

[133] F. W. Haberer, "Socialism and First Century Christianity," Moody Monthly, XXXIII (July, 1933), 482.

[134] [James M. Gray], Editorial comments on "Socialism and First Century Christianity," p. 483.

Russian Revolution. They felt that even the fragmentary evidence available was sufficient to indict the revolutionary government for cruelty, religious intolerance, and degradation of its people.[135] Such a system, they believed, had nothing to offer Americans. Melvin Grove Kyle likened Russian sympathizers to "dumb driven cattle," up to their knees in pasture while longing for the other side of the fence. Where but in the United States, he asked, could one see rich and poor side by side in a ten-cent store or laborers riding to work in their own cars?[136] Even in the midst of Depression unemployment W. B. Riley maintained that Americans were better off, for they enjoyed those liberties of religion and conscience which had been denied the Russians.[137]

Comparisons between the United States and Russia were of more than academic interest, for the first president of the Third Communist International had optimistically pre-

---

[135]"A Bishop Bows to Bolshevism," The King's Business, XV (March, 1924), 133-34; A. C. Gaebelein, "The Crimes of Russia," Our Hope, XXIX (June, 1923), 743; Leon Tucker, "A Pen Picture of Red Russia," The Wonderful Word, XVII (July, 1925), 440-41; Harold John Ockenga, "Do Men Have Rights?" Christian Faith and Life, XXXVIII (May, 1932), 263.

[136][Melvin Grove Kyle], Editorial, Bibliotheca Sacra, LXXXVII (January, 1930), 5-6.

[137]W. B. Riley, "Russian Communism or American Unemployment," The Christian Fundamentalist, V (July, 1931), 26-31, 35; "Our Constitution or Communism?" ibid., V (October, 1931), 132.

dicted in 1919 that within a year Europe would be communistic and within a few more years American capitalism would fall. In retrospect such prophecies appear ridiculous, but at the time they incited American radicals to redouble their efforts and caused other Americans to "see red" in the most unlikely places.[138]

Many fundamentalists took Communist predictions seriously, and occasionally called attention to its dangers to the home, school, and state.[139] A few, in fact, gradually became obsessed with this alleged peril. Arno C. Gaebelein discerned radical influence in the postwar industrial problems, and although his concern waned toward the end of the twenties, it revived with a vengeance during the Depression years, and increasingly ominous predictions poured from his pen.[140] William B. Riley voiced the same

---

[138] Michael Florinsky, Russia: A Short History (2d ed.; London: Macmillan Company, 1969), pp. 517, 519-20; Leuchtenburg, Perils of Prosperity, pp. 69-70.

[139] See, e.g., [Charles G. Trumbull], "The Antidote for Bolshevism," The Sunday School Times, LXI (June 7, 1919), 309-10; J. Frank Norris, "Robertson vs. Jim Ferguson; Rum, Romanism, Russianism the Issue," The Searchlight, VII (August 1, 1924), 1, 4; [James M. Gray], Editorials related to the Sacco-Vanzetti Case, Moody Monthly, XXVIII (October, 1927), 47-48; J. Davis Adams, "Awake! Citizens," Serving and Waiting, XX (September, 1930), 131.

[140] [A. C. Gaebelein], "That Other Great Danger," Our Hope, XXV (January, 1919), 429-30; "The Internal Conditions of the United States," ibid., XXIX (November, 1922), 292-93; "The Collapse of Evolution and Civilization," Our Hope, XXXVII (June, 1931), 741-42; cf. "Professor Einstein, the Scientist, Agnostic and Socialist," ibid., XXXVII (May, 1931), 672-77; Conflict of the Ages, pp. 112, 115.

alarm. He seldom commented on Communism in the early twenties, but by the end of the decade he was convinced that Americans were "soundly asleep on the rim of a social volcano," and that Communists were quietly fueling it through secularized education.[141]

The uncertainties of the Depression years, which undoubtedly aggravated the fears of Gaebelein and Riley, took their toll on other fundamentalists as well. Several periodicals devoted increased space to anti-Communist articles, drawing heavily upon the work of Elizabeth Knauss, a self-styled expert on the subject from Davenport, Iowa.[142] At least one dissenting voice was heard, however. William M. Yeomans warned his nervous colleagues that they were crying "Wolf!" and distracting Americans from the real sources of evil. Yeomans asserted:

> If we are threatened with . . . Socialistic or Communistic upheavals, it is not because of these foreign influences. It is because of our own sins. The social inequalities and injustices, the wickedness in high places, the atheism . . . , the inefficiency, the corruption and smug self-satisfaction of government, the aimlessness, formality and unconvincing voice of the

---

[141] Riley, "The Sacco-Vanzetti Excitement," p. 12; "Standardized Schools and Sovietism!" pp. 6-11; "Atheism and Intolerance in Russia," The Christian Fundamentalist, III (February, 1930), 552-53; "Bolshevism in America," The Bible Champion, XXXVI (May, 1930), 263-65.

[142] See, e.g., Elizabeth Knauss, "The Red Flag among American Young People," The Sunday School Times, LXXII (May 15, 1930), 333; "Communism and Disarmament," The Christian Fundamentalist, V (June, 1932), 422-24; "The Menace of Bolshevism," The Wonderful Word, XXII (September, 1930), 348-50.

> church . . . are sufficient . . . to beget unrest, resentment, violence, strife and even revolution.[143]

Fundamentalists usually condemned Communism on moral and religious grounds, and in doing so they frequently reserved a large share of criticism for modernism as well. The sympathy of modernists for the Russian experiment was well known,[144] and fundamentalists lost no time in tracing a logical progression from the one to the other. In robbing Christianity of an authoritative Bible and a transcendent God, modernism had also robbed society of its basis for ethics, authority, and cohesiveness. And in substituting a social for a personal gospel, it had embarked on a humanistic and political program that could easily produce affinities with radical social movements. In this way, they believed, modernism had allied itself with a revolutionary scheme which was bent on destroying society from its foundations up and reorganizing it on an anti-Christian pattern. Against such an alliance they felt it their duty to warn American churchgoers.[145]

---

[143] William M. Yeomans, "'Made in the U.S.A.,'" Serving and Waiting, XXIII (March, 1934), 264.

[144] As an example of many pro-Russian articles, see "Fighting Moscow in Detroit," The Christian Century, XLI (April 17, 1924), 493-94.

[145] [James M. Gray], "Modernism a Foe to Good Government," Moody Monthly, XXIV (July, 1924), 545-47; [A. C. Gaebelein], "The Father of Bolshevism," Our Hope, XXVI (October, 1919), 205-6; Conflict of the Ages, pp. 129-35; I. M. Haldeman, Dr. Harry Emerson Fosdick's Book: "The Modern Use of the Bible." A Review (Philadelphia: Sunday

From the foregoing analysis of fundamentalists' economic thought it becomes obvious that no simple economic classification will suffice. Being a loyal American, the fundamentalist tended to support the capitalistic system in general outline, even when its weaknesses were evident. He was willing to discuss the merits of socialism, but usually remained skeptical toward it. Being a loyal Christian, on the other hand, he believed in justice, and denounced evil wherever he discerned it--in the violent atheism of Russian Communism, the devouring greed of American big business, or the inflexible demands of unionized labor. Ultimately, he believed, no system was better than the individuals in it, so he concentrated on changing individuals through conversion and Christian indoctrination, whether employers or workers. In the end, therefore, his theological convictions exercised more influence on his economic views than did his attachment to an economic system.

This individual moral view of economics remained essentially unaltered by the Depression crisis. If the Depression increased the fundamentalists' suspicion of Communists, it also made them more skeptical toward capitalists. Louis Bauman suspected underhanded dealings as he

---

School Times Company, 1925), pp. 94-95. Fundamentalists especially charged that the idealistic pacifism of many modernists played into the hands of the Communists. See Gray's article above, p. 547; also "The Twelfth Annual Convention of the World's Christian Fundamentals Association," The Christian Fundamentalist, III (July, 1929), 248.

asked:

> . . . how is it that they can stand in the midst of all the superabundance of the fruits of the earth today, with all the present-day means of transportation at their command, with millions of unemployed hands begging for the privilege of doing something--how is it that these "men of renown" stand perplexed at the problems of employment and distribution?[146]

Businessmen's colossal failures also made fundamentalists wary of trusting their advice any longer. James M. Gray reminded them that, although most consumers still believed in the American system, they no longer trusted those who had manipulated it into the present chaos.[147] They had proved themselves to be unworthy stewards.

But moral failure was not limited to the self-centered businessman, according to the fundamentalists. It also lay with political leaders who lacked a sense of public responsibility, preachers who neglected their prophetic calling, and citizens who lost their balance in the pursuit and worship of money.[148] The Depression was therefore a

---

[146]Louis S. Bauman, "The Sad Failure of 'Men of Renown,'" The King's Business, XXII (November, 1931), 486.

[147][James M. Gray], "Consider the Consumer," Moody Monthly, XXXII (December, 1931), 160; "Our Smart Men?" ibid., XXXII (January, 1932), 231-32. See also William F. E. Hitt, "Why the Hard Times?" ibid., XXXIII (November, 1932), 105-6; William M. Yeomans, "'Their Ways Are Not Equal,'" Serving and Waiting, XXIII (August-September, 1933), 88.

[148]Tharp, "Man on the Median Line," p. 54; Donald Grey Barnhouse, "What the Church Can Do For the World in Depression," Revelation, II (December, 1932), 511; W. Courtland Robinson, "Hard Times and God," The Presbyterian, C (December 4, 1930), 3; J. Frank Norris, "Spiritual

divine judgment, sent to disclose America's spiritual defection and drive her back to God, just as were Israel's calamities in the days of the judges.[149]

But while fundamentalists pointed out America's spiritual failure, they did not neglect the more apparent physical need. They called on the churches to take the role of a modern "Good Samaritan," and J. Frank Norris' church in Fort Worth set the example by donating a large building and other resources to provide for the needy.[150] They recognized, moreover, that relief was of little use unless the economy was revived, and offered occasional suggestions for solving unemployment, redistributing wealth, and rectifying international financial problems.[151] Little of their

---

Lessons From the Twenty-Five Billion Dollar Crash," The Fundamentalist, VII (November 8, 1929), 1, 2, 7, 8; [James M. Gray], "Fundamentalism and Industrialism," Moody Monthly, XXXI (April, 1931), 390-91; [Melvin Grove Kyle], Editorial, Bibliotheca Sacra, LXXXIX (July, 1932), 257-58; A. Z. Conrad, "N.R.A. in Religion," Christian Faith and Life, XXXIX (October, 1933), 371-73.

149 [James M. Gray], "Business Is Sick," Moody Monthly, XXXI (October, 1930), 52; Horace F. Dean, "How Will the Winter of Depression End?" Serving and Waiting, XXII (July, 1932), 69, 83; Harold John Ockenga, "God and the Depression," Christian Faith and Life, XXXVIII (June, 1932), 306-9; Alva J. McClain, "The Message of Jonah and the Gourd," Serving and Waiting, XX (March, 1931), 301-2.

150 [Melvin Grove Kyle], Editorial, Bibliotheca Sacra, LXXXVIII (October, 1931), 384; Tharp, "Man on the Median Line," p. 53; J. Frank Norris, "The Church and the Poor," The Fundamentalist, XI (January 20, 1933), 3-4; "700 Free Meals Daily First Baptist Tabernacle," The Fundamentalist, X (December 23, 1932), 1.

151 See, e.g., Harold Paul Sloan, "The Christian

advice was sophisticated, and none of it challenged the existing political and economic structure. They preferred to believe, with Herbert Hoover, that solutions within the present framework, while slower, would leave fewer scars in the end.

Even while giving such advice, however, fundamentalists cautioned that any purely human remedy was inadequate. Political and economic measures could get the nation moving again, but they could never cure the moral infection that caused the disease. The real need was a spiritual revival. To the practical politician or businessman it may have seemed like pious cant or ostrich-like escapism to say, "Oh, that this nation in these trying days may come back to Him! Oh, that it may again know the saving grace of His Son! Then times will be better indeed."[152] But to the fundamentalist this was the only proper starting point for a permanent solution to any problem, whether individual or social. Spiritual revival brought moral rejuvenation, which in turn implied honesty, justice, selflessness, and cooperation--all essentials to social and economic stabil-

---

Church and the Unemployment Situation," Christian Faith and Life, XXXVII (February, 1931), 64-65; [James M. Gray], "Depression and the Way Out," Moody Monthly, XXXII (March, 1932), 328; J. Frank Norris, "Moratorium of President Hoover Has Brought New Hope," The Fundamentalist, IX (July 10, 1931), 1, 2, 6, 7.

[152]Edward C. Porter, "Christian Economy--A Homily for Thanksgiving Day," Moody Monthly, XXXII (November, 1931), 108.

ity.[153] Hence they approached the Depression in a manner completely consistent with their theology, relieving physical distress and allowing for institutional reforms, but finally depending on the spiritual cure of the gospel.[154]

This thoroughly religious approach was evident in fundamentalists' comments on national politics. They were disturbed that political leaders did not seem to recognize the moral dimension of the economic crisis. They made periodic requests for a national day of prayer, during both the Hoover and Roosevelt administrations, but these went unheeded. "The President and his associates have uttered not one single word in the nature of . . . national confession and humiliation," A. Z. Conrad complained early in 1934, "and no request has gone forth for the people of America to fall upon their knees . . . "[155] The self-

---

[153]Robinson, "Hard Times and God," p. 3; Sloan, "Christian Church and Unemployment," p. 65; Dean, "Winter of Depression," p. 83; Conrad, "N.R.A. in Religion," pp. 373-74.

[154]It is doubtful that the Depression brought the religious awakening fundamentalists hoped for. The Lynds' second "Middletown" study revealed that religious conditions were no better and that the hard times had, in fact, depleted church finances, hindered interdenominational cooperation, and accentuated conflicts over the purpose of the church. Meanwhile, doctrinal relaxation had continued. Robert S. and Helen M. Lynd, *Middletown in Transition* (New York: Harcourt, Brace and Company, 1937), pp. 297ff.

[155]A. Z. Conrad, "The 'Brain Trust' *versus* God," *Christian Faith and Life*, XL (April, 1934), 90; cf. "An Appeal to the President," *Moody Monthly*, XXXII (November, 1931), 111; Leon Tucker, "Please, Mr. President!" *The Wonderful Word*, XXVI (December, 1933), 420.

assurance and materialistic orientation of the "Brain Trust" seemed to bode ill for America's future. J. Gresham Machen warned that "practical" men seeking purely economic solutions were really as impractical as a man trying to start a car without an ignition spark, for they were overlooking the spiritual source of the nation's difficulties.[156]

Many fundamentalists also wondered where the innovative New Deal would lead politically. Although they tried to be openminded, some of them frankly predicted a loss in individual freedom. Louis Bauman called the government a "benevolent dictatorship," forced upon the nation by circumstances instead of arms.[157] Yet they viewed even this loss in the context of national spiritual failure. "The government is now trying to make us altruistic by law," wrote James M. Gray, "as it tried for years to make us sober by law. The pulpit lacked influence in both cases, and the strong hand of a dictator must now be tried."[158] If Americans lost some freedoms in the process of recover-

---

[156] J. Gresham Machen, The Christian Faith in the Modern World (Grand Rapids, Mich.: Wm. B. Eerdmans Publishing Company, 1947), p. 8.

[157] Louis S. Bauman, "Our Dictator-Shackled World," The King's Business, XXIV (June, 1933), 181.

[158] [James M. Gray], "Reaping What We Sowed," Moody Monthly, XXIV (December, 1933), 146; cf. Louis S. Bauman, "Is the Shadow of the Coming Dictator Falling Upon America?" The King's Business, XXIV (August, 1933), 263-64.

ing prosperity, they had only their foolish materialistic pursuits to blame.

It becomes evident from our study that we cannot adequately explain fundamentalism in terms of social or economic interests. We have discovered, instead, that its social thought was permeated at every point with abstract moral standards built on a theological foundation. If fundamentalists left no appreciable contribution as institutional reformers, it was not because they lacked interest in the problems, but because they were convinced they could solve them better by changing people. Most fundamentalists recognized value in legislation and social service, but they believed that value was limited by the spiritual level of society. When that spiritual level was raised through individual conversions and Christian teaching, the moral tone of their culture would rise accordingly. Some insisted that social amelioration should be reserved for the returning Christ alone, but most fundamentalists assumed at least a twofold ministerial responsibility to society: (1) to speak out plainly against social evils in order to stimulate their people to appropriate action; and (2) to present Christ's atoning work as the _sine qua non_ of personal and social transformation.

Fundamentalist attitudes toward social issues, while determined primarily by theology, were also conditioned by American traditions. The long-standing working relationship between evangelical Protestantism and the political system encouraged them to embark on crusades of moral legislation, but the wall between church and government discouraged them from plunging the church as an institution into reform activities. The traditions of political democracy and private enterprise also made them wary of untried political and economic innovations, especially in the wake of recent revolutionary movements abroad.

At certain points the adherence to these traditions led fundamentalists into contradictions. On one hand, they were willing to legislate against vice, liquor, and the teaching of evolution, but on the other, they were content to lecture the greedy capitalist about his sins without legislating changes in the system within which he operated. It is clear that the basically conservative social attitudes of the fundamentalists approximated more nearly those of the progressive era than those of the New Deal. This is readily understood when we remember that both progressives and fundamentalists owed much to earlier evangelical Protestantism. But while progressivism espoused its morals, fundamentalism retained its theology as well, and in that lay the only distinctiveness of fundamentalist social thought.

As long as they emphasized the social as well as the individual implications of that theology, fundamentalists retained a prophetic voice toward their society. But when, as in later decades, some allowed national traditions to replace theology as their chief concern, they became mere devotees of American culture religion and right-wing defenders of the status quo.

CHAPTER VII

CONCLUSIONS

The preceding analysis of fundamentalist social thought from 1918 to 1933 has provided a basis for challenging certain features of the common stereotype of a fundamentalist. While fundamentalism doubtless included rural and small-town Southerners and Midwesterners with little education, blindly loyal to the Constitution and capitalism, and suspicious of everyone with new ideas, these generalizations are not appropriate for the movement as a whole.

The common denominator which gave unity to fundamentalism cannot be found in social or cultural characteristics and ideas. Geographically, the movement appealed to persons from all areas of the country and even foreign countries, although its strongest support developed in the Middle Atlantic, East North Central, and Pacific regions. Intellectually, its leadership included men of varying capabilities, and competent scholars made common cause with sensational pulpiteers. In their attitudes toward minority groups, fundamentalists differed widely, but in general were considerably more moderate than the "hundred percent

Americans" of the war and postwar years. As advocates of social reform, they again were divided, with some taking a strong stand against public evils and others viewing social involvement as a prostitution of the church's calling. Even the crusades against liquor and evolutionary teaching did not enjoy the support of all. Economically, most fundamentalists were satisfied with the present system but reserved the right to criticize evils in capitalism, unionism, socialism, and communism equally. Both this lack of consensus and the complete silence of much fundamentalist literature on these issues indicate clearly that none of them gave unity to the movement.

Its unity, rather, lay in its biblically-based Christian theology. A sovereign and personal God, a written divine revelation, a perfect, virgin-born, crucified, and resurrected Savior, a life transformed by faith in Christ, and a hope of future eternal bliss all were threads woven tightly into the thinking of fundamentalists. This theological core was what led them to reject certain aspects of modern thought, even at the risk of being called unscholarly. It also moderated their nationalism and enabled most of them to avoid the worst features of the postwar intolerance engulfing the nation. Theology determined their general philosophy of social reform, which always retained personal conversion as the prerequisite for permanent social improvement. Theology was given generous application in the economic realm, leading fundamentalists to condemn greed and dishonesty wherever they saw it, to see the Depression as a moral crisis, and to propose a spiritual remedy for its solution. In brief, biblical doctrine colored the thinking of fundamentalists on any subject they discussed.

Nationalism was a secondary unifying force for fundamentalists, increasing their militancy as they saw the need to preserve Christian America from spiritual and political foes. Patriotism played a large role in fundamentalist opposition to Al Smith, to modernism, and to communism, as well as in the support of prohibition and anti-evolution laws. But this nationalism rarely operated apart from the theological emphases of the movement. While an idealistic view of America's history and destiny could easily become a new national religion for fundamentalists (and actually did for some of their successors) most of them resisted this temptation during the era under study. Instead, they warned that America could be a divinely used instrument only if her people returned to the God of their fathers.

From whatever standpoint one views fundamentalism, it retains no cohesiveness apart from its theology. Even its militant method, which was due partially to its cultural setting, is meaningless apart from the faith it was defending. That faith helped to shape the fundamentalist's view of his culture far more than his culture shaped his faith.

It is therefore historically inaccurate to apply the term "fundamentalist" to a social or cultural reactionary, for historical fundamentalism never developed a unified set of views on society or culture. Its only unity lay in its theology and its militant methods of promoting it.

This interpretation will not satisfy everyone, and many will continue to search in the social and cultural milieu of the twenties for further clues to the rise of this religious phenomenon. Yet religion itself might well be as autonomous a force in human behavior as are political or economic factors. Will Herberg has asserted that religion is "something that transcends the social and cultural framework in which it is embedded." He continues:

> When we deal with the religious situation, we are brought up short before the final mystery in a way that is even more immediate than in the ordinary affairs of life. No one who has given any serious thought to the problem of religion can have escaped this sense of depth beyond depth in dealing with his subject . . .[1]

Surely this is the case in the study of fundamentalism.

One last observation should be made. In a generation when much of American Protestantism had become captive to the culture it had helped to create, when Christianity was fast becoming synonymous with "the American way of life," and when the religious faith of many was little more than

---

[1]Will Herberg, Protestant-Catholic-Jew (Rev. ed.; Anchor Books; Garden City, N.Y.: Doubleday & Company, Inc., 1960), p. 4.

self-reliance or positive thinking,[2] fundamentalism by contrast purported to speak to American society on the basis of an external authority. Fundamentalists did not completely escape the influence of their culture, but their commitment to the Bible as the eternal voice of God to every culture made them less susceptible to the religious dilution, moral relativism, and extravagent optimism that characterized their liberal and passive contemporaries. And having avoided the worst effects of a culture religion themselves, they were able to carry out their self-imposed mission of warning prosperous, confident, complacent, self-righteous America that she still was accountable to a higher authority.

---

[2] Ibid., pp. 72-98; cf. Winthrop Hudson, American Protestantism (Chicago: University of Chicago Press, 1961), pp. 131-37; Robert S. and Helen M. Lynd, Middletown (New York: Harcourt, Brace and Company, 1929), p. 315.

APPENDIX A

PROMINENT FUNDAMENTALISTS, 1918-1933

BIEDERWOLF, WILLIAM EDWARD
- Born 1867, Monticello, Ind.
- Education
  - Wabash College, 1889-1890
  - Princeton University, A.B., 1892; A.M., 1894
  - Universities of Erlangen and Berlin (2 years)
- Church Affiliation
  - Presbyterian (U.S.A.), ordained 1897
- Pastor
  - Logansport, Ind., 1897-1900
- Chaplain, U.S. Army, 1898-1899
- Evangelist, various cities, after 1900
- President
  - Winona College, 1917-1919
- Dean
  - Winona School of Theology, 1922
- Other Activities
  - Director, American Mission to Lepers
  - Leader, Winona Lake Bible Conference
  - Author, several books
- Honors
  - D.D., 1931

BODDIS, GEORGE
- Born 1866, Wolverhampton, England
- Education
  - Pennington (N.J.) Seminary
  - Private theological study, 6 years
  - Philadelphia School of Elocution and Dramatic Art, 1898
  - Potomac University, A.M., 1912; Ph.D.
- Church Affiliation
  - Methodist Episcopal, ordained 1888
  - Northern Baptist, ordained 1894
- Pastor
  - Elam, Millersville, Lansdowne, Pa., 1888-1894
  - Philadelphia, Pa., 1894-1898
  - Coatesville, Pa., 1898-1905
  - Clarion, Pa., 1905-1907
  - Lambertsville, N.J., 1907-1919

Marcus Hook, Pa., after 1919
Instructor
Extension School, Potomac University, after 1914
Philadelphia School of the Bible, after 1921
Other Activities
Author, several brochures
Honors
S.T.D., Litt.D., LL.D.

BURRELL, DAVID JAMES
Born 1844, Mount Pleasant, Pa.
Education
Yale College, A.B., 1867
Union Theological Seminary (N.Y.), Graduate, 1870
Church Affiliation
Presbyterian (U.S.A.)
Home Missionary
Chicago, Ill., 1872-1876
Pastor
Dubuque, Ia., 1876-1887
Minneapolis, Minn., 1887-1891
New York, N.Y., 1891-1926
Other Activities
President, Hebrew-Christian Publication Society, New York
President, Anti-Saloon League of New York
Trustee, Biblical Seminary, New York City
A founder of American Bible League
Vice President, American Tract Society
Officer, Lord's Day Alliance
Author, many books and articles
Honors
Two D.D.'s, LL.D.

BUSWELL, JAMES OLIVER, JR.
Born 1895, Burlington, Wis.
Education
University of Minnesota, A.B., 1917
University of Chicago, A.M., 1924
McCormick Theological Seminary, B.D., 1923
Church Affiliation
Presbyterian (U.S.A.), ordained 1918
Chaplain, U.S. Army, 1917-1918
Pastor
Milwaukee, Wis. and Brooklyn, N.Y., 1918-1926
President
Wheaton College (Ill.), after 1926

CHAFER, LEWIS SPERRY
Born 1871, Rock Creek, Ohio
Education

Oberlin College, 1899-1902
Private theological studies, Buffalo, N.Y., 1900
Church Affiliation
Presbyterian (U.S.A.), ordained 1900
Evangelist, various cities, 1900-1914
Bible Teacher, various cities, 1914-1924
Founder, President
Evangelical Theological College (Dallas, Tex.), after 1924
Other Activities
Editor, Bibliotheca Sacra, after 1934
Member, Republican party, Dallas Athletic Club, Dallas Country Club
Composer, several hymns
Author, several books
Honors
D.D.

CONRAD, ARCTURUS ZODIAC
Born 1855, Shiloh, Ind.
Education
Carleton College, A.B., 1882; A.M., 1885
Union Theological Seminary (N.Y.), B.D., 1885
New York University, Ph.D., 1890
Church Affiliation
Presbyterian
Congregational
Pastor
Brooklyn, N.Y., 1885-1890
Worcester, Mass., 1890-1903
Boston, Mass., after 1905
Other Activities
Associate Editor, The Bible Champion
President, New England Home for Deaf Mutes
Preacher in England and Scotland various summers
Author, several books, many articles
Honors
D.D.

CRAIG, SAMUEL G.
Born 1874, Farm, De Kalb County, Ill.
Education
Tarkio College
Princeton University, A.B., 1895; A.M., 1900
Princeton Theological Seminary, B.D., 1900
University of Berlin, 1910-1911
Church Affiliation
Presbyterian (U.S.A.), ordained 1900
Pastor
Ebensburg, Pa., 1900-1909
Pittsburgh, Pa., 1912-1915

Editorial Work
  The Presbyterian, Philadelphia, Pa.
    Joint Editor, 1915-1918
    Contributing Editor, 1919-1924
    Editor, 1925-1930
  Christianity Today, Philadelphia, Pa.
    Editor, after 1930
Other Activities
  Trustee, Westminster Theological Seminary, 1929-1935
  Member, Republican party
  Author, one book, various articles
Honors
  Two D.D.'s

DIXON, AMZI CLARENCE
Born 1854, Shelby, N.C.
Education
  Wake Forest College, A.B., 1875
  Southern Baptist Theological Seminary
Church Affiliation
  Baptist (mainly Northern), ordained 1876
Pastor
  Chapel Hill, N.C., 1877-1880
  Asheville, N.C., 1880-1883
  Baltimore, Md., 1883-1890
  Brooklyn, N.Y., 1890-1896
  Boston, Mass., 1896-1901
  Chicago, Ill., 1906-1911
  London, England, 1911-1919
  Baltimore, Md., 1922-1925
Other Activities
  Author, many books

GAEBELEIN, ARNO CLEMENS
Born 1861, Greiz, Germany
Education
  German Gymnasium
  Johns Hopkins University
Church Affiliation
  Methodist Episcopal, ordained 1885
  Independent, after 1899
Pastor
  Baltimore, Md., 1894-1895
  New York, N.Y., 1896-1897?
  Hoboken, N.J., 1897?
Editor
  Our Hope, New York, N.Y., after 1894
Superintendent
  Hope of Israel Mission, New York, N.Y., 1894-1899
Lecturer, various U.S. and Canadian cities, after 1900
Other Activities

Special lecturer, Evangelical Theological College, Dallas, Tex., and Moody Bible Institute
Member, Mediaeval Academy of America, N.Y. Historical Society, Republican party
Author, many books
Honors
D.D.

GOODCHILD, FRANK MARSDEN
Born 1860, Philadelphia, Pa.
Education
Bucknell University, A.B., 1884; A.M., 1887
Crozer Theological Seminary, Graduate, 1887
Church Affiliation
Northern Baptist, ordained 1888
Pastor
Amenia, N.Y., 1887-1890
Philadelphia, Pa., 1890-1895
New York, N.Y., 1895-1924
Other Activities
Vice President, Baptist Union for Ministerial Education
President, Ministers' Home Society
Chairman of Board, American Baptist Home Missions Society
Member, boards of various religious organizations
Trustee, Northern Baptist Theological Seminary, Gordon Bible College, Philadelphia Baptist Institution
Member, Republican party
Contributing editor, _The Watchman-Examiner_
Honors
D.D.

GRAY, JAMES MARTIN
Born 1851, New York, N.Y.
Education unknown
Church Affiliation
Reformed Episcopal
Pastor
Brooklyn, N.Y.
Newburgh, N.Y.
Supply Chaplain
West Point Military Academy
Rector
Boston, Mass., 1879-1894
Teacher
Gordon Missionary Training School, Boston, Mass., 1889-1894
Lecturer
Northfield Conference, Northfield, Mass., 1893-1896
Summer Lecturer

Moody Bible Institute, Chicago, Ill., 1892-1903
Dean
Moody Bible Institute, 1904-1923
President
Moody Bible Institute, 1923-1934
President Emeritus
Moody Bible Institute, 1934-1935
Other Activities
President, Ministerial Alliance of Boston
Member, Executive Committee of Boston Monday Lectureship
Evangelistic work with D. L. Moody and under Presbyterian Church, U.S.A.
Consulting Editor, Scofield Reference Bible
Member, Old Testament Committee which prepared Tercentenary Edition of King James Bible
Editor, The Public Good, contributor to the Episcopal Recorder
Editor, Institute Tie, Christian Workers Magazine, Moody Bible Institute Monthly
Author, several books
Honors
D.D., LL.D.

HALDEMAN, ISAAC MASSEY
Born 1845, Concordville, Pa.
No college or seminary education
Church Affiliation
Northern Baptist, ordained 1870
Pastor
Brandywine, Pa., 1871-1875
Wilmington, Del., 1875-1884
New York, N.Y., after 1884
Other Activities
Member, Emergency Corps, 29th Pa. Regiment, Civil War
Member, Republican party
Author, several books, many pamphlets
Honors
D.D.

HORSCH, JOHN
Born 1867, Giebestadt, Germany
Education
Bavarian State Agriculture School, Diploma, 1886
Evangelical Theological Seminary (Ill.), Valparaiso University (Ind.), Baldwin-Wallace College, University of Wisconsin, 1888-1898
Church Affiliation
Mennonite
Publisher and church historian
Elkhart, Ind., 1887-1900

Berne, Ind., 1900-1908
Scottdale, Pa., 1908-1941
Other Activities
Author, many books and articles

KENNEDY, DAVID SCOTT
Born 1865, Philadelphia, Pa.
Education
University of Wisconsin, B.S., 1883
McCormick Theological Seminary, Graduate, 1886
Church Affiliation
Presbyterian (U.S.A.), ordained 1886
Pastor
Fort Wayne, Ind., 1886-1888
Allegheny, Pa., 1888-1911
Editor
The Presbyterian, Philadelphia, Pa., 1911-1927
Other Activities
Director, Western Theological Seminary
Trustee, Presbytery of Pittsburgh
President, Presbyterian Hospital, Pittsburgh, Pa.
Member, National Service Commission, Presbyterian Church, U.S.A.; Board of Freedmen, Pittsburgh; Republican party
Director, Lincoln University
Honors
D.D.

KEYSER, LEANDER SYLVESTER
Born 1856, Farm, Tuscarawas County, Ohio
Education
Ohio Northern University, 1875
Indiana State University, 1877-1878
Hamma Divinity School, B.D., 1883
Ohio Northern University, A.M., 1886
Wittenberg College, A.M., 1893
Church Affiliation
Lutheran (United), ordained 1879
Pastor
La Grange, Ind.; Elkhart, Ind.; Springfield, Ohio; Atchison, Kan.; Dover, Ohio, 1883-1911
Professor of Systematic Theology
Hamma Divinity School, Springfield, Ohio, 1911-1932
Professor Emeritus
Hamma Divinity School, after 1932
Other Activities
Lecturer on birds, and on scientific and theological subjects
Editor, The Lutheran Evangelist, 1895-1897
Associate Editor, The Bible Champion and Christian Faith and Life

Author, many books and articles
Honors
D.D.

KYLE, MELVIN GROVE
Born 1858, near Cadiz, Ohio
Education
Muskingum College, A.B., 1881; A.M., 1884
Allegheny Theological Seminary, Graduate, 1885
Church Affiliation
United Presbyterian, ordained 1886
Egyptologist and Lecturer on Bible Archeology 1908-1915
Professor of Biblical Theology and Archeology
Xenia Theological Seminary, Xenia, Ohio, 1915-1930
President
Xenia Theological Seminary, 1922-1930
Research lecturer, 1930-1933
Other Activities
Editor, Bibliotheca Sacra, 1921-1933
Editor, Archeological Dept., The Sunday School Times, 1911-1933
Member, Victoria Institute, London; American Oriental Society; Archeology Institute of America; Society of Bible Literature and Exegesis; Republican party
Moderator of United Presbyterian Conference, 1927
Author, several books, many articles
Explored several archeological sites in Palestine
Honors
D.D., LL.D.

LAWS, CURTIS LEE
Born 1868, Aldie, Va.
Education
University of Richmond
Crozer Theological Seminary
Church Affiliation
Northern Baptist, ordained 1892
Pastor
Baltimore, Md., 1893-1908
Brooklyn, N.Y., 1908-1913
Editor
The Watchman-Examiner, New York, N.Y., 1913-1940 (publisher after 1940)
Other Activities
Mason
Honors
D.D., LL.D.

MACARTNEY, CLARENCE EDWARD
Born 1879, Northwood, Ohio

Education
University of Wisconsin, A.B., 1901
Princeton University, A.M., 1904
Princeton Theological Seminary, Graduate, 1905
Church Affiliation
Presbyterian (U.S.A.), ordained 1905
Pastor
Paterson, N.J., 1905-1914
Philadelphia, Pa., 1914-1927
Pittsburgh, Pa., after 1927
Other Activities
Moderator, Presbyterian Church, U.S.A., 1924, 1925
Director, Westminster Theological Seminary
Author, many books and articles
Honors
D.D.

MACHEN, JOHN GRESHAM
Born 1881, Baltimore, Md.
Education
Johns Hopkins University, A.B., 1901; Graduate study, 1901-1902
Princeton University, A.M., 1904
Princeton Theological Seminary, B.D., 1905
University of Marburg, University of Gottingen, Graduate study, 1905-1906
Church Affiliation
Presbyterian (U.S.A.), ordained 1914
Instructor in New Testament
Princeton Theological Seminary, Princeton, N.J., 1906-1914
Assistant Professor of New Testament Literature and Exegesis
Princeton Theological Seminary, 1914-1929
Professor of New Testament
Westminster Theological Seminary, Philadelphia, Pa., 1929-1937
Other Activities
Member, Democratic party
Author, several books, many articles
Honors
D.D., Litt.D.
Phi Beta Kappa

MAGOUN, HERBERT WILLIAM
Born 1856, Bath, Me.
Education
Iowa (Grinnell) College, A.B., 1879; A.M., 1882
Johns Hopkins University, Ph.D., 1890
Church Affiliation
Congregational, licensed 1899

High School principal
Oskaloosa, Ia., 1879-1880
Grammar School principal
Bath, Me., 1880-1881
Acting Professor of Greek
Colorado College, 1890-1891
Clerical Work
Johns Hopkins University, Baltimore, Md., 1891-1892
Acting Professor of Greek and Latin
Oberlin College, Oberlin, Ohio, 1892-1895
Professor of Latin, Didactics, Greek
Redfield College, 1898-1904
Professor
Massachusetts College of Osteopathy, 1922-1927
Literary work after 1927
Other Activities
Lecturer
Associate Editor, Bibliotheca Sacra after 1908, and The Bible Champion, 1916-1922
Member, American Oriental Society, American Philological Association, Boston Congregational Club
Author, one book, many monographs and articles
Honors
Phi Beta Kappa

MASSEE, JASPER CORTENUS
Born 1871, Marshallville, Ga.
Education
Mercer University, A.B., 1892
Southern Baptist Theological Seminary, 1896-1897
Church Affiliation
Baptist (mainly Northern), ordained 1893
Pastor
Kissimmee, Fla., 1893-1896
Orlando, Fla., 1897-1899
Lancaster, Ky., 1899-1901
Mansfield, Ohio, 1901-1903
Raleigh, N.C., 1903-1908
Chattanooga, Tenn., 1908-1913
Dayton, Ohio, 1913-1919
Brooklyn, N.Y., 1920-1922
Boston, Mass., 1922-1929
Evangelist and Bible Teacher, after 1929
Other Activities
Author, many books and articles
Honors
LL.D.

MATTHEWS, MARK ALLISON
Born 1867, Calhoun, Ga.
No college or seminary education

Church Affiliation
Presbyterian (U.S.A.), ordained 1887
Pastor
Calhoun, Ga., 1888-1893
Dalton, Ga., 1893-1896
Jackson, Tenn., 1896-1902
Seattle, Wash., 1902-1940
Other Activities
Member, Tennessee Bar Association
Trustee, Seattle Chamber of Commerce
Mason
Prelate, Knights Templar in U.S.
Trustee, Whitman College, Whitworth College, San Francisco Theological Seminary
Honors
Two D.D.'s, two LL.D.'s

MUNHALL, LEANDER WHITCOMB
Born 1843, Zanesville, Ohio
Education
Largely self-educated
Chattanooga University, A.M.
Church Affiliation
Methodist Episcopal, ordained 1874
Evangelist, various cities, 1874-1930
Other Activities
Fought in Civil War (Union Army)
Editor, _The Methodist_, Philadelphia
Author, two books
Honors
Two D.D.'s

NORRIS, JOHN FRANKLYN
Born 1877, Dadeville, Ala.
Education
Baylor University, A.B., 1903
Southern Baptist Theological Seminary, Th.M., 1905
Church Affiliation
Southern Baptist, ordained 1899
Pastor
Mount Calm, Tex., 1899-1903
Dallas, Tex., 1905-1908
Fort Worth, Tex., 1909-1952
Detroit, Mich., 1935-1952
Other Activities
Editor, _Baptist Standard_, 1906-1909
Editor, _The Searchlight_ and _The Fundamentalist_, 1919-1952
President, Bible Baptist Seminary, Fort Worth
Radio ministry
Mason

PETTINGILL, WILLIAM LE ROY
Born 1866, Central Square, N.Y.
No college or seminary education
Church Affiliation
Northern Baptist, ordained 1899
Pastor
Wilmington, Del., 1903-1923
Co-founder
Philadelphia School of the Bible, Philadelphia, Pa., 1914
Dean
Philadelphia School of the Bible, 1914-1928
Bible teacher and writer, various locations, after 1928
Other Activities
Founder and editor, Serving-and-Waiting, 1911-1928, and Just a Word, 1928-1933
Consulting editor, Scofield Reference Bible
Vice President, Independent Fundamental Churches of America
Author, many Bible study books
Honors
Two D.D.'s

PHILPOTT, PETER WILLEY
Born 1865, Iona, Ontario, Canada
Education
School of Languages (Ontario)
Church Affiliation
Independent
Evangelist, 1894-1896
Pastor
Hamilton, Ontario, 1896-1922
Chicago, Ill., 1922-1929
Los Angeles, Cal., after 1929
Other Activities
Salvation Army work, 1884-1894
Active in recruiting for World War I, 1914-1917
Presiding judge, Military Conscription Court, 1917-1918
Trustee, Wheaton College
President, African Inland Mission for North America
Honors
D.D.

PRICE, GEORGE MCCREADY
Born 1870, Havelock, New Brunswick, Canada
Education
Battle Creek College, 1891-1893
Provincial Normal School (New Brunswick), Graduate, 1897
Loma Linda College, A.B., 1912

Pacific Union College, A.M., 1918
Church Affiliation
Seventh-Day Adventist
Teacher
New Brunswick, 1897-1902
Principal of Academy
Williamsdale, Nova Scotia, 1903-1904
Research
New York City, Washington, D.C., 1904-1905
Teacher
Loma Linda Medical College, Loma Linda, Cal., 1906-1912
Professor of English Literature
Fernando Academy (Cal.), 1912-1913
Professor of Chemistry and Physics
Pacific Union College, Angwin, Cal., 1920-1922
Professor of Geology
Union College, Lincoln, Neb., 1922-1924
Leave of Absence, 1924-1928
Professor of Geology and Philosophy
Emmanuel Missionary College (Mich.), after 1929
Other Activities
Member, Victoria Institute (London), American Association for the Advancement of Science, British Association for the Advancement of Science
Author, many books and articles, chiefly dealing with evolution

RADER, PAUL
Born 1879, Denver, Col.
Education
University of Denver
University of Colorado
Harvard University (post-graduate studies)
Church Affiliation
Methodist Episcopal
Congregational
Christian and Missionary Alliance
Independent
Member of Faculty
University of Puget Sound, Seattle, Wash.
Athletic Director
Hamline University, Minneapolis, Minn.
Pastor
Boston, Mass.
Pittsburgh, Pa., 1912-1915
Evangelist-pastor
Chicago, Ill., 1915-1921
Pastor
Chicago, Ill., 1921-1933
Other Activities

Author, one book

RILEY, WILLIAM BELL
Born 1861, Greene County, Ind.
Education
Valparaiso Normal School, Teacher's Course
Hanover College, A.B., 1885; A.M., 1888
Southern Baptist Theological Seminary, Graduate, 1888
Church Affiliation
Northern Baptist, ordained 1883
Pastor
Warsaw and Carrollton, Ky., 1885-1887
New Albany, Ind., 1887-1888
Lafayette, Ind., 1888-1891
Bloomington, Ill., 1891-1893
Chicago, Ill., 1893-1897
Minneapolis, Minn., 1897-1942
Founder and President
Northwestern Bible Training School, Minneapolis, 1902
Northwestern Evangelical Seminary, Minneapolis, 1935
Northwestern College of Liberal Arts, Minneapolis, 1944
Other Activities
Editor, *The Christian Fundamentalist*
Executive Secretary, World's Christian Fundamentals Association
Author, many books and articles
Honors
LL.D., D.D.

RIMMER, HARRY
Born 1890, San Francisco, Cal.
Education
Hahneman Medical College, 1912
Whittier College, 1915-1916
Bible Institute of Los Angeles, 1917-1918
Church Affiliation
Friends, ordained 1915
Presbyterian (U.S.A.)
Pastor
Los Angeles, Cal., 1916-1919
Conference Speaker
International Committee of Y.M.C.A., 1920-1925
Pastor
Duluth, Minn., 1934-1940
Other Activities
Lecturer on science and Bible
President, Research Science Bureau, after 1920
Author, many books and articles
Honors
D.D., Sc.D., LL.D.

ROOD, PAUL WILLIAM
Born 1889, Barnum, Minn.
Education
Theological Seminary, North Park College, Graduate, 1911
Church Affiliation
Mission, ordained 1915
Pastor
Chicago, Ill., 1911-1913
Minneapolis, Minn., 1913-1915
Seattle, Wash., 1915-1922
Turlock, Cal., 1922-1933
Chicago, Ill., 1933-1935
President
Bible Institute of Los Angeles, after 1935
Other Activities
President, World's Christian Fundamentals Association, after 1929
Director, North Park College, after 1935
Honors
D.D.

SHIELDS, THOMAS TODHUNTER
Born 1873, Bristol, England
Education unknown
Church Affiliation
Canadian Baptist, ordained 1897
Pastor
Delhi, Ontario; Hamilton, Ontario; London, Ontario, 1897-1910
Toronto, Ontario, after 1927
President
Toronto Baptist Theological Seminary, after 1927
Other Activities
Member, Board of Governors of McMaster University, 8 years
President, Canadian Protestant League, after 1941
Editor, *The Gospel Witness*, after 1922
Author, several books
Honors
Two D.D.'s

SHULER, ROBERT PIERCE
Born 1880, Grayson County, Va.
Education
Emory and Henry College, A.B., 1903
Church Affiliation
Methodist Episcopal, South, ordained 1900
Pastor
Pocohantas, Va.
Norton, Tenn.

Cumberland Gap, Tenn.
Elizabethtown, Tenn.
La Follette, Tex.
Grandview, Tex.
Temple, Tex.
Austin, Tex.
Paris, Tex.
Los Angeles, Cal., after 1920
Honors
Two D.D.'s, LL.D.

SLOAN, HAROLD PAUL
Born 1881, Westfield, N.J.
Education
University of Pennsylvania
Crozer Theological Seminary
Drew Theological Seminary, B.D., 1907
Church Affiliation
Methodist Episcopal, ordained 1908
Pastor
Red Bank, N.J., 1915-1918
Bridgeton, N.J., 1918-1924
Haddonfield, N.J., 1924-1934
Other Activities
District Superintendent, Camden District, 1934-1936
Preacher and lecturer at Princeton Seminary, Drew Seminary, Boston University
Editor, The Essentialist (6 years)
Editor, Christian Faith and Life, 1930-1932
Member, Advisory Council of League of Evangelical Students
Director, American Tract Society
Author, several books, many articles
Honors
S.T.D., D.D., LL.D.

STRATON, JOHN ROACH
Born 1875, Evansville, Ind.
Education
Mercer University, 1895-1898
Southern Baptist Theological Seminary, 1900-1902
University of Chicago
Boston School of Oratory and Expression
Church Affiliation
Northern Baptist, ordained 1900
Professor of Oratory and Interpretation of Literature
Mercer University (Ga.), 1899
Instructor
Baylor University, Waco, Tex., 1903-1905
Pastor
Chicago, Ill., 1905-1907

Baltimore, Md., 1908-1913
Norfolk, Va., 1914-1917
New York, N.Y., 1918-1929
Other Activities
Trustee, Anti-Saloon League of America
Author, several books, many articles
Honors
D.D.

THOMAS, WILLIAM HENRY GRIFFITH
Born 1861, Oswestry, England
Education
King's College (London), A.K.C., 1885
Oxford University, A.B., 1895; A.M., 1898; B.D., 1902; D.D., 1906
Church Affiliation
Church of England, ordained 1885
Curate
Clerkenwell, England
Oxford, England, 1888-1896
Vicar
Portman Square, England, 1896-1905
Principal
Wycliffe Hall, Oxford, England, 1905-1910
Professor of Old Testament Literature
Wycliffe College, Toronto, Ontario, 1910-1919
Professor of Systematic Theology
Wycliffe College, 1915-1919
Bible Speaker and Lecturer, 1919-1924
Other Activities
Author, many books and articles
Honors
Fellow, King's College, London

TORREY, REUBEN ARCHER
Born 1856, Hoboken, N.J.
Education
Yale University, A.B., 1875; B.D., 1878
University of Leipzig, University of Erlangen, Graduate study
Church Affiliation
Congregational, ordained 1878
Pastor
Garretsville, Ohio, 1878-1882
Minneapolis, Minn., 1883-1889
Superintendent
Moody Bible Institute, Chicago, Ill., 1889-1908
Pastor
Chicago, Ill., 1894-1905
Evangelist, 1901-1928
Dean

Bible Institute of Los Angeles, 1912-1924
Pastor
Los Angeles, Cal., 1915-1924
Other Activities
Superintendent, Minneapolis City Mission Society, 1886-1889
Superintendent, Chicago Evangelization Society, 1889-1908
Author, many books and articles

TRUMBULL, CHARLES GALLAUDET
Born 1872, Hartford, Conn.
Education
Yale University, A.B., 1893
Church Affiliation
Presbyterian (U.S.A.)
Editor
The Sunday School Times, Philadelphia, Pa., after 1903
Vice President, Secretary, Director
The Sunday School Times Company
Other Activities
Associate member, Victoria Institute
Member, Palestine Exploration Fund, Archaeological Institute of America
Fellow, American Geographic Society
Treasurer, Belgian Gospel Mission
Director, Pioneer Mission Agency, Keswick Colony of Mercy
Vice President, World's Christian Fundamentals Association
Vice President, Inland South American Missionary Union
Author, several books

TUCKER, WALTER LEON
Born 1871, Pleasanton, Kan.
Education
Bible Training School, Kansas City, Mo.
Moody Bible Institute
Church Affiliation
Baptist, ordained 1900
Pastor
Belton, Mo.; Kansas City, Mo.; Riverside, Cal.; Los Angeles, Cal., 1900-1915
Instructor
Bible Institute of Los Angeles, 1910-1913
Evangelist and Bible Lecturer, after 1915
Editor
The Wonderful Word, New York, N.Y.
Other Activities
Mason
Member, New York Automobile Club

Author, two books, many Bible studies

WILSON, ROBERT DICK
Born 1856, Indiana, Pa.
Education
College of New Jersey (Princeton), A.B., 1876; A.M., 1879; Ph.D., 1886
Western Theological Seminary, 1880-1881
University of Berlin, 1881-1883
Church Affiliation
Presbyterian (U.S.A.)
Instructor and Professor
Western Theological Seminary, Pittsburgh, Pa., 1880-1900
Professor of Semitic Philology and Old Testament Introduction
Princeton Theological Seminary, Princeton, N.J., 1900-1929
Professor of Old Testament
Westminster Theological Seminary, Philadelphia, Pa., 1929-1930
Other Activities
Member, Democratic party
Lecturer at various Bible conferences in U.S. and abroad
Delegate to International Congress of Orientalists, 1889, 1904, 1908
Author, several books, many articles
Honors
D.D., LL.D.

APPENDIX B

PROMINENT MODERNISTS, 1918-1933

AMES, EDWARD SCRIBNER
Born 1870, Eau Claire, Wis.
Education
Drake University, A.B., 1889; A.M., 1891
Yale Divinity School, B.D., 1892
Yale University, 1892-1894
University of Chicago, Ph.D., 1895
Church Affiliation
Disciples of Christ
Professor of Philosophy and Pedagogy
Butler College, Indianapolis, Ind., 1897-1900
Associate Professor of Philosophy
University of Chicago, 1900-1901
Pastor
University Church of Disciples of Christ, Chicago, Ill., after 1900
Various positions
Disciples Divinity House, Chicago, Ill., after 1901
Other Activities
Author, several books
Honors
LL.D.

BROWN, WILLIAM ADAMS
Born 1865, New York, N.Y.
Education
Yale University, A.B., 1886; A.M., 1888; Ph.D., 1901
Union Theological Seminary (N.Y.), Graduate, 1890
University of Berlin, 1890-1892
Church Affiliation
Presbyterian (U.S.A.), ordained 1893
Instructor, Provisional Professor, Professor of Systematic Theology
Union Theological Seminary, New York, N.Y., after 1892
Other Activities
Chairman, Committee on Educational Policy of Yale University
Acting Provost, Yale University, 1919-1920
Member, various committees on church co-operation, Society of Biblical Literature and Exegesis, Ameri-

can Philosophical Society, American Association for the Advancement of Science, Metropolitan Museum of Art, several clubs
Author, several books, many articles
Honors
Two D.D.'s

BURTON, ERNEST DE WITT
Born 1856, Granville, Ohio
Education
Denison University, A.B., 1876
Rochester Theological Seminary, Graduate, 1882
University of Leipzig, 1887
University of Berlin, 1894
Church Affiliation
Northern Baptist
Teacher
Academies and public schools, 1876-1879
Instructor of New Testament Greek
Rochester Theological Seminary, Rochester, N.Y., 1882-1883
Associate Professor and Professor of New Testament Interpretation
Newton Theological Institute, Newton, Mass., 1883-1892
Professor and Head of Department of New Testament Literature and Interpretation
University of Chicago, 1892-1925
President of University of Chicago, 1923-1925
Other Activities
Associate Editor and Editor-in-Chief, Biblical World, 1892-1913
Managing Editor, American Journal of Theology, 1907-1915
Chairman, China Education Commission, after 1921
Oriental Education Commissioner, University of Chicago, 1908-1909
Director, University Libraries, University of Chicago, after 1910
Author, many books
Honors
Three D.D.'s

BUTTRICK, GEORGE ARTHUR
Born 1892, Seaham Harbour, England
Education
Victoria University
Lancashire Independent Seminary
Church Affiliation
Congregational
Pastor
Quincy, Ill., 1915-1918

Rutland, Vt., 1918-1921
Buffalo, N.Y., 1921-1927
New York, N.Y., after 1927
Other Activities
Instructor in Homiletics, Union Theological Seminary, New York, N.Y.
Author, several books
Honors
Four D.D.'s

CADMAN, SAMUEL PARKES
Born 1864, Wellington, England
Education
Wesleyan College, Richmond, England
London University
Wesleyan (Conn.) University
Church Affiliation
Congregational
Pastor
New York, N.Y., 1895-1901
Brooklyn, N.Y., after 1901
Other Activities
President, Federal Council of Churches, 1924-1928
Lecturer at various seminaries
Author, several books, many articles
Honors
S.T.D., L.H.D., Litt.D., Ph.D., three LL.D.'s, two D.D.'s

CASE, SHIRLEY JACKSON
Born 1872, Hatfield Point, New Brunswick, Canada
Education
Acadia University, A.B., 1893; A.M., 1896
Yale University, B.D., 1904; Ph.D., 1906
University of Marburg, 1910
Church Affiliation
Northern Baptist
Instructor of New Testament
Yale Divinity School, New Haven, Conn., 1905-1906
Professor of History and Philosophy of Religion
Cobb Divinity School, Lewiston, Me., 1906-1908
Professor of New Testament and Church History
University of Chicago Divinity School, after 1905
Dean
University of Chicago Divinity School, after 1933
Other Activities
Editor, American Journal of Theology, 1919-1920, Journal of Religion, after 1927
Member, Society of Biblical Literature and Exegesis, American Society of Church History, American Historical Association

Author, various books and articles
Honors
D.D., D.C.L.

COE, GEORGE ALBERT
Born 1862, Monroe County, N.Y.
Education
University of Rochester, A.B., 1884; A.M., 1888
Boston University, S.T.B., 1887; Ph.D., 1891
University of Berlin, 1890-1891
Church Affiliation unknown
Professor
University of Southern California, Los Angeles, 1888-1890
Acting Professor and Professor of Philosophy
Northwestern University, Evanston, Ill., 1891-1909
Professor of Religious Education
Union Theological Seminary (N.Y.), 1909-1922
Professor of Religious Education
Teachers College, New York, N.Y., after 1922
Other Activities
Member, Religious Education Association (pres., 1909-1910), American Philosophy Association, American Psychology Association
Author, several books, many articles
Honors
LL.D.

COFFIN, HENRY SLOANE
Born 1877, New York, N.Y.
Education
Yale University, A.B., 1897; A.M., 1900
Union Theological Seminary (N.Y.), B.D., 1900
Edinburgh University
University of Marburg
Church Affiliation
Presbyterian (U.S.A.), ordained 1900
Pastor
New York, N.Y., 1900-1905
Associate Professor of Practical Theology
Union Theological Seminary, New York, N.Y., 1905-1926
Pastor
New York, N.Y., 1905-1926
President
Union Theological Seminary, after 1926
Other Activities
Author, many books
Honors
Five D.D.'s, three LL.D.'s, three Litt.D.'s, S.T.D., D.Theol., Th.D.

FAGNANI, CHARLES PROSPERO
Born 1854, New York, N.Y.
Education
City College of New York, A.B., B.S., 1873
Columbia Law School, LL.D., 1875
Union Theological Seminary (N.Y.), 1882
Church Affiliation
Presbyterian (U.S.A.), ordained 1882
Chapel Minister
New York, N.Y., 1882-1885
Pastor
Yonkers, N.Y., 1885-1886
Instructor in Hebrew
Union Theological Seminary, New York, N.Y., 1892-1899
Associate Professor of Old Testament Literature and Exegesis
Union Theological Seminary, 1915-1926
Professor Emeritus
Union Theological Seminary, after 1926
Other Activities
Author, several books
Honors
D.D.

FAUNCE, WILLIAM HERBERT PERRY
Born 1859, Worcester, Mass.
Education
Brown University, A.B., 1880; A.M., 1883
Newton Theological Institution, Graduate, 1884
Church Affiliation
Northern Baptist
Pastor
Springfield, Mass., 1884-1889
New York, N.Y., 1889-1899
President
Brown University, Providence, R.I., 1899-1930
Other Activities
President, World Peace Foundation
Lecturer, University of Chicago, 1897
Trustee, Newton Theological Institution, Worcester Academy, Rhode Island School of Design
Author, several books
Honors
Three D.D.'s, seven LL.D.'s

FOSDICK, HARRY EMERSON
Born 1878, Buffalo, N.Y.
Education
Colgate University, A.B., 1900
Union Theological Seminary (N.Y.), B.D., 1904
Columbia University, A.M., 1908

Church Affiliation
Northern Baptist, ordained 1903
Pastor
Montclair, N.J., 1904-1915
Instructor of Homiletics
Union Theological Seminary, New York, N.Y., 1908-1915
Professor of Practical Theology
Union Theological Seminary, after 1915
Pastor
New York City, after 1925
Other Activities
Ministry to World War I troops
Trustee, Colgate University, Barnard College
Member, Sons of American Revolution, Century Club
Author, many books and articles
Honors
Nine D.D.'s, three LL.D.'s, S.T.D.
Phi Beta Kappa

GILKEY, CHARLES WHITNEY
Born 1882, Watertown, Mass.
Education
Harvard University, A.B., 1903; A.M., 1904
Union Theological Seminary (N.Y.), B.D., 1908
Universities of Berlin and Marburg, 1908-1909
United Free Church College, Glasgow, New College, Edinburgh, Oxford University, 1909-1910
Church Affiliation
Northern Baptist, ordained 1910
Pastor
Chicago, 1910-1928
Professor of Preaching
University of Chicago Divinity School, after 1926
Dean of Chapel
University of Chicago Divinity School, after 1939
Other Activities
University preacher, various schools
Trustee, University of Chicago, 1919-1929, George Williams College, after 1929
Member, various clubs
Author, several books
Honors
Six D.D.'s
Phi Beta Kappa

GORDON, GEORGE ANGIER
Born 1853, Oyne, Scotland
Education
Bangor Theological Seminary, Graduate, 1877
Harvard University, A.B., 1881
Church Affiliation

Congregational, ordained 1877
Pastor
Temple, Me., 1877-1878
Greenwich, Conn., 1881-1883
Boston, Mass., 1884-1927
Other Activities
University preacher at Harvard and Yale
Lecturer at various universities
Member, National Institute of Arts and Letters, Massachusetts Historical Society
Fellow, American Academy of Arts and Sciences
President, Harvard Alumni Association, 1918
Author, several books
Honors
Four D.D.'s, two S.T.D.'s, two LL.D.'s

GRANT, PERCY STICKNEY
Born 1860, Boston, Mass.
Education
Harvard University, A.B., 1883; A.M., 1886
Episcopal Theological School, 1886
Church Affiliation
Protestant Episcopal, ordained Deacon 1886, Priest, 1887
Assistant Minister
Fall River, Mass., 1886
Minister
Fall River, Mass., 1887-1893
Rector
Swansea, Mass., 1890-1893
New York, N.Y., 1893-1924
Other Activities
Author, several books
Honors
S.T.D.

HILLIS, NEWELL DWIGHT
Born 1858, Magnolia, Iowa
Education
Lake Forest University, A.B., 1884; A.M.
McCormick Theological Seminary, Graduate, 1887
Church Affiliation
Presbyterian
Congregational, ordained 1887
Pastor
Peoria, Ill., 1886-1889
Evanston, Ill., 1889-1894
Chicago, Ill., 1895-1899
Brooklyn, N.Y., 1899-1924
Other Activities
Author, several books

Honors
D.D., L.H.D.

HORTON, WALTER MARSHALL
Born 1895, Somerville, Mass.
Education
Harvard University, A.B., 1917
Union Theological Seminary (N.Y.), B.D., 1920; S.T.M., 1923
Columbia University, A.M., 1920; Ph.D., 1926
Sorbonne, Strasburg, Marburg
Church Affiliation
Northern Baptist, ordained 1919
Instructor in Philosophy and Religion
Union Theological Seminary, New York, N.Y., 1922-1925
Associate Professor of Systematic Theology
Oberlin Graduate School of Theology, Oberlin, Ohio, 1925-1926
Fairchild Professor, after 1926
Other Activities
Member, American Theological Society, American Philosophy Association
Author, many books and articles
Honors
Phi Beta Kappa

HOUGH, LYNN HAROLD
Born 1877, Cadiz, Ohio
Education
Scio College, A.B., 1898
Drew Theological Seminary, B.D., 1905
New York University
Church Affiliation
Methodist Episcopal, ordained 1898
Pastor
Arcola, N.J., 1898-1904
Cranford, N.J., 1904-1906
King's Park, N.Y., 1906-1907
Brooklyn, N.Y., 1909-1912
Baltimore, Md., 1912-1914
Professor of Historical Theology
Garrett Biblical Institute, Evanston, Ill., 1914-1919
President
Northwestern University, Evanston, Ill., 1919-1920
Pastor
Detroit, Mich., 1920-1928
Montreal, Quebec, Canada, 1928-1930
Professor of Homiletics and Christian Criticism of Life
Drew Theological Seminary, Madison, N.J., after 1930
Dean
Drew Theological Seminary, after 1934

Other Activities
President, Detroit Council of Churches, 1926-1928
Member, Society of Biblical Literature and Exegesis, Chicago Society of Biblical Research, National Voters League, Midland Authors
Honors
Three D.D.'s, one Th.D., one Litt.D., three LL.D.'s, one L.H.D., one J.U.D.

KENT, CHARLES FOSTER
Born 1867, Palmyra, N.Y.
Education
Yale University, A.B., 1889; Fellow, 1889-1891; Ph.D., 1891
University of Berlin, 1891-1892
Church Affiliation unknown
Instructor
University of Chicago, 1893-1895
Associate Professor and Professor of Biblical Literature and History
Brown University, Providence, R.I., 1895-1901
Professor of Biblical Literature
Yale University, New Haven, Conn., 1901-1925
Other Activities
Director, National Council of Schools of Religion, 1922-1925
Member, Archeological Institute of America, American Oriental Society, Society of Biblical Literature and Exegesis, Religious Education Association, several clubs
Author, many books

KNUDSON, ALBERT CORNELIUS
Born 1873, Grandmeadow, Minn.
Education
University of Minnesota, A.B., 1893
Boston University, S.T.B., 1896; Student, 1896-1897
University of Jena, University of Berlin, 1897-1898
Boston University, Ph.D., 1900
Church Affiliation
Methodist Episcopal
Professor of Church History
Denver University, 1898-1900
Professor of Philosophy and English Bible
Baker University, Baldwin City, Kan., 1900-1902
Allegheny College, Meadville, Pa., 1902-1906
Professor of Hebrew and Old Testament Exegesis
Boston University School of Theology, 1906-1921
Professor of Systematic Theology
Boston University School of Theology, after 1921
Dean

Boston University School of Theology, 1926-1938
Dean Emeritus
Boston University School of Theology, after 1938
Other Activities
Fellow, American Academy of Arts and Sciences
Author, several books
Honors
D.D., Theol.D., LL.D.
Phi Beta Kappa

LAKE, KIRSOPP
Born 1872, Southampton, England
Education
Lincoln College, Oxford, A.B., 1895; A.M., 1897
Church Affiliation
Church of England
Curate
Durham, England, 1895
Oxford, England, 1897-1904
Professor
University of Leyden, Leyden, Holland, 1904-1913
Professor of Early Church History
Harvard University, Cambridge, Mass., 1914-1919
Professor of Ecclesiastical History
Harvard University, after 1919
Other Activities
Fellow, American Academy of Arts and Sciences
Author, many books
Honors
D.D.

LYMAN, EUGENE WILLIAM
Born 1872, Cummington, Mass.
Education
Amherst College, A.B., 1894; A.M., 1903
Yale Divinity School, B.D., 1899
University of Halle, University of Berlin, University of Marburg, 1899-1901
Church Affiliation
Congregational, ordained 1901
Professor of Philosophy
Carleton College, 1901-1904
Professor of Systematic Theology and Philosophy of Religion
Congregational College, Montreal, 1904-1905
Professor of Religion and Christian Ethics
Oberlin Graduate School of Theology, Oberlin, Ohio, 1913-1918
Professor of Philosophy of Religion
Union Theological Seminary, New York, N.Y., 1918-1940
Professor Emeritus

Union Theological Seminary, 1940-1942
Other Activities
Member, American Theological Society
Author, several books, many essays
Honors
Two D.D.'s, S.T.D.

MCGIFFERT, ARTHUR CUSHMAN, JR.
Born 1892, Cincinnati, Ohio
Education
Harvard University, A.B., 1913
Union Theological Seminary (N.Y.), B.D., 1917
Columbia University, A.M., 1917
American School of Archeology, 1913-1914
Harvard Divinity School, 1919
University of Zurich, 1919-1920
Church Affiliation
Congregational, ordained 1917
Minister
Lowell, Mass., 1920-1926
Professor of Christian Theology
Chicago Theological Seminary, 1926-1939
President and Professor of American Theology
Pacific School of Religion, Berkeley, Cal., after 1939
Other Activities
Chaplain during World War I
Member, Accrediting Association of Theological Schools
Author and editor, several books
Honors
D.D.
Phi Beta Kappa

MACINTOSH, DOUGLAS CLYDE
Born 1877, Breadalbane, Ontario
Education
McMaster University, A.B., 1903
University of Chicago, Ph.D., 1909
Church Affiliation
Northern Baptist, ordained 1907
Pastor
Marthaville, Ohio, 1897-1899
Instructor of Philosophy
McMaster University, 1903-1904
Professor of Biblical and Systematic Theology
Brandon College, 1907-1909
Assistant Professor and Dwight Professor of Systematic Theology and Philosophy of Religion
Yale University, 1909-1942
Other Activities
Chairman of Department of Religion, Yale Graduate School

Chaplain in England and France, 1916
YMCA Secretary in France, 1918
Author, several books
Honors
D.D., LL.D.

MATHEWS, SHAILER
Born 1863, Portland, Me.
Education
Colby College, A.B., 1883; A.M., 1887
Newton Theological Institution, Graduate, 1887
University of Berlin, 1890-1891
Church Affiliation
Northern Baptist
Associate Professor of Rhetoric, Professor of History and Political Economy
Colby College, Waterville, Me., 1887-1894
Associate Professor of New Testament History and Interpretation, Professor, Professor of Systematic Theology, Professor of History and Comparative Theology
University of Chicago Divinity School, 1894-1933
Jr. Dean
University of Chicago Divinity School, 1899-1908
Dean
University of Chicago Divinity School, 1908-1933
Dean Emeritus
University of Chicago Divinity School, 1933-1941
Other Activities
Editor, Biblical World and several other periodicals
Trustee, Church Peace Union, 1914-1941
President, Federal Council of Churches, 1912-1916
Author, many books
Honors
Five D.D.'s, LL.D., other honorary degrees

MERRILL, WILLIAM PIERSON
Born 1867, Orange, N.J.
Education
Rutgers College, A.B., 1887; A.M., 1890
Union Theological Seminary (N.Y.), B.D., 1890
Church Affiliation
Presbyterian (U.S.A.), ordained 1890
Pastor
Philadelphia, Pa., 1890-1895
Chicago, Ill., 1895-1911
New York, N.Y., after 1911
Other Activities
President, Board of Trustees, Church Peace Union, after 1915
Author, several books, many articles
Honors

Two D.D.'s, S.T.D., L.H.D.
Phi Beta Kappa

MOORE, EDWARD CALDWELL
Born 1857, West Chester, Pa.
Education
Marietta College, A.B., 1877
Union Theological Seminary (N.Y.), Graduate, 1884
Universities of Berlin, Gottingen, Giessen, 1884-1886
Brown University, Ph.D., 1891
Church Affiliation
Presbyterian (U.S.A.), ordained 1884
Pastor
Yonkers, N.Y., 1886-1888
Providence, R.I., 1889-1902
Professor of Theology, Professor of Christian Morals
Harvard Divinity School, Cambridge, Mass., 1902-1929
Professor Emeritus
Harvard Divinity School, after 1929
Other Activities
Lecturer at various schools
Fellow, American Academy of Arts and Sciences
Member, American Historical Association, Colonial Society of Massachusetts, American Commission for Relief in Near East, Council on Foreign Relations
Author, several books
Honors
D.D., LL.D., Th.D.

MORRISON, CHARLES CLAYTON
Born 1874, Harrison, Ohio
Education
Drake University, A.B., 1898
University of Chicago, Fellow in Philosophy, 1902-1905
Church Affiliation
Disciples of Christ, ordained 1892
Pastor
Clarinda, Iowa, 1892-1893
Perry, Iowa, 1894-1898
Chicago, Ill., 1898-1902
Springfield, Ill., 1902-1906
Editor
Christian Century, Chicago, Ill., after 1908
Other Activities
Lecturer on Christianity and public affairs, Chicago Theological Seminary, after 1931
Mason
Member, Union League Club, Republican party
Honors
Two D.D.'s, Litt.D., two LL.D.'s
Phi Beta Kappa

NEWTON, JOSEPH FORT
Born 1878, Decatur, Tex.
Education
Hardy Institute
Southern Baptist Theological Seminary
Church Affiliation
Independent, ordained 1893
Pastor
Paris, Tex., 1897-1898
St. Louis, Mo., 1898-1900
Dixon, Ill., 1901-1908
Cedar Rapids, Ia., 1908-1916
London, England, 1916-1919
New York, N.Y., 1919-1925
Philadelphia, Pa., 1925-1935
Other Activities
Associate Editor, *Christian Century*
Mason
Author, many books
Author, many pamphlets on patriotic and Masonic topics
Honors
Litt.D., D.D., LL.D.

NICHOLS, ROBERT HASTINGS
Born 1873, Rochester, N.Y.
Education
Yale University, A.B., 1894; Ph.D., 1896
Mansfield College (Oxford), 1899-1900
Auburn Theological Seminary, Graduate, 1901
Church Affiliation
Presbyterian (U.S.A.), ordained 1901
Pastor
Unadilla, N.Y., 1901-1902
South Orange, N.J., 1902-1910
Assistant Professor of Church History
Auburn (N.Y.) Theological Seminary, 1910-1913
Professor of Church History
Auburn Theological Seminary, after 1913
Other Activities
Editor, *Church History*
Member, American Society of Church History, American Historical Association, Presbyterian Historical Society, Republican party
Author, several books, many articles
Honors
D.D.
Phi Beta Kappa

PARKS, LEIGHTON
Born 1852, New York, N.Y.
Education

General Theological Seminary, B.D., 1876
Church Affiliation
Protestant Episcopal, ordained 1877
Rector
Boston, Mass., 1878-1904
New York, N.Y., 1904-1925
Other Activities
Author, several books
Honors
A.M., D.D., S.T.D.

POTTER, CHARLES FRANCIS
Born 1885, Marlborough, Mass.
Education
Brown University
Bucknell University, A.B., 1907; A.M., 1913
Newton Theological Institution, B.D., 1913; S.T.M., 1916
Church Affiliation
Northern Baptist
Pastor
Dover, N.H., 1908-1910
Mattapan, Mass., 1910-1914
Edmonton, Alberta, 1914-1916
Marlborough, Mass., 1916-1917
New York, N.Y., 1919-1925
Professor of Comparative Religion
Antioch College, New York, N.Y., 1927-1929
Pastor
New York, N.Y., 1927-1929
Other Activities
Author, several books

ROBBINS, HOWARD CHANDLER
Born 1876, Philadelphia, Pa.
Education
Yale University, A.B., 1899
Princeton Theological Seminary
Episcopal Theological School, B.D., 1903
Church Affiliation
Protestant Episcopal, ordained 1904
Curate
Morristown, N.J., 1903-1905
Rector
Englewood, N.J., 1905-1911
New York, N.Y., 1911-1917
Dean
Cathedral of St. John Divine, New York, N.Y., 1917-1929
Professor of Pastoral Theology
General Theological Seminary, New York, N.Y., after

1929
Other Activities
Member, Society of Mayflower Descendants, Society of Colonial Wars, National Institute of Social Sciences, Century Club
Author, many books
Honors
Seven D.D.'s, S.T.D.
Phi Beta Kappa

SMITH, GERALD BIRNEY
Born 1868, Middlefield, Mass.
Education
Brown University, A.B., 1891
Columbia University, A.M., 1898
Union Theological Seminary (N.Y.), B.D., 1898
Universities of Berlin, Marburg, Paris, 1898-1900
Church Affiliation
Northern Baptist, ordained 1902
Tutor in Latin
Oberlin Academy, 1891-1892
Instructor in math and modern languages
Worcester Academy, 1892-1895
Instructor, Assistant Professor, Associate Professor, Professor of Christian Theology
University of Chicago, 1900-1925
Other Activities
Lecturer at several universities
Managing Editor, American Journal of Theology, 1909-1920
Editor, Journal of Religion, 1921-1925
Member, Quadrangle and City Clubs
Author, several books
Honors
D.D.
Phi Beta Kappa

SMYTH, NEWMAN
Born 1843, Brunswick, Me.
Education
Bowdoin College, B.A., 1863; M.A., 1866
Andover Theological Seminary, Graduate, 1867
European study, 1868-1869
Church Affiliation
Congregational, ordained 1868
Pastor
Providence, R.I., 1867-1870
Bangor, Me., 1870-1875
Quincy, Ill., 1876-1882
New Haven, Conn., 1882-1907
Pastor Emeritus

New Haven, Conn., 1908-1925
Fellow of Yale
Yale University, 1899-1925
Other Activities
Fought in Civil War, 1864-1865
Author, several books
Honors
Three D.D.'s

SNOWDEN, JAMES HENRY
Born 1852, Hookstown, Pa.
Education
Washington and Jefferson College, A.B., 1875
Western Theological Seminary, Graduate, 1878
Church Affiliation
Presbyterian (U.S.A.), ordained 1879
Pastor
Huron, Ohio, 1879-1883
Sharon, Pa., 1883-1886
Washington, Pa., 1886-1911
Professor of Political Economics and Ethics
Washington and Jefferson College, Washington, Pa., 1893-1898
Professor of Theology and Apologetics
Western Theological Seminary, Pittsburgh, Pa., 1911-1929
Other Activities
Editor, Presbyterian Banner, 1898-1917 and after 1926
Author, many books
Honors
D.D., LL.D.

SOCKMAN, RALPH WASHINGTON
Born 1889, Mt. Vernon, Ohio
Education
Ohio Wesleyan University, A.B., 1911
Columbia University, A.M., 1913; Ph.D., 1917
Union Theological Seminary (N.Y.), Graduate, 1916
Church Affiliation
Methodist Episcopal
Pastor
New York, N.Y., after 1917
Other Activities
YMCA worker before and during World War I
Member, American Society of Church History
Author, several books, many articles
Honors
Three D.D.'s, LL.D.
Phi Beta Kappa

TITTLE, ERNEST FREMONT

Born 1885, Springfield, Ohio
Education
Ohio Wesleyan University, A.B., 1906
Drew Theological Seminary, B.D., 1908
Church Affiliation
Methodist Episcopal, ordained 1910
Pastor
Christiansburg, Ohio, 1908-1910
Dayton, Ohio, 1910-1913
Delaware, Ohio, 1913-1916
Columbus, Ohio, 1916-1918
Evanston, Ill., after 1918
Other Activities
Lecturer at several universities and theological schools
With Army YMCA in France six months in World War I
Trustee, Northwestern University
Mason
Author, several books
Honors
Three D.D.'s, two LL.D.'s
Phi Beta Kappa

TYSON, STUART LAWRENCE
Born 1873, Penllyn, Pa.
Education
Nashotah House, Wis., Graduate, 1895
St. John's College (Oxford), A.M., 1903; Post graduate, 1903-1907
Church Affiliation
Protestant Episcopal, ordained Deacon, 1895; Priest, 1897
Congregational, ordained 1925
Special Preacher
Oxford, England, 1899-1903
Assistant Pastor
Oxford, England, 1904-1907
Tutor
Oxford, England, 1903-1905
Professor of New Testament
Western Theological Seminary, Chicago, Ill., 1907-1908
Professor of New Testament and Liturgics
University of the South, Sewanee, Tenn., 1908-1913
Lecturer and Special preacher
New York, N.Y., 1913-1923
Lecturer, after 1923
Other Activities
Member, American Association for the Advancement of Science, Eugenics Research Association, American Eugenics Society, American Genetic Association, Oxford Union Society, Republican party

Author, one book
Honors
D.D.

VEDDER, HENRY CLAY
Born 1853, De Ruyter, N.Y.
Education
University of Rochester, A.B., 1873; A.B., 1876
Rochester Theological Seminary, Graduate, 1876
Church Affiliation
Northern Baptist
Editorial Staff
The Examiner, New York, N.Y., 1876-1892
Editor
The Examiner, New York, N.Y., 1892-1894
Baptist Quarterly Review, 1885-1892
Professor of Church History
Crozer Theological Seminary, Chester, Pa., 1894-1926
Editorial Staff
Chester Times, 1929-1935
Other Activities
Author, many books and articles
Honors
D.D.
Phi Beta Kappa

WIEMAN, HENRY NELSON
Born 1884, Richhill, Mo.
Education
Park College (Mo.), A.B., 1907
San Francisco Theological Seminary, 1910
Universities of Jena and Heidelberg, 1910-1911
Harvard University, Ph.D., 1917
Church Affiliation
Presbyterian (U.S.A.)
Professor of Philosophy
Occidental College, Los Angeles, Cal., 1917-1927
Professor of Philosophy and Religion
Divinity School, University of Chicago, after 1927
Other Activities
Lecturer at several universities and theological schools
Member, American Philosophy Association, American Theological Association, Quadrangle Club
Author, several books and articles
Honors
D.D., Litt.D.

APPENDIX C

INSTITUTIONS CONTRIBUTING TO GRADUATE EDUCATION OF 40 PROMINENT FUNDAMENTALISTS

Name of School	Fundamentalists Who Attended	
	No.	%
Princeton University	5	12.5
Princeton Theol. Sem.	5	12.5
Southern Baptist Theol. Sem.	5	12.5
Crozer Theol. Sem.	3	7.5
Union Theol. Sem.	2	5.0
University of Chicago	2	5.0
McCormick Theol. Sem.	2	5.0
University of Berlin	2	5.0
University of Erlangen	2	5.0
Allegheny Theol. Sem.	1	2.5
Bucknell University	1	2.5
Carleton College	1	2.5
Chattanooga University	1	2.5
Drew Theol. Sem.	1	2.5
Grinnell College	1	2.5
Hamma Divinity School	1	2.5
Hanover College	1	2.5
Harvard University	1	2.5
Johns Hopkins University	1	2.5
Muskingum College	1	2.5
New York University	1	2.5
Ohio Northern University	1	2.5
Oxford University	1	2.5
Pacific Union College	1	2.5
Potomac University	1	2.5
Theol. Sem., North Park College	1	2.5
University of Gottingen	1	2.5
University of Leipzig	1	2.5
University of Marburg	1	2.5
Wittenberg College	1	2.5
Yale Divinity School	1	2.5

APPENDIX D

INSTITUTIONS CONTRIBUTING TO GRADUATE EDUCATION OF 40 PROMINENT MODERNISTS

Name of School	Modernists Who Attended	
	No.	%
Union Theol. Sem. (N.Y.)	11	27.5
University of Berlin	10	25.0
University of Marburg	6	15.0
Yale University	6	15.0
Columbia University	5	12.5
Oxford University	4	10.0
Harvard University	3	7.5
University of Chicago	3	7.5
Newton Theol. Institution	3	7.5
Episcopal Theol. School	2	5.0
University of Paris	2	5.0
University of Jena	2	5.0
Yale Divinity School	2	5.0
Boston University	2	5.0
University of Edinburgh	2	5.0
Drew Theol. Sem.	2	5.0
Brown University	2	5.0
University of Rochester	2	5.0
Rochester Theol. Sem.	2	5.0
Acadia University	1	2.5
Amherst College	1	2.5
Andover Theol. Sem.	1	2.5
Auburn Theol. Sem. (N.Y.)	1	2.5
Bangor Theol. Sem.	1	2.5
Bowdoin College	1	2.5
Bucknell University	1	2.5
Drake University	1	2.5
General Theol. Sem.	1	2.5
Harvard Divinity School	1	2.5
Lake Forest University	1	2.5
Lancashire (Eng.) Indep. Sem.	1	2.5
McCormick Theol. Sem.	1	2.5
New York University	1	2.5
Princeton Theol. Sem.	1	2.5

Name of School	Modernists Who Attended	
	No.	%
Rutgers University	1	2.5
San Francisco Theol. Sem.	1	2.5
Southern Baptist Theol. Sem.	1	2.5
United Free Church College	1	2.5
University of Giessen	1	2.5
University of Gottingen	1	2.5
University of Halle	1	2.5
University of Heidelberg	1	2.5
University of Leipzig	1	2.5
University of Strasburg	1	2.5
University of Zurich	1	2.5
Western Theol. Sem.	1	2.5

BIBLIOGRAPHY

PRIMARY SOURCES

Books and Pamphlets

Barnes, Harry Elmer. The Twilight of Christianity. New York: Richard R. Smith, Inc., 1931.

Benson, Clarence H. A Popular History of Christian Education. Chicago: Moody Press, 1943.

Biederwolf, William E. Evangelism: Its Justification, Its Operation and Its Value. New York: Fleming H. Revell Company, 1921.

________. The New Paganism. Grand Rapids, Mich.: Wm. B. Eerdmans Publishing Company, 1934.

Chafer, Lewis Sperry. Grace. 8th ed. Findlay, Ohio: Dunham Publishing Company, 1947.

Conrad, A[rcturus] Z[odiac]. Comrades of the Carpenter. New York: Fleming H. Revell Company, 1926.

________. Jesus Christ at the Crossroads. New York: Fleming H. Revell Company, 1924.

Dixon, A[mzi] C. Evangelism Old and New. New York: American Tract Society, 1905.

________. Present Day Life and Religion. Chicago: The Bible Institute Colportage Association, 1905.

________. The Young Convert's Problems and Their Solution. New York: George H. Doran Company, 1906.

The Fundamentals: A Testimony to the Truth. 12 vols. Chicago: Testimony Publishing Company, [1910-1915].

Gaebelein, Arno Clemens, ed. Christ and Glory. New York: Publication Office "Our Hope," n.d.

________. The Conflict of the Ages. New York: Publication Office "Our Hope," 1933.

________. Half a Century: The Autobiography of a Servant. New York: Publication Office "Our Hope," 1930.

Gaussen, S. R. L. Theopneusty, or, The Plenary Inspiration of the Holy Scriptures. Translated by Edward Norris Kirk. New York: John S. Taylor & Co., 1844.

Grant, Madison. The Passing of the Great Race. New York: Charles Scribner's Sons, 1916.

Gray, James M. The Teaching and Preaching that Counts. New York: Fleming H. Revell Company, 1934.

Haldeman, I[saac] M. Dr. Harry Emerson Fosdick's Book: "The Modern Use of the Bible." A Review. Philadelphia: The Sunday School Times Company, 1925.

________. The Mission of the Church in the World. New York: The Book Stall, 1917.

________. Professor Rauschenbusch's "Christianity and the Social Crisis." New York: Charles C. Cook, n.d.

Horsch, John. The Failure of Modernism: A Reply to Harry Emerson Fosdick. Chicago: The Bible Institute Colportage Association, 1925.

________. Modern Religious Liberalism. Scottdale, Pa.: Fundamental Truth Depot, 1920.

Interchurch World Movement of North America. World Survey. Vol. 1. Revised ed. New York: Interchurch Press, 1920.

The International Jew: The World's Foremost Problem. Dearborn, Mich.: Dearborn Publishing Co., 1920.

Jones, Edgar De Witt. American Preachers of To-Day. Indianapolis, Ind.: The Bobbs-Merrill Company, 1933.

Keyser, Leander S. Contending for the Faith. New York: George H. Doran Company, 1920.

________. A Reasonable Faith. New York: Fleming H. Revell Company, 1933.

Kirkpatrick, Clifford. Religion in Human Affairs. New York: John Wiley & Sons, Inc., 1929.

Lake, Kirsopp. The Religion of Yesterday and Tomorrow. London: Christophers, 1925.

Light on Prophecy: The Proceedings and Addresses at the Philadelphia Prophetic Conference, May 28-30, 1918. New York: The Christian Herald, 1918.

Lippmann, Walter. American Inquisitors. New York: The Macmillan Company, 1928.

________. A Preface to Morals. New York: The Macmillan Company, 1929.

Lynd, Robert S., and Lynd, Helen Merrell. Middletown. New York: Harcourt, Brace and Company, 1929.

________. Middletown in Transition. New York: Harcourt, Brace and Company, 1937.

Macartney, Clarence E. Twelve Great Questions About Christ. New York: Fleming H. Revell Company, 1923.

Machen, J. Gresham. The Christian Faith in the Modern World. Grand Rapids, Mich.: Wm. B. Eerdmans Publishing Co., 1947.

________. Christianity and Liberalism. Grand Rapids, Mich.: Wm. B. Eerdmans Publishing Company, 1946.

________. God Transcendent and Other Selected Sermons. Edited by Ned Bernard Stonehouse. Grand Rapids, Mich.: Wm. B. Eerdmans Publishing Company, 1949.

________. What Is Christianity? Grand Rapids, Mich.: Wm. B. Eerdmans Publishing Company, 1951.

________. What Is Faith? New York: The Macmillan Company, 1925.

Massee, J[asper] C. Evangelistic Sermons. New York: Fleming H. Revell Company, 1926.

________. Revival Sermons. New York: Fleming H. Revell Company, 1928.

________. Sunday Night Talks. Chicago: The Bible Institute Colportage Ass'n., 1926.

________. The Ten Greatest Chapters In the Bible. Nashville, Tenn.: Sunday School Board of the Southern Baptist Convention, 1924.

_______. The Ten Greatest Christian Doctrines. New York: George H. Doran Company, 1925.

Mathews, Shailer. The Faith of Modernism. New York: The Macmillan Company, 1924.

Matthews, Mark A. Building the Church. New York: American Tract Society, 1940.

_______. Gospel Sword Thrusts. New York: Fleming H. Revell Company, 1924.

Mauro, Philip. "After This." Boston: Hamilton Bros., 1918.

_______. Evolution at the Bar. New York: George H. Doran Company, 1922.

_______. James: The Epistle of Reality. Boston: Hamilton Brothers, 1923.

_______. Man's Day. London: Morgan & Scott Ltd., 1908.

_______. Shall We Smite With the Sword? Boston: Scripture Truth Depot, n.d.

Mecklin, John Moffatt. The Ku Klux Klan: A Study of the American Mind. New York: Russell & Russell, Inc., 1963.

Ottman, Ford C. J. Wilbur Chapman: A Biography. New York: Doubleday, Page & Company, 1920.

Riley, W[illiam] B[ell]. The Bible of the Expositor and the Evangelist. 40 vols. Cleveland: Union Gospel Press, 1926-1938.

_______. The Perennial Revival: A Plea for Evangelism. Revised ed. Philadelphia: American Baptist Publication Society, 1916.

Shepherd, William G. Great Preachers As Seen By a Journalist. New York: Fleming H. Revell Company, 1924.

Sloan, Harold Paul. The Christ of the Ages. Garden City, N.Y.: Doubleday, Doran & Company, Inc., 1928.

_______. Historic Christianity and The New Theology. Louisville, Ky.: Pentecostal Publishing Company, 1922.

Snowden, James H. *Old Faith and New Knowledge*. New York: Harper & Brothers Publishers, 1928.

Stoddard, Lothrop. *The Rising Tide of Color*. New York: Charles Scribner's Sons, 1920.

Straton, John Roach. *The Gardens of Life*. New York: George H. Doran Company, 1921.

________. *The Menace of Immorality in Church and State*. New York: George H. Doran Company, 1920.

Thomas, W[illiam] H[enry] Griffith. *The Work of the Ministry*. London: Hodder and Stoughton, n.d.

Torrey, R[euben] A[rcher]. *The Fundamental Doctrines of the Christian Faith*. New York: George H. Doran Company, 1918.

________. *The Importance and Value of Proper Bible Study*. New York: Fleming H. Revell Company, 1921.

________. *Revival Addresses*. Chicago: Fleming H. Revell Company, 1903.

Vanderlaan, Eldred C. (ed.). *Fundamentalism versus Modernism*. New York: H. W. Wilson Company, 1925.

Wilson, Robert Dick. *Is the Higher Criticism Scholarly?* Philadelphia: The Sunday School Times Company, 1922.

Winrod, Gerald B. *Christ Within*. 3d ed. Wichita, Kans.: Defender Publishers, 1929.

________. *The Keystone of Christianity*. New York: Fleming H. Revell Company, 1930.

________. *Mussolini and the Second Coming of Christ*. Wichita, Kans.: Defender Publishers, 1928.

________. *Science, Christ and the Bible*. New York: Fleming H. Revell Company, 1929.

World Conference on Christian Fundamentals. *God Hath Spoken*. Philadelphia: Bible Conference Committee, 1919.

Periodicals and Newspapers

The Bible Champion, XXIV-XXXVI (1918-1930).

The Biblical Review, III-XVI (1918-1931).

The Biblical World, LII-LIV (1918-1920).

Bibliotheca Sacra, LXXV-XC (1918-1933).

The Christian Century, XXXIX-L (1922-1933).

Christian Faith and Life, XXXVII-XL (1931-1934).

The Christian Fundamentalist, I-VI (1927-1932).

Christian Fundamentals in School and Church (originally *School and Church*), II-IX (1919-1927).

The Christian Workers Magazine, XVII (1917).

Congressional Digest, V (1926).

The Essentialist, II-VI (1927-1930).

Evangelical Theological College Bulletin, 1926-1931.

The Forum, LXXI-LXXVI (1924-1926).

The Fundamentalist (originally *The Searchlight*), I-XI (1917-1933).

The King's Business, XIV-XXIV (1923-1933).

The Ladies' Home Journal, XLI-XLII (1924-1925).

The Literary Digest, LXXVI (1923).

The Missionary Review of the World, XXXII-LII (1919-1929).

Moody Bible Institute Monthly, XXI-XXXIV (1920-1933).

The Nation, CXVI-CXX (1923-1925).

The New Republic, XXX-XLII (1922-1925).

New York Herald Tribune, 1924-1926.

New York Times, 1918-1929.

Our Hope, XXI-XL (1914-1933).

The Presbyterian, LXXXVIII-CIII (1918-1933).

The Princeton Theological Review, XVI-XXVII (1918-1929).

Revelation, I-III (1931-1933).

The Scientific Monthly, XVI (1923).

Serving and Waiting, VII-XXIII (1917-1934).

The Sunday School Times, LX-LXXIII (1918-1931).

Survey, LII (1924).

The Watchman-Examiner, VI-X (1918-1922).

The Wonderful Word, IX-XXVI (1917-1933).

Manuscript Collections

Minnesota State Historical Society. Archives, Jewish Community Relations Council of Minnesota Papers.

Southern Baptist Convention Historical Commission. Archives, John Franklyn Norris Papers.

SECONDARY SOURCES

Books

Averill, Lloyd J. American Theology in the Liberal Tradition. Philadelphia: The Westminster Press, 1967.

Carter, Paul A. "The Fundamentalist Defense of the Faith." Change and Continuity in Twentieth-Century America: The 1920's. Edited by John Braeman, Robert H. Bremner, and David Brody. Columbus, Ohio: Ohio State University Press, 1968.

Coben, Stanley. "A Study in Nativism: The American Red Scare of 1919-20." New Perspectives on the American Past. 2 vols. Edited by Stanley N. Katz and Stanley I. Kutler. Boston: Little, Brown and Company, 1969.

Cole, Stewart G. The History of Fundamentalism. New York: Harper & Row, 1931.

Dabney, Virginius. Below the Potomac: A Book About the New South. New York: D. Appleton-Century Company, 1942.

Faulkner, Harold Underwood. The Quest for Social Justice, 1898-1914. New York: Macmillan Company, 1931.

Filene, Peter G. "An Obituary for 'The Progressive Movement.'" Twentieth-Century America: Recent Interpretations. Edited by Barton J. Bernstein and Allen J. Matusow. 2d ed. New York: Harcourt Brace Jovanovich, Inc., 1972.

Franklin, John Hope. "Postwar Upheaval: Racism and Riots." The Impact of World War I. Edited by Arthur S. Link. New York: Harper & Row, Publishers, 1969.

Furniss, Norman F. The Fundamentalist Controversy, 1918-1931. New Haven: Yale University Press, 1954.

Gabriel, Ralph Henry. The Course of American Democratic Thought. 2d edition. New York: The Ronald Press Company, 1956.

Gasper, Louis. The Fundamentalist Movement. The Hague: Mouton & Co., 1963.

Gatewood, Willard B., Jr., ed. Controversy in the Twenties: Fundamentalism, Modernism, and Evolution. Nashville, Tenn.: Vanderbilt University Press, 1969.

________. Preachers, Pedagogues, & Politicians: The Evolution Controversy in North Carolina, 1920-1927. Chapel Hill: University of North Carolina Press, 1966.

Giboney, Ezra P., and Potter, Agnes M. The Life of Mark A. Matthews. Grand Rapids, Mich.: Wm. B. Eerdmans Publishing Company, 1948.

Gilbert, Arthur. A Jew in Christian America. New York: Sheed and Ward, 1966.

Ginger, Ray. Six Days or Forever? Tennessee v. John Thomas Scopes. Boston: Beacon Press, 1958.

Goshen, Charles E. Drinks, Drugs, and Do-Gooders. New York: The Free Press, 1973.

Gusfield, Joseph R. Symbolic Crusade: Status Politics and the American Temperance Movement. Urbana, Ill.: University of Illinois Press, 1963.

Haller, John S., Jr. Outcasts from Evolution: Scientific

Attitudes of Racial Inferiority, 1859-1900. Urbana, Ill.: University of Illinois Press, 1971.

Handlin, Oscar. "American Views of the Jew at the Opening of the Twentieth Century." At Home in America. Vol. V of The Jewish Experience in America. Edited by Abraham J. Karp. 5 vols. Waltham, Mass.: American Jewish Historical Society, 1969.

Handy, Robert T., ed. The Social Gospel in America, 1870-1920. New York: Oxford University Press, 1966.

Hebert, Gabriel. Fundamentalism and the Church. Philadelphia: The Westminster Press, 1957.

Herberg, Will. Protestant-Catholic-Jew. Revised ed. Anchor Books. Garden City, N.Y.: Doubleday & Company, Inc., 1960.

Hicks, John D. Republican Ascendancy, 1921-1933. New York: Harper & Row, 1960.

Higham, John. "Social Discrimination Against Jews in America, 1830-1930." At Home in America. Vol. V of The Jewish Experience in America. Edited by Abraham J. Karp. 5 vols. Waltham, Mass.: American Jewish Historical Society, 1969.

________. Strangers in the Land: Patterns of American Nativism, 1860-1925. New Brunswick, N.J.: Rutgers University Press, 1955.

________. "The Tribal Twenties." Twentieth-Century America: Recent Interpretations. 2d ed. Edited by J. Barton Bernstein and Allen J. Matusow. New York: Harcourt Brace Jovanovich, Inc., 1972.

Hofstadter, Richard. Anti-Intellectualism in American Life. New York: Alfred A. Knopf, 1963.

________. The Paranoid Style in American Politics. New York: Alfred A. Knopf, 1965.

________. Social Darwinism in American Thought. Revised edition. Boston: The Beacon Press, 1955.

Hudson, Winthrop. American Protestantism. Chicago: The University of Chicago Press, 1961.

Jorstad, Erling. The Politics of Doomsday: Fundamentalists of the Far Right. Nashville, Tenn.: Abingdon

Press, 1970.

Karp, Abraham J. "At Home in America." At Home in America. Vol. V of The Jewish Experience in America. Edited by Abraham J. Karp. 5 vols. Waltham, Mass.: American Jewish Historical Society, 1969.

Kolko, Gabriel. The Triumph of Conservatism: A Reinterpretation of American History, 1900-1916. New York: Macmillan Company, 1963.

Leuchtenburg, William E. The Perils of Prosperity, 1914-32. Chicago: University of Chicago Press, 1958.

Levine, Lawrence W. Defender of the Faith. William Jennings Bryan: The Last Decade, 1915-1925. New York: Oxford University Press, 1965.

Lipset, Seymour Martin, and Raab, Earl. Politics of Unreason: Right-wing Extremism in America, 1790-1970. New York: Harper & Row, Publishers, 1970.

McLoughlin, William G., Jr. Modern Revivalism: Charles Grandison Finney to Billy Graham. New York: Ronald Press Company, 1959.

Masselink, William. Professor J. Gresham Machen. N.p.: n.publ., n.d.

May, Henry F. The End of American Innocence. New York: Alfred A. Knopf, 1959.

Miller, Robert Moats. American Protestantism and Social Issues, 1919-1939. Chapel Hill, N.C.: The University of North Carolina Press, 1958.

Mowry, George E. The Era of Theodore Roosevelt, 1900-1912. New York: Harper & Row Publishers, 1958.

________. The Progressive Era 1900-1918: Recent Literature and New Ideas. 2d edition. Washington, D.C.: Service Center for Teachers of History, 1964.

________, ed. The Twenties: Fords, Flappers & Fanatics. Spectrum Books. Englewood Cliffs, N.J.: Prentice-Hall, Inc., 1963.

________. The Urban Nation, 1920-1960. New York: Hill and Wang, 1965.

Murphy, Paul L. "Sources and Nature of Intolerance in the

1920's." The 1920's: Problems and Paradoxes. Edited by Milton Plesur. Boston: Allyn and Bacon, Inc., 1969.

Murray, Robert K. Red Scare: A Study of National Hysteria, 1919-1920. New York: McGraw-Hill Book Company, 1964.

Nye, Russel B. This Almost Chosen People. East Lansing, Mich.: Michigan State University Press, 1966.

Olson, Bernhard E. Faith and Prejudice. New Haven: Yale University Press, 1963.

Perkins, Dexter. The New Age of Franklin Roosevelt, 1932-45. Chicago: The University of Chicago Press, 1957.

Persons, Stow. "Religion and Modernity, 1865-1914." The Shaping of American Religion. Vol. I of Religion in American Life. Edited by James Ward Smith and A. Leland Jamison. 4 vols. Princeton, N.J.: Princeton University Press, 1961.

Riley, Marie Acomb. The Dynamic of a Dream: The Life Story of Dr. William B. Riley. Grand Rapids, Mich.: Wm. B. Eerdmans Publishing Company, 1938.

Roy, Ralph Lord. Apostles of Discord. Boston: Beacon Press, 1953.

Rudnick, Milton L. Fundamentalism and The Missouri Synod. St. Louis: Concordia Publishing House, 1966.

Runyan, William M. Dr. Gray at Moody Bible Institute. New York: Oxford University Press, 1935.

Sandeen, Ernest R. The Roots of Fundamentalism: British and American Millenarianism 1800-1930. Chicago: The University of Chicago Press, 1970.

Selznick, Gertrude J., and Steinberg, Stephen. The Tenacity of Prejudice: Anti-Semitism in Contemporary America. New York: Harper & Row, Publishers, 1969.

Shannon, David A. Between the Wars: America, 1919-1941. Boston: Houghton Mifflin Company, 1965.

Simpson, George Eaton, and Yinger, Milton. Racial and Cultural Minorities. 3d ed. New York: Harper & Row, Publishers, 1965.

Smith, Timothy L. Revivalism and Social Reform. New York: Abingdon Press, 1957.

Stark, Rodney, et al. Wayward Shepherds: Prejudice and the Protestant Clergy. New York: Harper & Row, Publishers, 1971.

Stonehouse, Ned B. J. Gresham Machen: A Biographical Memoir. Grand Rapids, Mich.: Wm. B. Eerdmans Publishing Company, 1954.

Timberlake, James H. Prohibition and the Progressive Movement, 1900-1920. Cambridge, Mass.: Harvard University Press, 1963.

Wiebe, Robert H. Businessmen and Reform: A Study of the Progressive Movement. Cambridge, Mass.: Harvard University Press, 1962.

_______. The Search for Order, 1877-1920. New York: Hill and Wang, 1967.

Reference Works

The Mennonite Encyclopedia. 4 vols. Scottdale, Pa.: Mennonite Publishing House, 1956.

The New Schaff-Herzog Encyclopedia of Religious Knowledge. 13 vols. Grand Rapids, Mich.: Baker Book House, 1950.

Schwarz, J. C., ed. Religious Leaders of America. Vol. II, 1941-1942. New York: By the Editor, 1941.

_______. Who's Who In the Clergy. Vol. I, 1935-1936. New York: By the Editor, 1936.

Twentieth Century Encyclopedia of Religious Knowledge. 2 vols. Grand Rapids, Mich.: Baker Book House, 1955.

Who's Who in America. Vol. 12, 1922-1923. Chicago: A. N. Marquis & Company, 1922.

Who's Who in America. Vol. 13, 1924-1925. Chicago: A. N. Marquis & Company, 1924.

Who's Who in America. Vol. 14, 1926-1927. Chicago: The A. N. Marquis Company, 1926.

Who's Who In America. Vol. 17, 1932-1933. Chicago: The A. N. Marquis Company, 1932.

Who's Who in America. Vol. 21, 1940-1941. Chicago: The A. N. Marquis Company, 1940.

Who Was Who In America. Vol. I, 1897-1942. Chicago: The A. N. Marquis Company, 1942.

Who Was Who In America. Vol. III, 1951-1960. Chicago: The A. N. Marquis Company, 1960.

Articles in Journals

Ahlstrom, Sydney E. "Continental Influence on American Christian Thought Since World War I." Church History, XXVII (September, 1958), 256-72.

Glad, Paul W. "Progressives and the Business Culture of the 1920's." The Journal of American History, LIII (June, 1966), 75-89.

Handy, Robert T. "Fundamentalism and Modernism in Perspective." Religion in Life, XXIV (Summer, 1955), 381-94.

Hays, Samuel P. "The Politics of Reform in Municipal Government in the Progressive Era." Pacific Northwest Quarterly, LV (October, 1964), 157-69.

Link, Arthur S. "What Happened to the Progressive Movement in the 1920's?" American Historical Review, LXIV (July, 1959), 833-51.

Lipset, Seymour Martin. "The Banality of Revolt." Saturday Review, LIII (July 18, 1970), 23-26, 34.

Mead, Sidney E. "Denominationalism: The Shape of Protestantism in America." Church History, XXIII (December, 1954), 291-320.

Miller, Robert Moats. "A Note on the Relationship between the Protestant Churches and the Revived Ku Klux Klan." Journal of Southern History, XXII (August, 1956), 355-68.

Moore, Le Roy, Jr. "Another Look at Fundamentalism: A Response to Ernest R. Sandeen." Church History, XXXVII (June, 1968), 195-202.

Rader, Benjamin G. "Richard T. Ely: Lay Spokesman for the Social Gospel." The Journal of American History, LIII (June, 1966), 61-74.

Rapson, Richard L. "The Religious Feelings of the American People, 1845-1935: A British View." Church History, XXXV (September, 1966), 311-27.

Smith, Willard H. "William Jennings Bryan and the Social Gospel." Journal of American History, LIII (June, 1966), 41-60.

Szasz, Ferenc M. "William B. Riley and the Fight Against Teaching of Evolution in Minnesota." Minnesota History, XLI (Spring, 1969), 201-16.

Welter, Rush. "The History of Ideas in America: An Essay in Redefinition." Journal of American History, LI (March, 1965), 599-614.

Unpublished Materials

Goldberg, Daniel. "A History of Baptist Higher Education in Iowa." Unpublished Th.M. thesis, Northern Baptist Theological Seminary, 1965.

Harrington, Carroll Edwin. "The Fundamentalist Movement in America, 1870-1920." Unpublished Ph.D. dissertation, University of California at Berkeley, 1959.

McBirnie, Robert Sheldon. "Basic Issues in the Fundamentalism of W. B. Riley." Unpublished Ph.D. dissertation, State University of Iowa, 1952.

www.ingramcontent.com/pod-product-compliance
Lightning Source LLC
LaVergne TN
LVHW061218100826
845148LV00004B/794

* 9 7 8 1 5 5 6 3 5 3 9 7 0 *